HAITI'S
PREDATORY REPUBLIC

HAITI'S PREDATORY REPUBLIC

The Unending Transition to Democracy

Robert Fatton Jr.

LYNNE
RIENNER
PUBLISHERS

BOULDER
LONDON

Published in the United States of America in 2002 by
Lynne Rienner Publishers, Inc.
1800 30th Street, Boulder, Colorado 80301
www.rienner.com

and in the United Kingdom by
Lynne Rienner Publishers, Inc.
3 Henrietta Street, Covent Garden, London WC2E 8LU

Library of Congress Cataloging-in-Publication Data
Fatton, Robert.
  Haiti's predatory republic : the unending transition to democracy / Robert Fatton, Jr.
    p. cm.
  Includes bibliographical references and index.
  ISBN 1-58826-060-7 (alk. paper)
  ISBN 1-58826-085-2 (pbk. : alk. paper)
    1. Haiti—Politics and government—1986– .
  F1928.2.F38   2002
  972.9407'3—dc21

                                                            2001048934

British Cataloguing in Publication Data
A Cataloguing in Publication record for this book
is available from the British Library.

Printed and bound in the United States of America

    The paper used in this publication meets the requirements
⊗   of the American National Standard for Permanence of
    Paper for Printed Library Materials Z39.48-1984.

    5   4   3   2   1

To Luc

Contents

Preface

This book is an analysis of Haiti's politics, from the fall of the Duvalier dictatorship on February 6, 1986, to Jean-Bertrand Aristide's second inauguration as president of the republic on February 7, 2001, to the attempted coup on December 17, 2001. It is the story of the gradual demise of a moment of utopia that had seemingly liberated a people from decades of oppression, squalor, and poverty and given them the conviction that "everything was possible." It is thus an exhilarating and yet depressing account.

It appeared that with the forced departure of Jean-Claude Duvalier the country would start a new history freed from its long legacy of despotism. Invigorated by the surge of popular power, Haitians of all social backgrounds hoped to embark on a democratic journey leading to economic development, political renewal, and social peace. A wave of national optimism and euphoria buried temporarily the conflicts between antagonistic actors, institutions, and social classes. These conflicts, however, quickly exploded in a series of confrontations between the army, which had inherited power from the dictator, and an increasingly assertive popular movement bent on both the *déchoukaj* (uprooting) of Duvalierists and the installation of a democratic regime. Ultimately, the military resorted to repression, violently aborting the elections of 1987 and organizing farcical ones in 1988 only to seize power again in a coup a few months later.

The army was, however, a profoundly divided institution; internecine struggles soon generated a series of coups and countercoups. Under massive domestic and international pressures, the men in uniform were compelled to exit the National Palace and facilitate the electoral return of civilians. The utopian vision, which had been blinded by the cynicism and repression of the military, reappeared again in the defiant eyes of the masses. Led by the charismatic and prophetic messianism of Father Jean-Bertrand Aristide, the huge majority of poor Haitians became Lavalas (the flood)—an unstoppable deluge. Elected in a landslide, Aristide assumed the presidency on February 7, 1991; embodying the hopes and aspirations of the *moun en deyo* (the marginalized and excluded) he *became* Lavalas.

Aristide was bent on turning the world upside down. He exposed the gigantic class divide separating Haitians, preached that *tout moun se moun* (all human beings are human beings), and advocated extraparliamentary methods of popular rule. He soon discovered, however, that Haiti's dominant class found this brand of politics to be thoroughly unacceptable. In September 1991, barely seven months after his presidential inauguration, Aristide was overthrown in a bloody coup and forced into exile.

Incapable of imposing its legitimacy at home and abroad, Raoul Cédras's new military dictatorship remained in power for three violent and repressive years. During this time, Aristide managed to sustain his domestic popularity and mobilize international public opinion against the junta. After a series of failed negotiations between the exiled president and the de facto regime of Cédras, 20,000 U.S. troops took over Haiti peacefully with the blessing of both Aristide and the United Nations. Ironically, Aristide, the advocate of liberation theology, the prophet of anticapitalism, and the nationalist leader, knew that to restore his presidency he had no choice but to depend, and depend utterly, on massive U.S. military assistance. The circumstances leading to Aristide's "second coming" changed him immensely. Constrained by the overwhelming U.S. presence and by the demands of the international financial institutions, he was forced to collaborate with former enemies and hesitant allies to implement policies he had hitherto rejected. He abandoned the priesthood to become a Machiavellian "prince," maneuvering unsuccessfully to recover the wasted time of exile by prolonging his presidency for three more years. In February 1996, bowing to external pressures, Aristide relinquished the reins of government to his former prime minister, René Préval. However reluctantly he may have done so, Aristide engineered the country's first peaceful electoral transition of power. The rituals of democracy were taking root in spite of manifest shortcomings and flaws.

The Préval presidency was marred by internal power struggles within Lavalas, culminating in a major split between Aristide and his erstwhile supporters. In addition, it symbolized the politics of *doublure*—meaning those holding public office were not those ruling the country. Indeed, secluded in his private residence in Tabarre, Aristide maintained his hegemonic presence; he was the power behind Préval's throne. The result was permanent crisis and political paralysis. The country suffered from increasing corruption, crime, and poverty. The euphoria of 1991 as well as the dreams rekindled by Aristide's return in 1994 gradually faded away, giving rise to popular apathy and cynicism. A series of rigged elections kept alive democratic rituals but undermined the victors' legitimacy. This lack of validation was particularly evident in the controversial 2000 parliamentary and presidential elections, won overwhelmingly by Aristide and his Fanmi Lavalas party. The opposition refused to recognize the legality of these ballots and sought to create an alternative government of national consensus. What it failed to acknowledge, however, was Aristide's continued popularity with *le peuple,* which still viewed him as the savior. The opposition could not accept the simple fact that Aristide remained an inescapable reality. Because the opposition had no popular roots, it was incapable of mobilizing the Haitian masses; it lacked a coherent program and comprised disparate groups ranging from Duvalierists to former Lavalasians and Marxists. What united these groups was neither ideology nor democratic principles, but a common visceral dislike for Aristide and an uncommon appetite for state power.

In this respect, both Lavalas and the opposition were prisoners of *la politique du ventre* (politics of the belly), a form of governability based on the acquisition of personal wealth through the conquest of state offices. In a country where destitution is the norm and private avenues to wealth are rare, politics becomes an entrepreneurial vocation, virtually the sole means of material and social advancement for those not born into wealth and privilege. Controlling the state turns into a zero-sum game, a fight to the death to monopolize the sinecures of political power. The tragedy of Haiti's systemic foundation is that it literally eats the decency and humanity of perfectly honest men and women, transforming them into *grands mangeurs* (big eaters)—a rapacious species of officeholders who devour public resources for their exclusive private gains. Rather than inviting moral redemption, the immense poverty plaguing the country has generated a generalized pattern of callous indifference and a thoroughly individualistic *sauve-qui-peut* (every man for himself) attitude. Deprivation is so overwhelming that to go on living, Haitians simply pay no attention to it. As the U.S. journalist Bob Shacochis states, the island's rich have always "pushed silently through the shoals of beggars, ignoring their extended hands."[1] As for the poor, the vicissitudes of eking out a meager existence have rarely afforded them the opportunity of changing their miserable circumstances. Historically, emancipation has assumed the form of personal gain or fulfillment to the detriment of any collective purposeful action.

Haiti provides a paradigmatic case of the difficulties—if not the impossibility—of establishing democratic rule in extremely poor nations plagued by a despotic inheritance. In this regard and more generally, this book is a contribution to the ongoing disciplinary efforts of various scholars to elaborate a theory of democratization. Much of what follows is a critique of the conventional wisdom that equates regular elections, elite control, and market rationality with democracy. In contradistinction I argue that democracy in its minimal liberal form is the result of a balance of forces between contending classes—the bourgeoisie and the working class—and that absent these classes, democracy is at best hesitant and indeed predatory. Predatory democracy is a regime in which very imperfect trappings of liberal democracy coexist with the Hobbesian struggle to monopolize the few sites of public power with access to wealth and privilege. It is true that constitutional constraints on executive authority exist and that the press remains free, but this struggle for office takes very brutal forms of intimidation and is ultimately determined by controversial and often fraudulent elections. Predatory democracy is thus a hybrid of authoritarianism and polyarchy. In this sense, while it represents a more accountable political system than the typical dictatorship, it suffers from the excesses of presidential monarchism and the intense competition for the appropriation of prebendary gains, both fundamental elements of despotic rule.

This book relies heavily upon, and could not have been written without, secondary sources; but it is also a journey into my own roots. Born into the Haitian elite and having deep personal ties of affection to it, I am well acquainted with its behavior, mentality, and prejudices. I have been privy to its "hidden discourse" and know what it really thinks; I have heard its "unspoken thoughts."[2] I thus know the chasm separating the words whispered in the intimate salons of Pétion Ville from those publicly voiced. I am disturbingly familiar with the elite's profound contempt for *le peuple*. I know it fears democracy, and I know the hostility it harbors toward the full exercise of universal suffrage. It is not that the Haitian dominant class is the "most repugnant elite," as the U.S. Embassy would have it; it is simply that if it wants to keep its position at the top of the social pyramid, it has little room in which to maneuver. Under present conditions, democracy—if it has any meaning—would inevitably challenge the structure of power and property rights, and this the dominant class knows and finds unacceptable. Its behavior differs little from that of any other dominant class confronted by an overwhelming and hostile popular wave. Thus, as one member of the old mulatto "aristocracy" told me, "We may be repugnant, but we are not the most repugnant elite, we are equally repugnant!"

Because I live in the privileged setting of academic life in the United States with the comfort that distance affords me, it is easy to pass moral judgment, but writing this book has been a profoundly painful and depressing intellectual and emotional process. It has entailed a difficult moral and political rupture with my own world, my own class; and yet, the vacuum that this rupture has created remains devastatingly empty. The hopes that the events of February 1986 and of February 1991 engendered have become so faint that intellectual honesty requires an acknowledgment of defeat.

This acute feeling of defeat and betrayal has generated among many activists a profound disenchantment. They sense that the ideals they fought for have become empty slogans for opportunistic politicians in search of personal power and wealth. This utter disgust drove Claude René, an early Lavalas militant, to suicide; in his testament, where he declared his repulsion of both the opposition and the government, he put it simply: "M soti nan malpwote a. Je laisse la nausée" [I am exiting the stinking sewage. I am departing from the nausea].[3] René's suicide is an extreme reflection of the deep disillusion of many erstwhile Lavalasians. It is a dark reminder that Haiti is dabbling with catastrophe and near the abyss. In these baleful times there is some solace, however, in sharing Antonio Gramsci's belief in the "pessimism of the intellect, and optimism of the will." The book is thus grounded in a cautious pessimism.

*　　*　　*

I want to thank the University of Virginia for its financial support, without which this book would still be in my imagination. This support enabled me to devote a full year to research and writing, unencumbered by the duties and obligations of "normal life." I also want to express my gratitude to the editors of *Comparative Politics* and *New West Indian Guide* for permission to include in this book material that had been published in different forms in their respective journals.

I am indebted to Alex Dupuy, Carolle Charles, Bob Maguire, and Henry "Chip" Carey for their intellectual contributions, particularly during our numerous "Haiti panels" at the annual meetings of the Latin American Studies Association. Whether he knows it or not, my brother Bernard has been an inspiration, offering pointed and fraternal criticisms that altered my views on key issues. I suspect he would have wanted more alterations, but I am willing to take full blame for whatever remains that is wrongheaded. In addition, I was tremendously lucky to have as an editor a novelist—my good friend Blaire French. If my prose has some clarity and if the text is comprehensible to more than a few, it is in large measure because of her considerable help and talent. I am equally indebted to Carrol Coates, who in the midst of more important works of translation found the time and the energy to translate the numerous French quotations and documents into superb English. Finally, I want also to thank many comrades and contacts in Haiti whom I prefer not to identify. They represented an indispensable source of knowledge and information.

I cannot, however, end this preface without acknowledging my deep and loving debt of gratitude to Cindy Hoehler-Fatton, my wife and intellectual and academic companion, for putting up with my "Haiti obsession" at a time when she was herself completing a manuscript. She spent a disproportionate number of hours on motherhood, freeing me much too generously from the obligations of fatherhood. I thus apologize to Luc, my son, for

my numerous leaves of absence and promise him more afternoons of "base-
ment soccer." Finally, Vanessa, I hope that this book will not discourage
you from continuing to fight against the ugly structures of oppression on
which rest regrettably much of the foundations of human relations both at
home and abroad. I am afraid that I have been a bad example, resembling
one of those philosophers Marx denounced for having only interpreted the
world when the point is to change it. Having dedicated two previous books
to my wife and daughter, it is only fair that this one be for Luc.

Notes

1. Bob Shacochis, "There Must Be a God in Haiti," in Edward Abbey, ed., *The Best of Outside: The First 20 Years* (New York: Vintage Departures, 1998), p. 306.

2. James C. Scott, *Domination and the Arts of Resistance* (New Haven: Yale University Press, 1990).

3. "Claude René se Suicide et Laisse son Testament Politique," Haiti Online, October 8, 2000.

A despot may go away, but no dictatorship comes to a complete end with his departure. A dictatorship depends for its existence on the ignorance of the mob; that's why all dictators take such pains to cultivate that ignorance. It requires generations to change such a state of affairs, to let some light in. Before this can happen, however, those who have brought down a dictator often act, in spite of themselves, like his heirs, perpetuating the attitudes and thought patterns of the epoch they themselves have destroyed. This happens so involuntarily and subconsciously that they burst into righteous ire if anyone points it out to them. . . . It is one of the most difficult things in the world . . . to change the past.

—Ryszard Kapuściński, *Shah of Shahs*

1

Introduction

The Democratization Paradigm

Democratization has become a fashionable and indeed hegemonic paradigm in political science.[1] While proponents of democratization do not necessarily share the same principles, the paradigm embodies a spectrum of thought corresponding to a certain logic and a common set of formulations. It represents what Joseph Schumpeter termed a "classical situation" to designate "the achievement of substantial agreement after a long struggle and controversy—the consolidation of the fresh and original work which went before."[2] Schumpeter adds, however, that a "classical situation" like a paradigm is "an expository device. Though certainly based upon provable facts, neither must be taken too seriously or else what is intended to be a help for the reader turns into a source of misconceptions."[3] My rendering of the paradigm minimizes heuristic differences and maximizes common attributes. At its most basic level, democratization refers to the complicated process transforming authoritarian regimes into democracies.

As an ideal type, the paradigm of democratization comprises the following major propositions:

1. In general, democratization is prompted by an organic crisis of authoritarian society. The crisis is caused by a series of problematic phenomena, each powerful enough to disrupt the social continuity of life, and each aggravating the others. Economic decline, the eruption of people's power, the fragmentation of the dictatorial bloc, and external shocks combine—with varying degrees of intensity—to generate the democratizing moment.

2. Democratization is a complicated process of bargaining among competing political elites, resulting in "pacts" of transition leading to a historical rupture with authoritarianism and an eventual consolidation of democracy.

1

3. These pacts are concluded in a climate of "insulation" from popular pressures preventing the rise of "extremist" demands and favoring the triumph of the "political center."[4] The primary objective is a peaceful transition that can only be achieved through compromise with authoritarian forces. The compromise guarantees a lasting survival of, and a continued political role for, such forces in the postdictatorial phases.

4. "Economic reforms," the implantation of market rationality and the further integration of domestic forces of production into world capitalism, are essential preconditions for the successful consolidation of democracy.

5. Finally, democratization requires the retreat of the state, the development of civil society, and the preservation of the existing distribution of wealth, income, and status.

In the paradigm's perspective, democratization is at most a change of regime rather than a structural transformation of the state. It is a kind of regime discontinuity within the obdurate parameters of systemic continuity. Thus, the paradigm tends to gloss over the significant "impairments" to democratic practice caused by the persisting vitality of authoritarianism during the periods of transition and consolidation. Impairments, as Charles Lindblom has argued,

> are both *deliberate* . . . and *inadvertent*. . . . They can employ either *word and symbol* . . . or *deed*. . . . They can *inculcate* . . . or *obstruct or confuse* the forming of attitudes, beliefs, and volitions. . . . They include both positive acts or *commissions* . . . and *omissions*.[5]

The lingering legacy of authoritarianism has the deliberate effect of not only protecting key figures of the dictatorial coalition from popular justice, but also of including them in vital veto-empowered institutions of the new regime. It has inadvertent consequences insofar as it curtails the democratic horizon by forcing citizens to tolerate persistent authoritarian idioms and practices in the name of democracy itself. The legacy contributes to making the "constitution of tyranny"[6] an integral part of the new regime. As Catherine Conaghan and James Malloy have argued, the dismaying "democratic despotism" characterizing the new democracies of the central Andes is not a "regional pathology" but a "bolder [version] of some of the same problems at play in a variety of contemporary democracies."[7]

In the paradigm's view, democracy cannot tolerate too many popular pressures; it cannot be too democratic. A democracy that responds to demands "from below" soon becomes "overloaded" and faces a "crisis of governability" degenerating into incivility. What the democratization paradigm advocates is thus "responsible" techniques of governance resting on "a subtle screening of participants and demands."[8] In this perspective, a successful democratization requires the marginalization of extremists to facilitate the emergence of a moderate center capable of negotiating with soft-liners and hard-liners a pact of democratization. The "satisficing" precondition of such a pact is, however, the survival of the authoritarian legacy. All political players must feel that the pact grants them "some important satisfactions and [shields them from] the worst possible dissatisfactions."[9]

The fear of mutually assured destruction may also contribute to a satisficing solution as a relative balance of power between authoritarian and democratizing blocs forces them into a compromise. In Samuel Huntington's words,

> The risks of confrontation and of losing thus impel government and opposition to negotiate with each other; and guarantees that neither will lose everything become the basis for agreement. Both get the opportunity to share in power or to compete for power. Opposition leaders know they will not be sent back to prison, government leaders know they will not have to flee into exile. Mutual reduction in risk prompts reformers and moderates to cooperate in establishing democracy.[10]

But how can democracy be established if the success of democratization depends on the preservation of some of the most critical institutions, actors, and cultural syndromes of the ancien régime? And how or when can a democracy be consolidated if its foundations rest on a despotic legacy? There is little agreement on these issues, even if consolidation tends to be associated with the routinization of electoral politics and a subsequent alternation of regime.[11] The paradigm fails to specify clearly when the transition ends and the consolidation begins and whether the huge authoritarian detritus that the transition carries will continue to weigh heavily on consolidation.

Thus, the theory of democratization suffers from its incapacity to explain convincingly how a democracy can tolerate, let alone institutionalize, the authoritarian legacy and still remain a democracy. The logic of democratization theory is paradoxical; it suggests that democracy cannot crystallize without compromises with the authoritarian bloc. In turn, these compromises ensure the powerful continuity of despotic structures, institutions, and agents as well as the relative freezing of existing class alignments and distributive systems. As Adam Przeworski has emphasized,

> A transition to democracy can be made only at the cost of leaving economic relations intact, not only the structure of production but even the distribution of income. Freedom from physical violence is as essential a value as freedom from hunger, but unfortunately authoritarian regimes often produce as a counter-reaction the romanticization of a limited model of democracy. Democracy restricted to the political realm has historically coexisted with exploitation and oppression at the workplace, within the schools, within bureaucracies, and within families.[12]

Democratization thus routinizes the legitimation of the authoritarian legacy and its accompanying inequities of resources, power, and status.[13] It constitutes "a continued, insistent, and ubiquitous process of elite communication and intimidation to protect advantages against slow erosion—constant elite struggle to win minds to a commitment to such values as order, obedience, the status quo, deference, political docility, and inequalities of income and wealth."[14]

The problem with the democratization paradigm is that ultimately its concept of democracy is both minimalist and inadequate. It is minimalist, because it does not go beyond a type of electoral politics based on compromising pacts between and within elites;[15] it is inadequate because analytically it privileges the study of regimes while downplaying or ignoring the significance of state and class power. In fact, democratization theory conflates state and regime as if a change of regime entails a necessary change of state. The two, however, are clearly distinct. In *Latin America in the Time of Cholera*, James Petras and Morris Morley describe the conceptual distinction between state and regime:

> The state includes the permanent political institutions of society: the military, the judiciary, the civil bureaucracy, the top officials in the central bank, etc. Moreover, these permanent political institutions are integrated with the system of class rulership; together, they form "the state." . . . Regimes, on the other hand, are composed of the transitory officials who occupy the executive and legislative branches and who usually devise policies within the parameters of the state and interests of the dominant classes. When regimes differ substantially from states, a crisis emerges—which is usually resolved by the overthrow of the regime by the state.[16]

Thus, a change of regime is necessary but not sufficient for a change of state. The conflation of state and regime explains why democratization theory can equate democracy with the emergence of new civilian regimes whose very birth and continued survival require the persistence of authoritarian institutions and norms. Dominant classes and their allies in the state and civil society tolerate and/or support democratization precisely because the change of regime it entails is quite compatible with the powerful continuity of despotic forms of class and state power. Similarly, in the post–Cold War period, imperial nations—particularly the United States—have come to accept these political calculations and welcome now ongoing processes of democratization. They know that such processes may contribute to political stability and thus minimize the likelihood of costly and dangerous military interventions. Moreover, a change of regime imperils neither the existing structures of production nor the hegemonic and strategic interests of imperial nations. It is a change that is quite compatible with the powers-that-be in the domestic as well as international arena.[17]

In fact, in the last few years, the World Bank and the International Monetary Fund (IMF) have adopted the concept of "governance" as a means of inducing borrowing countries into developing more "accountable" and "market-friendly" environments.[18] The concept is strikingly similar to the democratization paradigm. This trend within international lending institutions, however, is no coincidence since many of the Bank's "organic intellectuals"[19] are the prime theorists of democratization. Suffice it to say that both governance and democratization paradigms advocate the privatization of public assets, the shrinking of state activities, the implantation of a regime of austerity, and a further integration of national economies into world capitalism.[20] That such measures may be incompatible with democratization itself is an indication of the "benignity"[21] with which both paradigms portray policies that accentuate inequities and privilege the privileged.[22]

To that extent, democratization has obdurate class limitations even if it implies the implantation of electoral politics and the ushering in of a new regime with the support of transnational actors. It does not result in a change of state; at best, it emasculates some of the most nefarious organs of repression and opens up a space for greater popular participation and the taming of the inherited culture of terror; at worst, it institutionalizes the veto power of the old dictatorial coalition, rewarding torturers, putschists, and coup leaders.[23] Democratization can thus routinize the authoritarian legacy and ultimately legitimize the silent violence of daily material deprivation afflicting oppressed majorities.

Moreover, democratization, particularly in situations of acute scarcity, is endangered by the social aspirations and processes of class formation plaguing the very antiauthoritarian coalition responsible for the overthrow of dictatorial rule. The coalition's conquest of power may simply result in an internecine struggle for the totalitarian monopolization of the political arena. Having few if any private avenues for social mobility, those who had hitherto been excluded now use their control of the state to acquire large prebends and become a new ruling class. The environment of scarcity within which democratization occurs fuels within the antiauthoritarian coalition a savage struggle for the limited spaces of power; new alliances are formed only to be abruptly broken, old friends turn into enemies, and "democrats" reunite with associates of the former tyrant. The sole objective is the capture of the state and its offices. Rather than being a civil competition, electoral politics becomes a fight to the finish in which fraud and manipulations become the rule.

Successful entrepreneurs of democratization can thus hide behind its facade to organize prefabricated elections with the intent of supplanting the dislodged old guard and enriching themselves. To that extent, democratization in poor countries represents more a circulation of small groups of elites seeking to climb into the dominant class than a major social transformation. Privilege, prestige, and wealth remain exclusive. The new resembles the old. The virtual lack of class analysis in democratization theory generates an emphasis on elite strategies and leadership that downplays questions of structural power and inequities. From this perspective, then, democratization is the affair of elites who initiate and control the process over which the working class and other subordinate groups have little if any influence. As Ruth Berins Collier has argued,

> The dominant framework used in theoretical and comparative accounts . . . has not only adopted an actor-based rather than a structural perspective, but it has tended to privilege certain kinds of actors: individual elites rather than *collective* actors, strategically defined actors rather than *class*-defined actors, and state actors more than *societal* actors. As a framework, it almost precludes the problematization of the role of working-class and mass action. Indeed, in most theoretical and comparative accounts, the working class and its organizations receive relatively little (if any) attention.[24]

Moreover, the exit of class from democratization theory obscures the reality that in the postauthoritarian period the old dominant class continues to exercise significant power. It also hides the ferocious processes of class formation that democratization itself engenders. It seems clear that the anti-dictatorial coalition is not merely animated by democratic ideals; its members are also bent on gaining power and wealth. These two motivations are not necessarily mutually supportive; more often than not they stand in direct contradiction. The antidictatorial coalition is therefore not automatically democratic; its struggle against tyrannical rule may well be rooted in its pursuit of narrow material and political interests. Once the dictatorship is overthrown, the conflicts over who rules and for what purposes can propel internecine wars within the democratizing bloc. This is especially the case in poor countries where control of the state is the means to acquire and monopolize wealth. In such instances, those who fought for democracy because of their own marginalization can easily become the new marginalizers, recreating the old authoritarian patterns. The process of class formation within the democratizing coalition can thus be intense and cause the development of a new despotism. In short, by failing to take class seriously, democratization theory ignores the reconfiguration of class power and thus the limitations of democracy itself. Hence, the theory suffers from a "benign" notion of democracy that empties the concept of any real meaning.

A meaningful notion of democracy has to include much more than the mere exercise of voting for politicians, albeit in free and competitive elections; it has to take into account the social, cultural, and material environment within which citizens make their choices. As Robert Dahl has pointed out, capitalism tends to "produce inequalities in social and economic resources so great as to bring about severe violations of political equality and hence of the democratic process."[25] Huge inequalities of class power causing acute material deprivations can only make a mockery of civic liberties; they deny the full enjoyment of equal opportunities for political participation without which democracy is an empty shell.[26] A substantive conception of democracy is thus required; not only for theoretical reasons, but also because it will offer an ideal type with which we can assess the extent of democratization and measure the distance that remains to be covered before the journey is truly completed.

A substantive conception of democracy requires a participatory structure of governance where rulers are fully accountable to citizens and where the economic sphere comes under popular control. It must include more than the electoral mechanisms guaranteeing the possibility of regime alternation and the institutional checks safeguarding individual rights from the overpowering reach of the state. Thus, a meaningful democracy must subject civil society and the market to norms of popular accountability. To do otherwise is to subscribe to an unwarranted separation of politics and economics, as if one had little or no effect on the other.

Current definitions of democracy, however, tend to posit the necessity of this separation, for they assume that the logic of markets and "marketization" is coterminous with the logic of democracy and democratization. As Ellen Meiksins Wood has explained,

> [In] the conceptual framework of liberal democracy, we cannot talk, or even *think*, about freedom *from* the market. We cannot think of freedom from the market as a kind of empowerment, a liberation from compulsion, an emancipation from coercion and domination. . . . The very condition that makes it possible to define democracy as we do in modern liberal capitalist societies is the separation and enclosure of the economic sphere and its invulnerability to democratic power. Protecting that invulnerability has even become an essential criterion of democracy. This definition allows us to invoke democracy *against* the empowerment of the people in the economic sphere. It even makes it possible to invoke democracy in defence of a *curtailment* of democratic rights in other parts of "civil society" or even in the political domain, if that is what is needed to protect property and the market against democratic power.[27]

Democracy, at a minimum, therefore entails an expansion of popular control over the economic realm; without such control, democracy is at best limited in scope and incapable of reducing the vast inequities generated by the market and civil society. It is within this framework of understanding that any assessment of democratization must proceed.

Haiti's Problematic Democratization

In this book, I analyze the process of democratization that has marked the modern history of Haiti. I examine the 1986 fall of the Duvalier dictatorship, the subsequent rise, collapse, and "resurrection" of the freely elected populist regime of Jean-Bertrand Aristide, and the political convulsions following Aristide's peaceful passage of power to René Préval's government in 1995. Finally, I explore the vicissitudes of Aristide's 2000 reelection to the presidency and their potential impact on his legitimacy and capacity to rule effectively.

I suggest that the transition from authoritarianism to populism was a function of the ascendancy of civil society and, in particular, popular civil society. A variety of voices, groups, and organizations slowly established their independence from, and ultimately contributed to the fall of, the Duvalierist dictatorship. To paraphrase Moshe Lewin, this societal "maze" found new ways of "keeping private" what it had hitherto been unable to keep private and "socialized" what it had wanted to protect from the regimenting and excessive reach of the state.[28] "Private spaces" reemerged from a long period of repression and reinvigorated civil society's resistance to authoritarian rule. Thus, the prime characteristic of civil society is its capacity to fight the intrusion of the state; and it is this perspective that informs my usage of the term throughout these pages.

Not surprisingly, Lewin's definition of civil society provides a heuristic tool to illuminate the Haitian landscape:

> [Civil society is] . . . the aggregate of networks and institutions that either exist and act independently of the state or are official organizations capable of developing their own, spontaneous views on national or local issues and then impressing these views on their members, on small groups and, finally, on authorities. These social complexes do not necessarily oppose the state, but exist in contrast to outright state organisms and enjoy a certain degree of autonomy. The possibility of serious dissidence from various levels of society cannot be excluded.[29]

Thus, the development of pluralist and self-organizing civic associations bent on defending their own corporate interests against the exactions of the state has the potential to erode and perhaps block any authoritarian temptation. Independent households, religious and legal associations, literary circles, press clubs, and a plethora of other voluntary organizations reinforce the growth of an arena of citizens' power, where private social forces build autonomous trenches to stop and/or mold the advance of the state. This aggregate of private forces engaged in nonstate activities standing paradoxically in the way of the state constitutes civil society.

Civil society, however, is not a tabula rasa; the political and cultural processes defining the wider social domain condition its practices. While subaltern classes may hope and believe that civil society is an arena where they can construct their own autonomous communities, they cannot free themselves totally from the watching eyes and political weight of dominant groups. "Popular" civil society is simply too weak to escape from ruling-class surveillance and its opportunistic patronage. To this extent, civil society has a contradictory role. On the one hand, it creates opportunities for the flowering of subordinate class organizations; on the other hand, it privileges the superior associational capacity of the dominant class. By creating a realm of unofficial initiatives, movements, and organizations that operate independently of the state, civil society enhances the power of those having the capacity to use their material means to construct their own "private spaces." Inevitably, in a poor country like Haiti, civil society becomes a prime arena for advancing the interests of the dominant class.[30] It is true that it embodies a novel framework of representation, but it brings with it the baggage of a profoundly class-divided nation. It is a new edifice, but it has old foundations. It represents a major discontinuity with the dictatorial past, but its roots are enmeshed in a web of political, historical, and cultural continuities.

Thus, while the emergence of civil society in Haiti has disturbed hierarchies of power and traditional codes of conduct, it has failed to eradicate them. In fact, it looked impotent in the face of Haiti's redictatorialization. Civil society was simply unable to undermine the old balance of class power as well as the vital repressive organs of the Duvalierist state that survived the departure of Jean-Claude Duvalier. The 1991 coup that overthrew President Aristide reflected the persisting capacity of the Haitian dominant class to unleash the most brutal violence against those forces that threatened to turn the change of regime into a change of state.

In this book, I modify the classical Marxian usage of "dominant class" in hopes of capturing better Haitian specificities.[31] I will use the term to imply a group of people sharing a similar interest in appropriating the economic surplus from below while preserving and/or enhancing their political rule from above. The group, however, is not always united; in times of normalcy—that is, when subordinate classes do not challenge its rule—it can fight over the distribution of the spoils of state power. Moreover, matters of race, color, and religion do intrude and generate divisions and certain antagonisms. This has meant that I see the Haitian dominant class as comprising two broad factions: the "possessing" class and the ruling class proper.

As I argue in Chapter 2, the possessing class is that class that derives its wealth primarily from the private sector through "comprador" and small manufacturing and banking activities. Generally, while it has strong licit and illicit linkages to the state, it does not control directly its apparatus.

Those who have direct political control of the state represent what I define as the ruling class proper. They use the state as a private means of enrichment to acquire prebendary gains. They extract resources not only from their exploitation of subordinate classes but also from informal and formal taxation of the possessing class. In fact, if it wants to continue to do business and/or move into new ventures, the possessing class, more often than not, has to buy "protection" from the ruling class. There is thus a conflictive relationship between the two factions of the dominant class. These very real tensions dissipate, however, when subordinate classes mobilize to challenge the existing distribution of power, privilege, and property. At this point, the dominant class becomes united in its opposition to any fundamental change from below.

Not surprisingly, I argue that the Cédras dictatorship reflected the brutal condensation of the interests of the Haitian dominant class. Thus, only force could have dislodged the coup leaders and their allies. The U.S. military intervention, Operation Uphold Democracy, that restored President Aristide to his office in October 1994, demonstrated once more that violence remained decisive in Haitian politics and represented the only viable means of ending redictatorialization.

The intervention, however, has had contradictory consequences. While it resuscitated the difficult process of democratization and facilitated the relative neutralization of the repressive organs of the state, it protected the old balance of class power and set constraining parameters for economic transformation. The result is a change of regime rather than the creation of a new state. In addition, the Lavalas[32] regime that crystallized in the aftermath of Operation Uphold Democracy soon began to exhibit the traditional patterns of nepotism and clientelism of the past. After a decade of power, it generated a new class of *grands mangeurs*, who are literally getting fat through the corrupt exploitation of their public offices for private gains.[33]

The term became all the rage during the 1997 carnival season, when huge dancing crowds chanted accusatory songs against the Haitian political class for "getting fat" at the expense of the poor majority.[34] Vilified as obese characters who had been deformed by the corruptions of power, the *grands mangeurs* became the target of popular mockery and insults: "Gad grosé kravat yo . . . Gad grosé tét bèf yo . . . Gad grosé bank yo" and "Yo manje jistan yo gonfle" [look at their huge ties . . . watch their humongous sports utility vehicles . . . look at their fat bank accounts . . . they eat to the point of ballooning].[35] Thus, *grands mangeurs* not only refers to the voracious appetite for the personal consumption of state resources but it symbolizes the intimate relationship between the acquisition of power and growing physical corpulence. In a country where malnourishment and hunger are a permanent predicament for the vast majority, the conquest of public office is a meal ticket to corpulence, a sign of growing status and privilege.

Constrained by the trappings of democratization, Lavalas "big eaters" may not be as rapacious as their Duvalierist predecessors, but they indicate the persistence of old patterns of abuse. In fact, these patterns are rooted in the early days of independence and reached their paroxysm with Duvalierism; they form the Haitian political "habitus"—the system of "dispositions acquired through experience" that shapes particular types of behavior at particular historical moments.[36] The predatory behavior and messianic pretensions of the Haitian political class that have marked the history of the country since its inception have not spared the Lavalas regime.

Upon his return from exile and following the example set by his predecessors—including Toussaint Louverture, Jean-Jacques Dessalines, and indeed François Duvalier—Aristide claimed with increasing vigor that his own person embodied the popular will and that God had sanctified his mission. As he put it in his autobiography, "The people's sufferings are my own. I have shared them for so long that there can never be a gap between the president and the aspirations of the majority of Haitians."[37]

Ruling increasingly like an imperial president, Aristide sought to suppress challenges to his supremacy and stifle the autonomous development of popular forms of power. Bent on monopolizing the political arena and convinced of his unique and direct relationship with the masses, he had little sympathy for structured parties and programs. He favored "movements" and "fluidity," provided they found inspiration in his own words and vision. Aristide's overwhelming charisma, as well as the growing class ambitions of the cadres of the "February 1991 generation," fueled powerful centrifugal forces. Ideological differences, personal animosities, and material aspirations, contained by the common struggle against the military dictatorship, burst out in the wake of the compromises and difficulties of Aristide's presidential succession.

With the election of René Préval in December 1995, power was soon displaced from the National Palace to Tabarre.[38] Plagued by internecine disputes, the Lavalas movement exploded. Voicing their disenchantment with Aristide's monarchical messianism and demagogic tendencies, a growing number of senior Lavalasians deserted him to create new parties and *groupuscules*.[39] On the one hand, there was Aristide and his Fanmi Lavalas, and on the other, there was the opposition—fragmented, dispirited, and in search of a viable strategy. By 2000 the high hopes generated by February 1991 were fading; the country was engulfed in an acute crisis of governance, the economy was in shambles, and poverty had reached alarming proportions. While Aristide continued to master the game, very little of the energy and popular support that carried him to the presidency a decade earlier remained. The nation was exhausted; within the political class there was only cynicism and opportunism, and among the masses there was, as there had always been, the permanent and harsh struggle for daily survival. Without the narco-resources generated by the growing cocaine trade[40] and the remittances of the diaspora, the economy would have collapsed.[41] Popular power, at least in its autonomous forms, was dissolving, giving way to Chimères, Zinglendos, and other violent and deadly squads.[42]

The crisis was thus systemic, affecting all spheres of society. Democratization was giving birth to what I shall call a predatory rather than an "unconsolidated" democracy. Unconsolidated democracies are, in Philippe Schmitter's words,

> condemned to democracy without enjoying the consequences and advantages that it offers. They are stuck in a situation in which all the minimal procedural criteria for democracy are respected. Elections are held more or less frequently and more or less honestly. The various liberal freedoms exist—multiple political parties, independent interest associations, active social movements, and so on—but without mutually acceptable rules of the game to regulate the competition between the political forces. The actors do not manage to agree on the basic principles of cooperation and competition in the formation of governments and policies. Each party considers itself uniquely qualified to govern the country and does what it can to perpetuate itself in power. Each group acts only in the furtherance of its own immediate interests, without taking into consideration its impact upon the polity as a whole. Whatever formal rules have been enunciated (in the constitution or basic statutes) are treated as contingent arrangements to be bent or dismissed when the opportunity presents itself.[43]

While Haiti has all the features of an unconsolidated democracy, it suffers from more acute symptoms of democratic dysfunctionality. In fact, its politics is increasingly based on the criminalized zero-sum game of a predatory democracy. The game is characterized by brutal forms of intimidation in which emerging and antagonistic factions of the Lavalas petite bourgeoisie, assisted by armed gangs, struggle to monopolize the few sites of public power giving access to wealth and privilege. Lavalas is not, however, the only faction appropriating the means of violence; all groups possessing resources have created their own autonomous "security" apparatuses and forces.[44]

There is thus a dispersion of the means of coercion that generates private armies that can ultimately escape from their creators' control. These private security apparatuses fill the vacuum generated by the absence of effective centralized state power. Paradoxically, they are also the prime vehicle for the political fight over the private capture of the state, a necessary means to claim absolute control of political offices and the prebends of privatization and illicit trade. The extreme scarcity of resources transforms the fight into a Hobbesian war between small personalistic clans of big men. Etzer Charles captures the essence of the phenomenon in his important book *Le Pouvoir Politique en Haïti:*

> The underdevelopment from which Haiti is suffering has transformed the apparatuses of the political system into a veritable field of action in which the elites of the petty bourgeoisie may be found seeking their fortune and social ascension. For these elites, who generally have knowledge at their disposal, the state apparatus becomes the only path that they must follow in order to reach the high spheres of the social hierarchy and enjoy all its privileges.
>
> From that point onward, the dialectic of social dynamisms between different classes is fully confirmed. The political universe seems to be a veritable arena where classes, fragmentary parts of classes, clans, etc. confront each other with the principle, "to each his turn."[45]

The principle of "to each his turn" has deformed the process of democratization into a *politique du ventre* whereby the different factions of the Lavalas bloc have been literally eating each other to digest the limited fruits of power.[46] As a result, the bloc exploded into multiple *groupuscules,* each seeking complete supremacy and each resorting to the old authoritarian repertoire inherited from the Haitian political habitus. This habitus reflects the historical tendency of most Haitian leaders to look at political power as an indivisible quantity that can be won collectively but that must be kept individually and exercised absolutely. With rare exceptions, Haiti's numerous constitutions, beginning with the very first one promulgated in 1801 under the leadership of Toussaint Louverture,[47] have all ratified the providential authoritarianism of a single all-powerful individual. Toussaint's 1801 charter set the tone for future generations and declared him governor general of the island "for life." While life mandates were not a universal feature of all Haitian constitutions, they shaped political customs and expectations and legitimated the dictatorship of personal rule.[48]

Most Haitian leaders have firmly believed in the messianic nature of their authority and lorded it over *le peuple* with the most acute paternalism. Jean-Jacques Dessalines, the military commander of the rebellious slaves and first ruler of an independent Haiti, nurtured the roots of the patronizing type of personal authoritarianism that Toussaint had implanted. On the very day he was named governor general for life, he warned his compatriots against any form of dissent:

> And you, people. Remember that I sacrificed everything to fly to your defense—my parents, children, fortune, and that I am now rich only by

dint of your freedom; that my name has become anathema to all those peoples desiring slavery, and that the despots and tyrants pronounce my name only to curse the day that I was born; and if you either refuse or accept with reluctance the laws dictated to me for your well-being by the spirit that watches over your destiny, you will deserve the fate of ungrateful people.[49]

It is in this same vein that one must view René Préval's declaration that "nou pran pouvwa, nou pran'l net" [we have taken power, and we will keep it forever].[50] Power cannot be shared; it is the springboard to material well-being and class climbing for the relatively marginalized but educated petite bourgeoisie from whose ranks come most Haitian politicians. The quest for office responds, therefore, to the desire to meet primary needs and ultimately to satisfy the aspirations of becoming bourgeois. Again, Charles's words are worth quoting at length:

[The] desire to get rich and to belong to the dominant class becomes the motivation of every political attitude for many people. It follows that every individual placed at a level that is more or less high in the hierarchy of power thinks only of using that power in order to gather as much money as possible, of living in opulence, and thus displaying his greatness or, better still, his newly acquired status as a "bourgeois." "To each his turn"; his turn to get rich, is the principle that seems to direct administrative action in the upper spheres. This principle, recognized and accepted by all the holders of power, seems to be the very rule of political morality. Thus, throughout the circuitous paths of the political system, there is continual confrontation among all those aspiring to change class. And, in order to succeed, any means is valid: misappropriation of funds, influence peddling, despoiling, etc.[51]

Corruption is thoroughly pervasive; it is the grease that oils the political system and facilitates access to bureaucratic and elected positions. Except for the 1990 ballots that carried Aristide to power, elections have become increasingly predetermined and fraudulent affairs in which those selected by the president's party are virtually assured of entering the ranks of a new aspiring ruling class.[52] While citizens continue to go to the polls, the exercise is a mere facade that poorly masks the grossly deceitful modes of organizing, supervising, and counting the votes. The semblance of democratic rituals and practices characterizing the formal structures of governance has obscured the real sites of power where the dominant actors make critical policies "offstage." It is in this anonymous, opaque, and hidden world that power holders establish the rules of the game, select their cadres, acquire illicit resources, and manipulate their Chimères. In this world political acts are disguised and subvert public pronouncements and images. In a predatory democracy things are simply not what they seem. As the Creole proverb puts it, "Tout sa ou wè, sé pa sa" [everything you see is an illusion].

Those who rule are not necessarily those who have power, and those who have power are not necessarily those who rule. Thus, the supreme executive position of René Préval masked the persisting dominion of Tabarre. As Jean-Claude Jean and Marc Maesschalck explain,

> René Préval is a double, president by default. He has the responsibilities without the power. To the contrary, ex-President Aristide holds the real power, but not the responsibilities. Haiti exists at the present moment in a unique situation of dissociation between the real center of power and the formal sites where it is exercised (the presidency, the position of prime minister, the parliament). In consequence, any attempt to resolve this crisis must take into account this real dissociation between power and responsibility.[53]

The disjunction between reality and appearance is a fundamental facade of predatory democracy. Behind it hides a criminalized zero-sum game of power dominated by intense processes of class formation where factions of the petite bourgeoisie fight for political supremacy, where elected officials at the highest level are controlled by opaque private forces, where elections are held regularly and are usually fraudulent, and where public administrators claim to save the constitution by continuously violating its spirit and its laws. And yet, a predatory democracy is not a completely closed system of power; it offers some space for maneuvering. The opposition and its political parties are not completely silenced, civil society is not extinguished, and a free press remains vocal. There is room for popular struggles portending potential alterations in the nature of the state. In spite of tenuous attachments to democratic practices, many peasant organizations, trade unions, and professional groups have kept their independence and still speak truth to power. Representing a persistent challenge to the hegemonic pretensions of Fanmi Lavalas, these movements make a return to a full dictatorship unlikely. While they cannot guarantee the birth of a functioning polyarchy, they may at least facilitate the transition from predatory to unconsolidated democracy. Thus, in spite of severe social and material constraints stemming from the existing domestic balance of class power and the external patterns of acute dependence, the future of Haitian society is not entirely foreclosed.

In this perspective, democratization can bring about a change of state, even if its integument and the constellation of forces that generated it in the first place make such an outcome unlikely. Democratization can thus open a Pandora's box and go beyond the constraining walls of predatory democracy behind which both material scarcity and the despotic legacy seem destined to confine it. In spite of its critical limitations, democratization does affect the balance of class power; it is not mere sham. When dominant classes cannot contain it, democratization can unleash liberating movements of resistance against enduring forms of exploitation, domination, and privilege. Democratization matters, but it has to be viewed in its constraining historical boundaries. While democratization is generally initiated as a result of popular pressures against an entrenched dictatorship, it is the dictatorship itself—in a compromising alliance with "reformist" political elites—that channels democratization into forms of representation preserving the lingering authoritarian legacy.

Moreover, any significant transformation in the structures of power and property rights faces additional obstacles in poor countries like Haiti because the working class is miniscule and fragile and thus can have only a marginal impact on power holders. In fact, if Barrington Moore's famous bon mot—"no bourgeois, no democracy"—is correct, it necessarily implies its antinomy: "no working class, no democracy."[54] A classical bourgeoisie cannot stand in midair; its successful existence presupposes a working class from which it extracts the economic surplus required for capitalist economic activities. Thus, the debate about whether it is the working class or the bourgeoisie that is responsible for democratic rule is artificial; the two classes are opposite sides of the same coin. Their conflicts and struggles are the very stuff generating the historical compromises from which ultimately results democracy.[55] As Dietrich Rueschemeyer, Evelyne Huber Stephens, and John D. Stephens have argued,

> The chances of democracy . . . must be seen as fundamentally shaped by the balance of class power. It is the struggle between the dominant and subordinate classes over the right to rule that—more than any other factor—puts democracy on the historical agenda and decides its prospects. Capitalist development affects the chances of democracy primarily because it transforms the class structure and changes the balance of power between classes.[56]

In Haiti, however, such balance of power has not crystallized because capitalist development has produced a bourgeoisie and a working class that are both at best utterly small, embryonic, and fragile. Their unreservedly precarious existence explains in part the weak and indeed predatory character of the country's democracy. The very secondary role of the tiny working class in the struggle for democracy has meant that the populist and opportunist tendencies of the petite bourgeoisie have had free rein. In their quest for political supremacy, different factions of the petite bourgeoisie took charge of the democratizing process and marginalized the working class as well as other forces "from below." The subordinate bloc gradually lost its autonomous capacity to pressure power holders. Instead, the burdens of extreme scarcity prevented it from sustaining its efforts and defending its own interests. Exhausted, demoralized, and indeed starving, the bloc fragmented and its strength dissipated. Whatever was left of the bloc became an appendage of other social forces. As Jean and Maesschalck have explained,

> Destabilized at the most profound level of their being by misery, confronted daily with their despairing situation, many militants are unable to invest in long-term construction. Even if they show a desire to do so, they have neither the strength nor the means. From this stems the tendency to lapse into *sterile activism,* to put their efforts into acts that are as dangerous as they are spectacular and with an impact that rarely extends beyond the short term and the ephemeral.[57]

The Haitian case indicates that popular pressures are decisive in the crystallization of the moment of democratization. Unlike the long-term processes of implementation and consolidation, the moment of democratization, however "electrical" and dramatic, is an ephemeral historical event that promises much but offers little by itself. It signals the exit of the dictator and his most immediate cronies and the beginning of a complicated period of political uncertainties. By compelling the dominant classes and middle sectors to opt for democratization, popular pressures and mass mobilizations are the determining force engendering the crisis that provokes the fall of authoritarianism. In the aftermath of the democratizing moment, however, these popular forces gradually lose steam and are eventually co-opted by better organized and financially more independent social forces.

Formerly excluded parties and leaders of the dominant classes and middle sectors begin to reimpose their power, a task facilitated by the material scarcity and political exhaustion facing subordinate groups. Indeed, these emerging *chefs* can literally buy popular support to advance their own strategic interests. Such support derives from the opportunistic response of poor people for access to basic resources such as food, employment, and health; it has little to do with political loyalty.

The relative decline of popular forces weakens the democratic impulses of democratization, which becomes the affair of the dominant classes and the petite bourgeoisie. The tensions and conflicts between dominant classes and working classes that have traditionally resulted in the development and consolidation of liberal democracy have now been displaced by struggles between ascendant and falling groups of the dominant classes and middle sectors. The outcome is the predatory type rather than the liberal form of democracy rooted in the classical struggle between bourgeoisie and proletariat.[58]

Haiti's predatory democracy is thus the result of two fundamental factors embedded on the one hand in the persisting legacy of a dictatorial habitus, and on the other in the fragility and indeed virtual absence of both a productive bourgeoisie and a large working class. These two factors are mutually reinforcing and have tended to generate a perverse dictatorial cycle from which Haitian society has yet to extricate itself. The utter underdevelopment of the bourgeoisie and working class has contributed to the profound backwardness of the economy, which in turn has nurtured *la politique du ventre* and its accompanying authoritarian propensities. This has meant that subordinate classes are busy eking out a miserable existence; they have little time or energy to mobilize as a collective agent bent on democratizing a system that has consistently condemned them to a life of squalor. In the rare historical moments when they do, they soon find themselves exhausted, marginalized, and co-opted into patterns of individualized patronage and clientelism.

Once popular forces are displaced from the strategic and central position of the democratizing game, democratization loses the player who benefits most from democracy itself. To that extent, the democratic project is undermined in the postauthoritarian period by the relative absence of popular forces in the sites of power. On the other hand, while a "maximalist" presence of popular forces at the moment of democratization facilitates and accelerates the exit of the dictatorial bloc, it may well precipitate a restoration of despotism during the early phase of democratic consolidation. Privileged groups may feel threatened by a mobilized mass of poor people making its claim for full citizenship; they may simply abandon their already precarious support for democratic rule, foment a coup, and return to authoritarianism.

In fact, the Haitian case demonstrates that if the coercive balance of power favors dominant classes—as it always tends to do—a maximalist posture of popular forces is likely to generate a military end to democratization. It is only when the army is thoroughly emasculated and/or when dominant and subordinate classes confront each other with roughly equivalent coercive means that real and meaningful democratization becomes possible. The possibility, however, is not overwhelming; an equilibrium of terror may invite a descent into hell, leading to chaos, violence, and even civil war. In addition, the contending parties may miscalculate their own as well as their adversaries' strength and engage in ill-conceived and ill-timed strategies. For instance, blinded by its huge popular support, the Lavalas movement underestimated in 1991 the dominant classes' capacity and determination to use brutal force to preserve existing alignments of power and wealth. The coup that brought down Aristide clearly indicated that while Lavalas had the masses on its side, it lacked the coercive means to carry out its own project or to compel the opposition into submission or compromise. Simply put, the monopoly of violence was still in the hands of the dominant classes and their allies in the military; to that extent, the coup was to be expected.

Democratization is therefore a very constrained phenomenon: dominant classes are committed to it to the degree to which its costs at the moment of its instauration and during the period of its implementation and consolidation are not too high. These classes will halt democratization once they perceive—objectively or in the imaginary—that popular forces challenge the distribution of resources, the structure of ownership, or the acquisition of privilege. Democratization's success is ultimately dependent on establishing a new and more accountable political dispensation that leaves virtually untouched the methods and legal framework governing the production and the appropriation of the economic surplus. To a significant extent, democratization embodies a decisive measure of political containment representing the conservative adjustment of the dominant classes to popular challenges. It symbolizes what I have termed elsewhere a passive revolution—a reconfiguration of, rather than a rupture with, the ancien régime.[59] Like all reconfigurations, however, it may engender unintended outcomes and thus have potential perils for the continued rule of the ruling class.

In making their history, human beings open up surprising alternatives at unexpected moments; they engender a protean politics that occasionally defies the binding structures of anticipated outcomes. This is so because social structures are never fixed. Social structures dialectically create the norms and institutions of their own self-reproduction while simultaneously unleashing conditions of their own potential dissolution and transcendence. Ralph Dahrendorf has argued for the applicability of this dialectical approach on a very wide scale: "The idea of a society which produces in its structure the antagonisms that lead to its modification appears an appropriate model for the analysis of change in general."[60] A real democratization of Haitian society is thus possible even if the existing constellation of forces makes it unlikely. The task of this book is to study the social origins, aspirations, and limitations of this democratization. While past and present are bleak, the future remains relatively undetermined, and thus there exists the faint hope for a thorough transformation of Haiti's political and economic landscape.

Notes

1. Some of the most important writings of the democratization theory include Guiseppe Di Palma, *To Craft Democracies* (Berkeley: University of California Press, 1990); Francis Fukuyama, *The End Of History and the Last Man* (New York: Free Press, 1992); Axel Hadenius, *Democracy and Development* (Cambridge:

Cambridge University Press, 1992); Stephan Haggard and Robert R. Kaufman, *The Political Economy of Democratic Transitions* (Princeton: Princeton University Press, 1995); Samuel Huntington, *The Third Wave* (Norman: University of Oklahoma Press, 1991); Juan Linz, "Transitions to Democracy," *Washington Quarterly* 13, no. 1 (1990): 143–164; Terry Lynn Karl, "Dilemmas of Democratization in Latin America," *Comparative Politics* 23, no. 1 (1990): 1–21; Guillermo O'Donnell and Philippe C. Schmitter, *Transitions from Authoritarian Rule: Tentative Conclusions About Uncertain Democracies* (Baltimore: Johns Hopkins University Press, 1986); Adam Przeworski, *Democracy and the Market* (Cambridge: Cambridge University Press, 1991); Georg Sorensen, *Democracy and Democratization* (Boulder: Westview Press, 1993); Alfred Stepan and Cindy Skach, "Constitutional Frameworks and Democratic Consolidation," *World Politics* 46, no. 1 (October 1993): 1–22. All of these works downplay class and emphasize the role of leadership and elites in the process of democratization. There are, however, a few important exceptions in the literature that privilege class: Dietrich Rueschemeyer, Evelyne Huber Stephens, and John D. Stephens, *Capitalist Development and Democracy* (Chicago: University of Chicago Press, 1992); and Ruth Berins Collier, *Paths Toward Democracy* (Cambridge: Cambridge University Press, 1999), p. 8. It is interesting to note that Guillermo O'Donnell, in his recent book, *Counterpoints* (Notre Dame: University of Notre Dame Press, 1999), autocriticizes his previous work and shows the structural limitations of democratization.

2. Joseph A. Schumpeter, *History of Economic Analysis* (New York: Oxford University Press, 1954), p. 51.

3. Ibid., p. 52.

4. Stephen Horblitt, "Barriers to Nonviolent Conflict Resolution," in Georges A. Fauriol, ed., *Haitian Frustrations: Dilemmas for U.S. Policy* (Washington, D.C.: Center For Strategic and International Studies, 1995), pp. 129–142. In *The Political Economy of Democratic Transitions,* Haggard and Kaufman (p. 173) clearly favor the creation of "broad-based catchall parties" because they tend to "move to the center" and are unlikely to "gravitate toward radical, polarizing solutions or to back strikes, demonstrations, and protests that complicate the ability of government to act."

5. Charles E. Lindblom, *Inquiry and Change* (New Haven: Yale University Press, 1990), pp. 66–67.

6. Brian Loveman, *The Constitution of Tyranny: Regimes of Exception in Spanish America* (Pittsburgh: University of Pittsburgh Press, 1993).

7. Catherine M. Conaghan and James M. Malloy, *Unsettling Statecraft* (Pittsburgh: University of Pittsburgh Press, 1994), p. 221. Summarizing their findings on the emerging democracies of the central Andes, Conaghan and Malloy suggest that these regimes are characterized by a "democratic despotism" (pp. 220–221):

> The marginalization of the legislature; the arrogance and autonomy of the executive branch; the growing disjunction between electoral choice and public policy; the weakness of political parties; the devaluation of "politics" and the entrenchment of economics as the framing discipline of public policy; the forced contraction, through neoliberal policies, of the public sphere (and by extension, the contraction of what may be defined as rights)—all these phenomena constitute important features of these regimes. To focus solely on elections as the defining feature of these regimes misses much of how they operate. Elections are not a problem; the problem with Latin American democracy is what happens after elections. The real deficit within these democracies has to do with the absence of governmental responsiveness and accountability to the public.

8. Michael Crozier, in M. Crozier, Samuel Huntington, and J. Watanuki, *The Crisis of Democracy* (New York: New York University Press, 1975), p. 12.

9. O'Donnell and Schmitter, *Transitions from Authoritarian Rule,* p. 70.

10. Huntington, *The Third Wave,* p. 161.

11. According to the much quoted definition of Linz, "Transitions to Democracy," p. 158,

> [A consolidated democracy] is one in which none of the major political actors, parties, or organized interests, forces, or institutions consider that there is any alternative to democratic processes to gain power, and that no political institution or group has a claim to veto the action of democratically elected decision makers. This does not mean that there are no minorities ready to challenge and question the legitimacy of the democratic process by nondemocratic means. It means, however, that the major actors do not turn to them and they remain politically isolated. To put it simply, democracy must be seen as the "only game in town."

While this definition is simple, almost simplistic, it verges on tautology; it essentially says that democracy is consolidated because the political actors who matter are committed to it. It is difficult to see how it could be otherwise. See also Haggard and Kaufman, *The Political Economy of Democratic Transitions,* pp. 15–16. Samuel Valenzuela, "Democratic Consolidation in Post-Transition Settings," in Scott Mainwaring, Guillermo O'Donnell, and J. Samuel Valenzuela, eds., *The New South American Democracies in Comparative Perspective* (Notre Dame: University of Notre Dame Press, 1992), p. 69, offers a more convincing definition:

> [A] democracy is consolidated when elections following procedures devoid of egregious and deliberate distortions designed to underrepresent systematically a certain segment of opinion are perceived by all significant political forces to be unambiguously the only means to create governments well into the foreseeable future, and when the latter are not subjected to tutelary oversight or constrained by the presence of reserved domains of state policy formulation.

12. Adam Przeworski, "Some Problems in the Study of the Transition to Democracy," in Guillermo O'Donnell, Philippe C. Schmitter, and Laurence Whitehead, eds., *Transitions from Authoritarian Rule: Comparative Perspectives* (Baltimore: Johns Hopkins University Press, 1986), p. 63.

13. Luis Carlos Bresser Pereira, José Maria Maravall, and Adam Przeworski, *Economic Reforms in New Democracies: A Social-Democratic Approach* (Cambridge: Cambridge University Press, 1993).

14. Lindblom, *Inquiry and Change,* p. 89.

15. For instance, in *The Third Wave,* Huntington argues that the "common institutional core" of democratic regimes is the fact that their "principal officers of government are chosen through competitive elections in which the bulk of the population can participate" (p. 109). Moreover, as he acknowledges, "Negotiations and compromises among political elites were at the heart of the democratization processes. The leaders of the key political forces and social groups in society bargained with each other, explicitly or implicitly, and worked out acceptable if not satisfying arrangements for the transition to democracy" (p. 165).

16. James Petras and Morris Morley, *Latin America in the Time of Cholera* (New York: Routledge, 1992), pp. 1–2.

17. William Robinson, *Promoting Polyarchy* (Cambridge: Cambridge University Press, 1996). As Robinson argues (p. 6),

All over the world, the United States is now promoting its version of "democracy" as a way to relieve pressure from subordinate groups for more fundamental political, social and economic change. The impulse to "promote democracy" is the rearrangement of political systems in the peripheral and semi-peripheral zones of the "world system" so as to secure the underlying objective of maintaining essentially undemocratic societies inserted into an unjust international system. The promotion of "low-intensity democracy" is aimed not only at mitigating the social and political tensions produced by elite-based and undemocratic status-quos, but also at suppressing popular and mass aspirations for more thoroughgoing democratization of social life in the twenty-first-century international order. Polyarchy is a structural feature of the emergent global society.

18. World Bank, *Governance and Development* (Washington, D.C.: World Bank, 1992). See also Susan George and Fabrizio Sabelli, *Faith and Credit: The World Bank's Secular Empire* (Boulder: Westview Press, 1994), pp. 142–161.
19. On the notion of "organic intellectuals," see Antonio Gramsci, *Selections from the Prison Notebooks,* edited and translated by Quintin Hoare and Geoffrey Nowell Smith (London: Lawrence and Wishart, 1971). As Colin Leys, *The Rise and Fall of Development Theory* (Bloomington: Indiana University Press, 1996), wrote (p. vii),

The USA is a superpower with imperial interests, a markedly military history and a tradition of intolerance towards the left. These things inevitably influence American political science: the congruence between the standpoint of so much mainstream American political science and US foreign policy (including the neo-liberal reconstruction of the world order in the 1980s) is a significant fact to which attention should be drawn.

20. Robert Cox with Timothy J. Sinclair, *Approaches to World Order* (Cambridge: Cambridge University Press, 1996), pp. 528–529.
21. I borrow the concept of "benignity" from Lindblom, *Inquiry and Change* (p. 201), to convey the idea that conventional social science has a propensity to turn "the everpresent irrationality, coerciveness, inhumanity, and ugliness of many social processes into a picture of benignity."
22. George and Sabelli, *Faith and Credit,* pp. 58–72; see also Bresser Pereira, Maravall, and Przeworski, *Economic Reforms in New Democracies.*
23. Huntington's "least unsatisfactory" solution to what he calls the "torturer problem" is encapsulated in his slogan "Do not prosecute, do not punish, do not forgive, and, above all, do not forget" (*The Third Wave,* p. 231).
24. Berins Collier, *Paths Toward Democracy,* p. 8.
25. Robert Dahl, *A Preface to Economic Democracy* (Cambridge: Polity Press, 1985), p. 60.
26. David Held, *Models of Democracy* (Cambridge: Polity Press, 1987).
27. Ellen Meiksins Wood, *Democracy Against Capitalism* (Cambridge: Cambridge University Press, 1995), p. 235.
28. Moshe Lewin, *The Gorbachev Phenomenon* (Berkeley: University of California Press, 1988), p. 80.
29. Ibid.
30. Not surprisingly, in class-divided Haiti, contending actors have claimed to represent "civil society." While the Initiative de la Société Civile has tended to embody the interests of the dominant classes and received support from powerful international forces, the Société Civile Majoritaire has recently emerged as a rival

organization professing to defend the *moun andeyo.* See "À qui Appartient la 'Société Civile'?" *Haiti Progrès,* June 13–19, 2001.

31. My modifications have been influenced by the writings of Jon Elster and Ralph Miliband. See Jon Elster, *Making Sense of Marx* (Cambridge: Cambridge University Press, 1985), pp. 318–397; Ralph Miliband, *Marxism and Politics* (Oxford: Oxford University Press, 1977).

32. *Lavalas,* the Creole word for flood, symbolizes the loosely structured mass movement of the poor that sought to uproot Duvalierism.

33. The term *grands mangeurs* became very popular during the 1997 carnival. See "Carnaval Grands Mangeurs," *Haïti en Marche,* February 12–18, 1997, pp. 1–8; and *Haïti en Marche,* Feburary 19–25, 1997, p. 12.

34. I use the term "political class" to denote all individuals holding or pursuing political office irrespective of party affiliation or ideological affinity.

35. "Carnaval Grands Mangeurs," p. 8.

36. Pierre Bourdieu, *In Other Words: Essays Towards a Reflexive Sociology* (Stanford: Stanford University Press, 1990), pp. 9, 61, 77.

Gérard Barthélémy, "Le Discours Duvalieriste Après les Duvalier," in Gérard Barthélémy and Christian Girault, eds., *La République Haïtienne* (Paris: Karthala, 1993), p. 180, uses "reflexes" to describe the same phenomenon:

> Il y a d'abord un certain nombre de phénomènes, d'habitudes et de croyances qui appartiennent au comportement politique général, depuis 1804. Ces tendances fortes de la vie politique nationale ne sont l'apanage d'aucune formation en particulier. Il s'agit de comportements profonds, propres à une origine et à une histoire particulières dont l'évolution, à long terme, est en marche bien que de façon très lente: c'est pourquoi nous les désignons sous le terme de "réflexes."

[First, there are a certain number of phenomena, habits, and beliefs that belong to the domain of general political behavior since 1804. These strong tendencies of national political life are not the prerogatives of any education in particular. They are deep behaviors belonging to a particular origin and history of which a long-term evolution is in progress, although at a very slow rate: that is why we refer to them using the term "reflexes."] (Translated by Carrol Coates)

37. Jean-Bertrand Aristide, *Aristide: An Autobiography* (Maryknoll, N.Y.: Orbis, 1993), p. 154.

38. Tabarre is the area in Port-au-Prince where Aristide's private residence is located. The expression has become a code word denoting the real site of Haitian political power.

39. Many key figures who had supported Aristide's election to the presidency and his restoration to power after the military coup of 1991 abandoned and criticized him for his *dérive totalitaire.* Among the most important are Gérard Pierre-Charles, leader of Organisation du Peuple en Lutte (OPL); Evans Paul, leader of the Front National pour le Changement et la Démocratie (FNCD); Micha Gaillard of Kongré Nasyonal Mouvman Demokratik (KONAKOM); Chavannes Jean-Baptiste, head of the Mouvement des Paysans de Papaye (MPP); Hervé Denis, a former prime minister designate; Jean Casimir, a former Aristide ambassador to the United States; and Paul Déjean, a cabinet member in Aristide's own government. Raoul Peck, a former minister of culture in the Préval administration, condemned what he perceived to be Aristide's corruption and authoritarianism in a biting book that captures the views of many erstwhile comrades of "Titid": *Monsieur le Ministre . . . Jusqu'au Bout de la Patience* (Port-au-Prince: Éditions Velvet, 1999). A critical but less vitriolic analysis of Aristide's politics and style can be found in an important

book by Robert Malval, who was Aristide's prime minister during his years in exile in Washington: *L'Année de Toutes les Duperies* (Port-au-Prince: Éditions Regain, 1996).

40. U.S. officials estimate that in 2000 over 15 percent of all the cocaine consumed in the United States transited through Haiti. See *New York Times,* October 27, 1998; and July 30, 2000.

41. Anthony V. Catanese, *Haitians: Migration and Diaspora* (Boulder: Westview Press, 1999), pp. 113–120. According to Catanese, international remittances to Haiti amounted to 10 to 15 percent of the nation's gross domestic product (GDP) (p. 118). A more recent estimate by the Multilateral Investment Fund puts the level of remittances at 17 percent of the GDP (see "Migrants Spur Growth in Remittances," *Financial Times,* May 16, 2001).

42. *Chimères* and *Zinglendos* are Creole words used to describe violent and intimidating gangs. "Zinglendos" represents the new type of criminals who have emerged in the post-Duvalier period. The Zinglendos tend to be organized in armed gangs bent on the making of easy money through robberies of all kinds and drug trafficking. Their methods are extremely brutal, varying from intimidation to murder. The danger is that the Zinglendos will increase their power by becoming the armed wings of different political parties and of drug lords.

Chimères, on the other hand, have been associated with groups of lumpen connected to Aristide's Fanmi Lavalas party; their function is to menace the opposition into silence. A senior member of Fanmi Lavalas told me, however, that he first encountered the Chimères in 1997 when he was campaigning in Cité Soleil, the largest slum of Port-au-Prince. He was informed by Lavalasian popular organizations that he could campaign in the Cité only if he was prepared to negotiate with the Chimères. Initially then, the Chimères seem to have enjoyed some autonomy from Lavalas. It is clear, nonetheless, that Lavalas had a privileged negotiating position with them. The Chimères would simply oppose the entrance of anti-Aristide forces into what they considered their "territory." The Chimères are thus a political entity associated with Lavalas; Zinglendos, on the other hand, seem to be criminal elements linked to the drug trade and the old Duvalierist repressive security apparatus. Apparently, however, the distinction between the two groups is gradually vanishing. See Jean-Michel Caroit, "En Toute Impunité les Chimères Font Régner la Terreur en Haïti," *Le Monde,* April 11, 2000, p. 4.

43. Philippe C. Schmitter, "Transitology: The Science or the Art of Democratization?" in Joseph S. Tulcin with Bernice Romero, eds., *The Consolidation of Democracy in Latin America* (Boulder: Lynne Rienner, 1995), p. 16.

44. This is not to say that privileged classes enjoy this situation; on the contrary, they would prefer to have an efficient and rational police force capable of imposing order on society. The failure of state power has, however, compelled these classes into spending enormous resources for their private safety. The pervasive presence of security services is symptomatic of the dominant classes' incapacity to impose their hegemony; it is also the simple reflection of the inevitable violence resulting from the dichotomic social structure dividing the Haitian population into a huge majority condemned to a life of massive destitution and a tiny minority enjoying the benefits of ostentatious consumption.

45. Etzer Charles, *Le Pouvoir Politique en Haïti de 1957 à Nos Jours* (Paris: Karthala, 1994), p. 24. Translated from the original French by Carrol Coates:

> Le sous-développement dont souffre Haïti . . . a transformé les appareils du système politique en un véritable champ d'action où se retrouvent les élites de la petite

bourgeoisie, en quête de fortune et d'ascension sociale. Pour ces élites disposant généralement du savoir, l'appareil d'État devient le seul chemin par où elles doivent passer pour parvenir aux hautes sphères de la hiérarchie sociale et jouir de tous les privilèges.

Dès lors, la dialectique des dynamismes sociaux entre classes différentes s'affirme pleinement. L'univers politique apparaît comme une véritable arène où s'affrontent les classes, les fractions de classe, les clans, etc., avec pour principe: "à chacun son tour."

46. Jean François Bayart, *L'État en Afrique: La Politique du Ventre* (Paris: Fayard, 1989); the book was translated into English as *The State in Africa: The Politics of the Belly* (New York: Longman, 1993). Bayart's definition of the politics of the belly characterizing postcolonial Africa fits well with Haitian realities (p. xviii):

It refers chiefly to the food shortages which are still so much part of life in Africa. Getting food is often a problem, a difficulty and a worry. Yet, very often, the term "eating" conveys desires and practices far removed from gastronomy. Above all, it applies to the idea of accumulation, opening up possibilities of social mobility and enabling the holder of power to "set himself up." Women are never very far from the scenario. . . . The politics of the belly are also the politics of intimate liaisons, and mistresses are one of the cogs in the wheel of the postcolonial State. "Belly" also of course refers to corpulence—fashionable in men of power. It refers also to nepotism which is still very much a social reality with considerable political consequences. And, finally, in a rather more sinister way, it refers to the localization of forces of the invisible, control over which is essential for the conquest and exercise of power.

47. Louis Joseph Janvier, *Les Constitutions d'Haïti (1801-1885)* (Paris: C. Marpon and E. Flammarion, 1886), pp. 1–25.

48. Claude Moïse, *Constitutions et Luttes de Pouvoir en Haïti,* Vol. 1, *La Faillite des Classes Dirigeantes (1804-1915)* (Montreal: CIDIHCA, 1988; 1990); *Constitutions et Luttes de Pouvoir en Haïti,* Vol. 2, *De l'Occupation Etrangère à la Dictature Macoute (1915-1987)* (Montreal: CIDIHCA, 1990); *Une Constitution dans la Tourmente* (Montreal: Éditions Images, 1994).

49. As cited in Moïse, *Constitutions et Luttes de Pouvoir en Haïti,* Vol. 1, p. 30. Translated from the original French by Carrol Coates:

Et toi peuple. . . . Rappelle-toi que j'ai tout sacrifié pour voler à ta défense, parents, enfants, fortune, et que maintenant je ne suis riche que de ta liberté; que mon nom est devenu en horreur à tous les peuples qui veulent l'esclavage, et que les despotes et les tyrans ne le prononcent qu'en maudissant le jour qui m'a vu naître; et si jamais tu refusais ou recevais en murmurant les lois que le génie qui veille à tes destinées me dictera pour ton bonheur tu mériteras le sort des peuples ingrats.

50. Author's translation; as quoted in Hervé Denis, "Pour que Gagne Haïti," *Haiti Online,* September 5, 2000; see also "René Préval: Lavalas Pran Pouvwa, li Pran'l net," *Le Matin* (Port-au-Prince), August 30, 2000.

51. Charles, *Le Pouvoir Politique en Haïti de 1957 à Nos Jours,* p. 27. Translated from the original French by Carrol Coates:

[Le] désir de s'enrichir et d'appartenir à la classe dominante devient pour beaucoup de gens le mobile de toute attitude politique. Il s'ensuit alors que tout individu placé a un niveau plus ou moins élevé de la hiérarchie du pouvoir ne pense qu'à utiliser ce dernier pour amasser le plus d'argent possible, vivre dans l'opulence et manifester ainsi sa grandeur, ou mieux, sa nouvelle situation de "bourgeois." "À chacun son tour," son tour de s'enrichir, tel est le principe qui semble guider l'action administrative dans les hautes sphères. Ce principe, reconnu et admis par l'ensemble des dirigeants, semble être même une régle de la morale politique. Aussi à travers tous les circuits du système politique, c'est l'affrontement continuel entre ceux qui aspirent à un transfert de classe. Et pour y parvenir, tous les moyens sont bons: concussion, traffic d'influence, spoliation, etc.

52. Henry F. Carey, "Electoral Observation and Democratization in Haiti," in Kevin J. Middlebrook, ed., *Electoral Observation and Democratic Transitions in Latin America* (San Diego: Center for U.S.-Mexican Studies, 1998), pp. 141–166. As Carey put it, "Marx's dictum about history repeating itself seems to apply to foreign electoral observation in Haiti: the 1987 election massacres were a tragedy, while the 1990–91, 1995, and 1997 elections were a farce."

53. Jean-Claude Jean and Marc Maesschalck, *Transition Politique en Haïti* (Paris: L'Harmattan, 1999), p. 110. Translated from the original French by Carrol Coates:

René Préval est un président de *doublure,* un président par défaut. Il a les responsabilités, mais pas le pouvoir. A l'inverse, l'ex-président Aristide détient le pouvoir réel, mais il n'a pas les responsabilités. Haïti vit à l'heure actuelle une situation singulière de dissociation entre le centre réel du pouvoir et ses lieux formels d'exercise (présidence, primature, parlement). Par conséquent, toute tentative de résolution de cette crise doit tenir compte de cette dissociation de fait entre pouvoir et responsabilité.

54. Barrington Moore Jr., *Social Origins of Dictatorship and Democracy* (Boston: Beacon Press, 1966), p. 418.

55. Miliband, *Marxism and Politics,* pp. 86–89.

56. Rueschemeyer, Huber Stephens, and Stephens, *Capitalist Development and Democracy,* p. 47.

57. Jean and Maesschalck, *Transition Politique en Haïti,* p. 84. Translated from original French by Carrol Coates:

Déstabilisés au plus profond de leur être par la misère, confrontés quotidiennement au désespoir de leur situation, beaucoup de militants ne sont pas en mesure d'investir dans la construction du long terme. Même s'ils en manifestent le désir, ils n'en ont ni la force ni les moyens. D'où la tendance à verser dans *l'activisme stérile,* à s'investir dans des actions aussi dangereuses que spectaculaires, dont l'impact dépasse rarement le court terme et l'éphémère.

58. Moore, *Social Origins of Dictatorship and Democracy;* see also Miliband, *Marxism and Politics.*

59. Robert Fatton Jr., *The Making of a Liberal Democracy: Senegal's Passive Revolution, 1975–1985* (Boulder: Lynne Rienner, 1987).

60. Ralph Dahrendorf, *Class and Class Conflict in Industrial Society* (Stanford: Stanford University Press, 1959), pp. 125–126.

2

Class, State, and Civil Society in Haiti

The Predatory State and the Rise of Civil Society

The Haitian state has historically represented the paradigmatic predatory state.[1] Constituting the "agency of a group or class," the predatory state, as Douglas North has argued, functions primarily

> to extract income from the rest of the constituents in the interest of that group or class. [It enforces] a set of property rights that maximize the revenue of the group in power, regardless of its impact on the wealth of the society as a whole ... [and] regardless of its effects upon efficiency.[2]

The predatory state is thus a despotic structure of power that preys on its citizens without giving much in return; its total lack of accountability suppresses even the murmurs of democracy. Civil society as well as political society are forced underground; they inhabit what James Scott has called the "infrapolitical" world.[3] This is the "unobtrusive realm of political struggle ... [where no] ... public claims are made, no open symbolic lines are drawn. All political actions take forms that are designed to obscure their intentions or to take cover behind an apparent meaning."[4]

Until the fall of Jean-Claude Duvalier's dictatorship in 1986, the predatory character of the Haitian state inhibited the development of a democratic culture and compelled it into remaining a "hidden transcript." Civil society and subordinate classes were "backstage" and expressed only in coded words their outrage at the official justice and authority of those lording it over them. The fall of the dictatorship, however, indicated that subordinates hitherto quiet had finally mustered the means, the resources, and the courage to break their silence. They exploded onto the public stage as a collective historical actor in one of "those rare moments of political electricity when, often for the first time in history, the hidden transcript is spoken directly and publicly in the teeth of power."[5]

The marginalized masses—the *moun andeyo*—were finally demanding their humanity.[6] This demand differentiated the uprising against Duvalier from the numerous moments of popular wrath that have characterized Haitian history.[7] In other words, while the revolt of the masses is certainly not a new phenomenon and is indeed a recurring event in the turbulent politics of the island, the *moun andeyo's* persistent call for a recognition of their dignity as human beings constitutes a rupture with the past. Having been excluded from the national community, the *moun andeyo* gained their voices; no longer silent, they began to claim their rights to be full citizens. Their struggles for a political, moral, and cultural presence are well encapsulated in the *"tout moun se moun"* slogan made popular by Aristide.[8] The idea that every human being was indeed a human being who deserved respect represented a revolutionary awakening; it challenged the utterly hierarchical fabric of Haitian society.

Tout moun se moun exploded on the political stage and signaled the vocal awakening of those who had hitherto been excluded from the political, social, and economic game. As Franklin Midy explains,

> By regaining their freedom of political speech and their right to answer, those who were excluded in Haiti regained their humanity and their citizenship; they became historical actors and the subjects of History. Moreover, they broke the monopoly of speech held by "the elite" up to that time and that of power over the right to speak, a monopoly meaning that the "chief's" word, or that of the "authorities," could not be gainsaid, thus guaranteeing their monopoly over power. There was a subversion of the relationship of unilateral and unidirectional communication, which was a relationship of power, a relationship of subordination.[9]

Breaking the silence acquired the potency of open revolt and soon became the *déchoukaj*, the attempted popular uprooting of Duvalierism and Duvalierists.[10] The confrontation between state and civil society, rulers and ruled, was no longer confined to the subordinates' "infrapolitics"; it became a very public expression of defiance to those in power. Haitian civil society awakened from the experience of "state terror," and the public declaration of its "hidden transcripts" symbolized its transformation into an effective political force.

In this vein, the Haitian process of democratization reflected civil society's *débordement* of the state. By *débordement* I mean the capacity of civil society to defy and ultimately overwhelm the predatory state and its *projet disciplinaire* through illegal mass political defiance and protest.[11] *Débordement* does not, however, entail a necessary transformation of the state; ruling classes can contain it and limit its impact to a mere change of regime. Moreover, internecine conflicts can fragment the antiauthoritarian coalition into small and opportunistic coteries of self-seeking "big men." In short, civil society's *débordement* of the state is synonymous neither with revolution nor democracy. While it may unleash an uncertain democratization, it is unlikely to generate the profound transformation of the state. Thus, civil society is a potentially liberating factor in any political calculus; but it is not always civil, let alone progressive. It can be quite uncivil; it is replete with antinomies. Embedded in the coercive social discipline of the market, civil society is virtually bound to come to the defense and promotion of private rights and sectional claims.

In spite of a strong popular basis, Haitian civil society has remained since Duvalier's fall the preserve of middle and privileged classes whose organizations—rooted in external sources of power and finance—have transformed the country into the République des Organisations Nongouvernementales (ONGs) Rather than constituting a coherent social project, Haitian civil society has tended to embody a disorganized plurality of mutually exclusive projects that are not necessarily democratic. As a plural realm, it broadly comprises three different blocs or spaces articulating respectively the interests of (1) the neo-Duvalierist authoritarian coalition, (2) the neoliberal reformist bloc, and (3) the populist Lavalasian sectors.[12]

These blocs are not frozen entities; they are internally fragmented, and members of each can move from one to the other. In fact, a strong political opportunism has marked the history of these three blocs, and there is an astonishing circulation of leaders, class factions, and parties from one sector to another. Dramatic about-faces reflecting very sudden changes of allegiance are common among the political elites and class groupings. Defection and expulsion from "political families" as well as reintegration and co-optation into them are prime characteristics of the conflictive nature of Haitian civil society. For instance, while the "old" ruling class and reactionary segments of the "possessing" class[13] have been the basis of the neo-Duvalierist coalition, and although they supported wholeheartedly the coup of 1991, some of their key figures gradually made their peace with Aristide once he returned to power.[14] Similarly, the "reformists" of the "possessing class," who had initially backed the Lavalas movement, turned their backs on the president and his successor, René Préval, fearing a lapse into a new dictatorship. In addition, the lumpen, which had served as the *macoutiste*[15] foundation of the Duvalier dictatorship and the "attachés" of the Cédras junta, became the Zinglendos of criminal bands and the Chimères of an increasingly militarized Lavalas. Different factions of social classes had thus taken on different and contradictory positions depending on how distinct historical conjunctures affected their immediate interests. Ideological principles and loyalties were hesitant, ephemeral, and ultimately irrelevant in the political struggle. What mattered was how to be proximate to, and stay in the sites of, state power.

This tactical flux in allegiances explains why after brutally annulling the 1987 elections, General Namphy's military junta was able to enter into a short-lived pact with the reformist Leslie Manigat. The pact led to Manigat's fraudulent election as president in January 1988. A few months later, Manigat's attempts at cleaning up the military provoked his overthrow.[16] Similarly, what President Aristide called a "marriage" between Lavalas and the army broke up with the coup of September 1991. The divorce had the clear signature of General Raoul Cédras, Aristide's own hand-picked chief of staff.

In addition, before the coup, the united front of the left, which had catapulted Aristide to the presidency in 1990, fragmented under the pressures and temptations of power. In the weeks preceding Aristide's overthrow, certain key figures of the Lavalas alliance defected to join the opposition. For example, Senator Thomas Eddy Dupiton, an important leader of the Front National pour le Changement et la Démocratie (FNCD), distanced himself from the democratic forces and began flirting with the neo-Duvalierists.[17] In the aftermath of the coup, Dupiton and other erstwhile figures of the Lavalas movement cemented an opportunistic promilitary alliance with neo-Duvalierist and neoreformist blocs. The alliance facilitated the junta's installing as prime minister neoreformists Jean-Jacques Honorat and then Marc Bazin, who were respectively determined to either prevent altogether Aristide's return or to negotiate his restoration as an utterly emasculated president. Such pacts between seemingly antagonistic groups and personalities betray the profound political opportunism of Haiti's political class.

Little changed when Aristide returned to power in October 1994; in fact, new and even more unnatural partnerships have crystallized. The Organisation Politique Lavalas (OPL), which regrouped most factions of the Lavalas movement in a successful but controversial effort to win the parliamentary elections of 1995, soon split into two major camps. Aristide's Fanmi Lavalas and Gérard Pierre-Charles's Organisation du Peuple en Lutte both began to cooperate with former members of the military as well as with conservative oligarchic families and neo-Duvalierist forces.

In their intense competition to remain or conquer state power, the neo-Duvalierist, neoliberal, and Lavalasian blocs have all felt compelled to engage in continuous and unprincipled struggles, negotiations, and compromises. They have tended to promote their narrow short-term interests at the expense of any long-term program of social change. Their commitment to democratic practice has been hesitant—more a means to obtain power than an end in itself. While the neo-Duvalierist and neoliberal blocs tended to have more material resources and organizational skills, they lacked the power of numbers and the aura of democratic legitimacy characterizing the poorly structured and fragmented Lavalas movement. Not surprisingly, in their efforts to palliate their respective deficiencies, the blocs sought to cement the most surprising alliances.

By generally reflecting the lopsided balance of class, racial, and gender power, the agencies of civil society inevitably privileged the privileged and marginalized the marginalized. Civil society's plurality does not entail an automatic and equal representation of the whole polity. Civil society is not an all-encompassing movement of popular empowerment and economic change. It is simply not a democratic deus ex machina equalizing life chances and opportunities; crippled by material limitations and class impairments it should not be confused with a "civic community." The latter, as Robert Putnam defines it, is "marked by an active, public-spirited citizenry, by egalitarian political relations, by a social fabric of trust and cooperation. . . . Citizens in a civic community, though not selfless saints, regard the public domain as more than a battle-ground for pursuing personal interest."[18]

It is clear, however, that the seeds of the civic community cannot be planted without a dense civil society regrouping a vast network of associational life. Moreover, if these seeds are to flourish in Haiti, they must privilege the Lavalasian civil society—the popular civil society of the subordinates. Born of the difficult struggles against the Duvalier dictatorship, and expressing a sense of communal defense against the abuses of state power, popular civil society has certain social-democratic impulses, which are almost always expressed in a contradictory and demagogic populism.

Notwithstanding such impulses, the Lavalasian cadres realized once they captured power that the harsh realities of the world and domestic economies would force them into accepting the necessity of both restoring the fiscal health of the state and introducing market reforms.[19] Lavalas, and Aristide in particular, rejected, however, what Adam Przeworski and his colleagues have described as the "technocratic style of policy making [that] weakens nascent democratic institutions." They attempted with varying degrees of success to emphasize the fact that "without a social policy that protect[ed] at least those whose subsistence [was] threatened by the reforms, the political conditions for the continuation of reforms [would] become eroded."[20]

Upon seizing power, Lavalasian civil society called for the establishment of three different types of citizenship resembling closely those identified by T. H. Marshall more than forty years ago.[21] First, the movement demanded political citizenship—"the right to participate in the exercise of political power." Second, it sought civil citizenship—"the rights necessary for individual freedom." And finally, it claimed social citizenship—"the right to a modicum of economic welfare and security [and the] right to share to the full in the social heritage and to live the life of a civilized being according to the standards prevailing in society."[22]

Moreover, Lavalas injected into Marshall's idea of citizenship a populist vision of participatory democracy transcending mere parliamentarism and privileging initiatives "from below." It is true that in practice this meant often a form of "mob rule" that intimidated not only enemies but also potential allies. At its best, however, it aspired to suppress the obdurate class impairments of the minimal liberal state. It was an attempt, albeit clumsy and demagogic, to articulate the democratic collective rights of traditionally marginalized classes. In fact, historically, these classes have been the most forceful promoter, defender, and supporter of democracy, not because of some special vocation or superior moral qualities, but rather because they have a vested interest in democratic rule. History has taught them the simple lesson that without such rule, they will be consistently excluded from political participation; absent democracy, they will be condemned to suffer the most acute moral indignities and material deprivations that such exclusion entails.

Haiti's democratic transition qua change of regime would have never materialized without the protests, the strikes, and the energy of the Lavalasian movement. The movement represented the determinant social force that compelled predatory rulers into accepting pacts to form a politically more accountable regime and ultimately to organize free elections. This is not to say that the Lavalas subordinate classes are incapable of undemocratic and indeed despotic, cruel behavior; on the contrary, the incidence of violence by and against the lumpen poor and the practice of necklacing show that they do engage in atrocities and can be mobilized for the worst kind of brutality. It is also true that their poverty invites unpredictability; the highest bidder can buy them for noble as well as despicable acts. After all, for mere pittances, Macoutes[23] perpetrated savageries against their own brothers and sisters of the subordinate classes.[24] As Amy Wilentz put it,

> [The] lumpen are traditionally fickle. At moments of great historical change they may support you for your ideas, for your words. But many among them can be bought. In times of plenty they are loyal, but when was the last time Haiti had experienced a time of plenty? And in times of penury their support can be and often is purchased by the highest bidder— and for very little. For a dollar they'll demonstrate. For twenty, maybe less, they'll torture, they'll burn, they'll kill, they'll assassinate.[25]

Thus, the participation of subordinate classes in savage moments of cruelty indicates clearly that they have no spontaneous or necessary democratic vocation. They are more interested in democracy than any other class, because they have more to gain from it; but they can hardly claim a higher morality. They simply do not have the monopoly on virtue.

Moreover, subordinate classes carry the burden of their political habitus: they believe in the emancipatory powers of a providential, messianic leader. It is a belief that has undermined political organization and parties.

It facilitates the rise of "patrons" and demagogues and obliterates the need for institutional structures of governability. "One-manism" becomes the dangerous norm. It is not surprising, therefore, that given his humble roots, fiery homilies against Duvalierism, and brave struggle against injustice, Jean-Bertrand came to symbolize the prophet whom God entrusted with leading his people to rise against their oppressors. Bypassing forms of collective accountability and decisionmaking, Aristide condensed unto himself whatever transformative project the Lavalasian bloc may have had.

Faced with the prospects of defeat in the presidential elections of 1990, the bloc abandoned the long-term strategy of building a coherent mass-popular party, dumped its lackluster candidate, and opted for the charismatic anti-Duvalierism personified by Aristide.[26] While this choice ensured victory at the polls, Lavalas became so closely identified with Aristide that it lost its autonomy. By idealizing him as the savior, the movement nurtured unintentionally the cult of his personality and ultimately imparted to him supernatural powers. Aristide's courageous struggle against Duvalierism and his ability to survive numerous attempts on his life gave him an aura of mystical invincibility and a unique popular legitimacy.[27] In addition, Aristide was a man of the people: he was born into the peasantry, he knew the vicissitudes and hardships of poverty, and his ascension to the clergy transformed him into the voice of the poor. He came to symbolize the fight against *macoutisme* and the embodiment of popular aspirations. The main slogan of his presidential campaign unambiguously stated, "Titid ak nou, nou se Lavalas" [together with Titid, together we are Lavalas]. Aristide was the prophet as well as the prince. He was indeed Lavalas.[28]

This personification of Lavalas had its dangers; it contained the seeds of a possible new *dérive totalitaire* (drift toward totalitarianism). Aristide could easily assume a presidential monarchism bent on suppressing any alternative, independent power. As Jean and Maesschalck have argued,

> Even if "Lavalas" is a popular phenomenon, the "source" of the tendency resides in a personal initiative founded on "charismatico-religious" leadership. Despite its complexity and contradictions, the entire movement is built on one person, the only one capable of giving it impetus and possibly a new start. There is thus a relationship of complete dependence with respect to the leader. But the latter engages in antiorganizational practices that have already been recognized: among his entourage, no group has been able to assume an autonomous status and to develop freely. This leader spontaneously opposes any form of control over his power. His action is stimulating for individuals and can produce mass effects, but it has a destructuring effect on a group striving to form and to organize on an objective basis. . . .
>
> This religious relationship with the leader has a wait-and-see attitude with relationships based on confidence and any questioning of leaders, autonomy of those acting, and critical conscience being perceived as

treachery. The priest-president has neutralized the development of enlightened political judgment among the masses. He has transformed a demanding people into a well-behaved mass trusting in the occurrence of miracles.[29]

Thus, the personalization of power has gravely undermined the coher-
ence, independence, and organizational drive of the Lavalas movement.
Paradoxically, the emergence of Aristide as the messianic leader has emasculated the transformative potential of subordinate classes who are now a
disorganized mass awaiting personal salvation. This creates a serious danger, because a meaningful democracy is impossible without strong institutions that have precedence over any individual leader. In fact, in Haiti as
elsewhere, democratic accountability depends on political parties and other
associations privileging the mobilization and organization of subordinate
classes. Clearly, accountability can be established neither on the basis of
these classes' occasional public eruption at election time nor on their exclusion from the sites of power.

Subordinate classes must be the prime agent of any democratic alternative; they are, by far, the largest and most exploited social group. It is true
that class does not exhaust the multiplicity of possible forms of individual
identity and that it does not constitute the only exploited collective agent.
In Haiti, race and gender have also historically represented identities of
oppressed categories. Class represents, however, the only agency capable
of uniting the disparate interests of the marginalized. Moreover, subordinate classes, in spite of their uncertainties, remain the group most objectively committed to the realization of democracy because of their productive relations and life experiences.[30] Of all social actors, as Dietrich
Rueschemeyer, Evelyne Huber Stephens, and John D. Stephens have
argued, it is the subordinate classes, and in particular the working class,
that have the most interest in the expansion and preservation of democratic
practice.[31]

The problem, however, is that in a poor and nonindustrialized country
like Haiti, the working class is virtually nonexistent. Representing only 9
percent of the labor force, the working class numbers fewer than 200,000
people out of a total population of over 7 million inhabitants.[32] Mostly concentrated in Port-au-Prince, the working class is organized in three main
unions: the Centrale Autonome des Travailleurs Haïtiens (CATH), the
Fédération des Ouvriers Syndiqués (FOS), and the Confédération des
Travailleurs Haïtiens (CTH). CATH, FOS, and CTH claim to have respectively 176,000, 200,000, and 3,000 members; the vast majority, however,
are peasants.[33] While the working class knows that it needs democracy to
survive and improve its conditions, its small size and ideological divisions
have significantly limited its impact on the process of democratization. In

turn, these limitations have contributed to both debilitating democratization itself and generating the conditions for predatory democracy. To put it bluntly, democracy is impossible without the empowerment of subordinate classes, in particular the working class.

Neither predatory rulers of the neo-Duvalierist bloc, nor "reformist" members of the dominant classes, nor middle sectors of the petite bourgeoisie have ever favored such empowerment; subordinate classes have had to wrest it from them. At best, the neo-Duvalierist bloc tolerated liberalization as a means of containing democratization, which was ultimately forced on them by Lavalas. Liberalization, as Samuel Huntington has remarked, "is the partial opening of an authoritarian system short of choosing governmental leaders through freely competitive elections."[34] While it falls short of full-scale democratization, which entails at a minimum the replacement of a dictatorial regime by a government "selected in a free, open, and fair election," it can engender a series of unexpected political consequences.[35] Liberalization encompasses more than just a "partial opening"; it is both an expansion of individual and group rights and the curbing of arbitrary power.[36] These processes have, however, a very uncertain trajectory; the full journey to democratization can be halted at any moment by the still powerful dictatorial coalition.

In this sense, the fall of Jean-Claude Duvalier did not imply a necessary "extrication" from authoritarianism;[37] the defeat of the dictatorship was not an inevitable guarantee of a successful democratization; democratization failed miserably in 1987 and 1991 when Haitian society fell into the abyss of electoral violence and military coups. The collapse of the Duvalier tyranny and the process of liberalization that it triggered unleashed pent-up centrifugal forces and degenerated into civil strife, criminal violence, personalistic confrontations, and ultimately the brutal coup of 1991. The Haitian experience indicates clearly that in the absence of a massive foreign military intervention, the fear of the ugly realities of a hellish war of all against all does not compel political actors into accepting democratizing pacts "satisficing" the interests of everyone without "maximizing" those of any.[38] Hence, liberalization need not terminate in democratization and a change of regime, let alone a transformation of the state. It creates uncertainty.

Democratic Uncertainty and the Balance of Class Power

Since the fall of Duvalier in 1986, Haitian liberalization has navigated between the Scylla of unsettling and unpredictable democratic outcomes and the Charybdis of coups and violent chaos. The uncertainties of democratic elections with their potential to upset power holders caused the brutal putschism of neo-Duvalierist forces opposing the implantation of more accountable forms of governance. As Alex Dupuy has pointed out,

> Haiti never had democratic regimes precisely because the most important political forces—the military, the prebendary state bourgeoisie, and the private sector bourgeoisie—always believed that they had more to gain under a dictatorship and more to lose under a democracy. The latter would inevitably have meant competition for public office and the right to rule legitimately. A democracy would also have raised issues of the effectiveness of government, public accountability, fairness, justice, and equality—all or any one of which would have threatened the interests of the beneficiaries of the prebendary state system. . . . [The] likelihood of a successful transition to democracy in Haiti, even to a democratic government that would seek to preserve the interests of the powerful and propertied elites, was very remote. This was so if only because democracies, no matter how conservative and repressive they may be, are unpredictable: They may create opportunities for social forces that stand to benefit more from such a regime to advance their interests and challenge established privileges.[39]

In Haiti, the dominant class ultimately feared the regulated uncertainties of constitutionalism; it realized that in free and fair elections it might surrender its immediate control of the state apparatus to representatives of popular classes and/or a hitherto marginalized segment of the petite bourgeoisie. The island's dominant class is composed of a ruling class proper—a class that controls the state apparatus to enrich itself through prebendary gains—and a "possessing" class that accumulates wealth mainly through comprador activities. By possessing class, I imply the French concept of *classe possédante*, a class that has accumulated wealth through private ventures and independently of direct state predations.[40] In Haiti, mulattoes and "Arabs," two groups whose racial heritage and complexion make them unlikely political rulers, have dominated this class. As Etzer Charles points out,

> [The possessing class] is by and large a bourgeoisie of foreign origins, coming from different places, particularly from the U.S.A., Italy, Lebanon, Syria, etc. A number of present-day bourgeois—almost all of them, in fact—arrived in the country penniless and have managed to amass capital and thereby become a dominant class, thanks to their dynamism.[41]

To pursue its extractive practices, however, the possessing class is compelled to buy protection from the ruling class.[42] Made up of heterogeneous groups with an unlikely capacity to control effectively the commanding heights of the state, the possessing class exhibits conjunctural patterns of servility toward the ruling class. Such servility is rooted in the "alien" nature of the possessing class, whose mulatto and "Arab" origins preclude it from direct control of the state apparatus and force it into making large "donations" to political power holders. For instance, François Duvalier was known to have extorted money from the possessing families in exchange for their personal freedom and their continued economic activities. Similarly, the coup that overthrew Aristide was financed by many of these same families.[43] Charles describes well the possessing class's servility:

> What particularly characterized the situation of the business bourgeoisie with respect to those in power was its silence or political powerlessness, an expression of real submission to the group in power. For (almost) the entire period [of Duvalier], this bourgeoisie suffered various fiscal measures without demonstrating the least opposition. Blackmail, persecution, and other means of pressure were often used by authorities to obtain money from members of the bourgeoisie. The latter experience a state of domination that, even as it harms their direct interests, leads them by that very phenomenon to seek the protection of the wielders of power.[44]

Not surprisingly, in an attempt to minimize its insecurity and the costs of its dependence on the ruling class, the possessing class has privileged international cultural and financial linkages. Always connected to the outside world through flights of capital and ownership of foreign properties, the possessing class is a class in "transit" in Haiti. While it can and does play its exit option in times of emergency, its status is one of acute dependence on the Haitian ruling class.

Since the ascendancy of François Duvalier in 1957, the ruling class has been composed of ever changing segments of the black petite bourgeoisie; whichever segment of it was on top, however, managed to monopolize the coercive means of power. Thus, what the ruling class lacked in institutional stability and homogeneity was compensated for by its control and exercise of brutal force. The ruling class's systematic practice of extortion rests on this control and willingness to use naked violence. For the ruling class, politics is the means of material appropriation. Charles writes,

> In fact, their power and their wealth do not repose on possession of the means of production, but on their position and their activities within the political arena. Their ability to remain, or not, within the circle of the dominant class depends on the evolution of the game or of the political struggle.[45]

Both the possessing and ruling classes have no social project, except the day-to-day struggle of keeping themselves in positions of power, wealth, and prestige. Having neither a national vision nor a coherent ideology, their time horizon never goes beyond the immediate short term. Ruling and possessing classes are not always in alliance; whatever unity they achieve is rooted in an opportunistic convergence of interests. They form an uneasy partnership in which each has its own sphere of concerns, but this partnership tends to coalesce when faced by a challenge from below.[46]

Not surprisingly, the dominant class opposed the overwhelming victory of Jean-Bertrand Aristide in the 1991 presidential elections because it marked the ascendancy of Lavalas and the potential political transformation of the status quo. Fearing such transformation and viscerally opposed to everything that Aristide represented, the dominant class abandoned any pretense of constitutionalism to support the military coup that overthrew the Lavalas government in September 1991. The coup indicated that the equilibrium of forces had not been established. The dominant class could depend on the ultimate power of the coercive apparatus of the state to block what it perceived to be a significant threat to its vital interests. Indeed, the military had profound grievances against Aristide himself, whom they perceived as interfering with their corporate preserve.[47] On the day of his inauguration, Aristide purged the officer corps of most of its top commanders and soon created a special presidential security force (the SSP) to ensure his own survival. The army saw in these two events a direct challenge to its institutional integrity and therefore had its own independent reasons to overthrow the president.[48] It is clear, however, that an opportunistic convergence of interests united the dominant class and the military. Both feared the ascendancy of Aristide's political class and the unpredictable outcome of its rule, and both had the material and coercive resources to put an end to the Lavalasian experiment. Indeed, despite their overwhelming superiority in numbers, the subordinate classes lacked the organization, resources, and weaponry to counteract the putschism of the dominant class.

If liberal democracy was to succeed at all in Haiti, however, it had to equalize, structure, and regulate political unpredictability and uncertainties. Democracy could not tolerate the erratic, capricious, and arbitrary absolutism that had historically characterized Haitian presidential monarchism. Democratic governance required a different sort of uncertainty, an uncertainty contained within and structured by a predictable system of rules. Most critically, political actors had—at a minimum—to be convinced that the uncertainties of defeat did not outweigh the gains of a possible future victory. The precondition for the establishment of such convictions was the institutionalization of uncertainty within a predictable framework within which outcomes would neither be permanent nor arbitrary.

As Przeworski has explained, liberal democracy is "a system of ruled open-endedness, or organized uncertainty."[49] The incentives to join with this system are themselves contingent upon the capacity of political forces to mobilize, neutralize, or overcome state and class power. Rueschemeyer, Huber Stephens, and Stephens have demonstrated clearly in their important study *Capitalist Development and Democracy* that it is power relations that most importantly determine whether democracy can emerge, stabilize, and then maintain itself even in the face of adverse conditions.

There is first the balance of power among different classes and class coalitions. This is a factor of overwhelming importance. It is complemented by two other power configurations—the structure, strength, and autonomy of the state apparatus and its inter-relationships with civil society and the impact of transnational power relations on both the balance of class power and on state-society relations.[50]

In the Haitian context, the process of democratization would have been aborted without the full impact of transnational power relations. The U.S. military occupation of the island was determinant in reinstalling Jean-Bertrand Aristide to the presidency from which he had been overthrown in 1991. Thus, it has become clear that predatory rulers can no longer depend on external forces to maintain their rule. The end of the Cold War has meant the significant emasculation of foreign support for dictatorships and the global ideological ascendancy of liberal democratic values.[51]

The U.S. intervention signaled that the only existing superpower has the intention of enhancing the spread of liberal-market societies in its immediate "zone of influence." Using its military might and intelligence services as well as its own nongovernmental organizations, the United States has facilitated and continues to influence powerfully the ongoing Haitian democratic transition. The presence of international "monitors" has also served to legitimize or censure electoral outcomes.[52] External factors remain decisive and in some instances determine the shape of Haitian politics, all the more so given that the country's material well-being is utterly dependent on the whims of the world economy and the demands of foreign financial organizations.

International factors therefore impinge massively upon both the productive capacity and the structure of governance of Haiti, but they cannot obliterate the internal logic of the country. Reflecting the domestic balance of class power and the clashes of civil society, the internal logic has shaped and continues to shape the process of democratization.

This process reveals that unlike the predators of the neo-Duvalierist bloc, the reformist sectors of the dominant class and the middle sectors were prepared to go beyond liberalization; they sought to establish a liberal democracy—a regime in which political leaders are freely elected to uphold individual rights, the sanctity of private property, and the pursuit of market gains. These sectors were thus an important force in the democratizing coalition. Their commitment to democracy was, however, largely opportunistic; it tended to reflect both their incapacity to share power with the intransigent neo-Duvalierist predators and their growing exclusion from a shrinking pool of prebendal gains. Hence, the quasi-bourgeois bloc that comprised the reformist wing of the dominant class and the middle sectors depended paradoxically on Lavalasian support to realize its own class project. Necessity transformed it into an agent of liberal democratization.

In the immediate aftermath of Jean-Claude Duvalier's fall, the quasi-bourgeois bloc pushed for a minimal liberal democracy with the support of a mobilized popular civil society;[53] but once the predators had vacated the seats of power and a founding election had taken away their right to rule, the bloc began to undermine the very minimal rights of liberal democracy. Feeling threatened by an increasingly assertive popular civil society and fearing the personal ascendancy of Aristide, the reformists and the middle sectors welcomed General Cédras's coup of 1991. They became prevaricated allies and formed the social basis of the military dictatorship that overthrew the Lavalas regime. This transformation was no surprise, for the reformists and the middle sectors have always resisted the ascendancy of popular forces. They have always feared that the rise of these forces would tilt the balance of class power too far away from what they perceived to be their fundamental interests.

The balance of class power is thus determinant in the making of a democracy. The denser and more hegemonic and popular a civil society is, the more likely the implantation and consolidation of democracy. In fact, it is only when the forces of civil society and in particular popular civil society are institutionalized that consolidation can have a real chance of materializing. Such institutionalization makes possible the emergence of "political society," which in turn is a prerequisite for the establishment of a long-lasting democracy. Political society is the "arena in which the polity specifically arranges itself for political contestation to gain control over public power and the state apparatus."[54] As Alfred Stepan has explained,

> [A] full democratic transition must involve political society, and the composition and consolidation of a democratic polity must entail serious thought and action about those core institutions of a democratic political society—political parties, elections, electoral rules, political leadership, intraparty alliances, and legislatures—through which civil society can constitute itself politically to select and monitor democratic government.[55]

Thus, unless civil society can generate—specially "from below"—an effective political society, extrication from authoritarian rule can easily degenerate into a process of "redictatorialization." This clearly is the lesson of the 1991 coup that overthrew the freely elected Aristide regime. Should subordinate classes fail to create their own political organizations, the balance of power will inevitably favor predatory rulers and middle sectors whose commitment to democracy is always ambiguous and tenuous.

The dominant class, and in particular its young entrepreneurial wing, has understood well the virtues of mobilizing its own associations and groups to create a civil society of the privileged to block the ascendancy of more popular forces. In its most visible attempt to capture the political initiative, it called for a major rally against "insecurity and anarchy" on May 28, 1999. The rally was rapidly aborted for fear that it might have degenerated into a violent confrontation between detractors and supporters of Aristide. Rally organizers led by Olivier Nadal, president of the Haitian Chamber of Commerce, denounced Lavalasian partisans for disrupting and silencing "civil society," while counterdemonstrators voiced their outrage at what they perceived to be a "provocation" by members of the elite and old Duvalierist stalwarts.[56] The rally demonstrated that "civil society" has become a code word without any precise meaning to be manipulated by all actors to advance their own political agenda in the name of democracy. Civil society is therefore not the magical civic arena from which democracy will emerge. It reflects the political tensions and social polarization of the wider society. It may indeed be quite uncivil.[57]

The creation of a more peaceful climate requires the creation of effective political parties capable of becoming the prime agents of mediation among state, civil society, and political society. Mass parties representing and articulating the interests of their respective constituencies, particularly subordinate classes, are a sine qua non for the establishment of a balance of power from which democracy can emerge.[58] Haiti's democratization, however, has given birth to social movements rather than mass parties, to "onemanism" instead of collective structuration. The parties that have crystallized have tended to be based on clientelistic and personalistic criteria. In fact it may well be more appropriate to describe them as *groupuscules;* Kern Delince has argued convincingly that they represent "voluntary association[s] of political activists, constituted at the initiative of an influential leader, with the aim of participating in national politics. . . . [The *groupuscule*] is an *ad hoc* social grouping, which specializes in the accomplishment of a specific and temporary objective."[59]

Paradoxically, such *groupuscules* may—in the short term—mitigate the opposition of predators, reformist bourgeois, and middle sectors to the process of democratic transition and consolidation. Weak or nonexistent radical mass parties channel the mobilization of subordinate classes into divisive clientelistic and particularistic networks, reassuring dominant elites that the electoral process poses no major threat to their fundamental interests. The consolidation of democracy is therefore a delicate and contradictory process requiring simultaneously a balance of power between dominant and subordinate classes and the political overrepresentation of ruling-class interests through the relative deactivation or fragmentation of radical mass parties.

As Rueschemeyer, Huber Stephens, and Stephens have argued, comparative historical experiences of successful democratizations show that

> [political parties] played crucial roles in mobilizing pressures from subordinate classes and mediating such pressures in ways which reduced the threat level to elites. . . . The dominant classes accommodated to democracy only as long as the party system effectively protected their interests. Strong clientelistic, non-ideological multi-class parties as well as strong conservative parties could perform this function. . . . [Where] such parties were lacking or lost their capacity to protect the economic interests of the dominant classes, the latter appealed to the military for intervention to prevent or to end democratic rule.[60]

Liberal democracy is thus full of constraints and limitations to the exercise of popular power; it impairs the ascendancy of subordinate classes and privileges the interests of dominant classes. Its structures are biased structures, always curbing the scope and expansion of democratic practice.[61] Not surprisingly, when in the process of democratization subordinate classes create their own organizations and parties, they reinforce unintentionally the moderating impulse inherent in democratization. Their capacity to create effective and autonomous trade unions, political parties, and other associational agencies is contingent on the existence of certain spaces of political freedom. The prerequisite of these conditions is the establishment of at least a minimal liberal democracy, and this in turn requires liberalizing coalitions with reformists and the middle sectors.

As President Aristide found out in his "second coming," the democratic project of subordinate classes cannot be realized without such coalitions. In Haiti, coalitions of this type are necessary because the power of subordinate classes is severely debilitated by three fundamental realities: (1) their daily struggles for survival in conditions of extreme deprivation, (2) their limited organizational resources, and (3) their long habituation to the subalternity of "infrapolitics." Moreover, the limited size of the Haitian working class and the difficulties of institutionalizing peasant interests contribute to the further erosion of the already debilitated power of subordinate classes.

The democratic project is thus undermined by the political weakness of civil society. Under current conditions, it can crystallize only with the combined mobilization of the reformists, the middle sectors, and the popular sectors. The mix, however, is full of ambiguities and contradictions and is by no means assured. The initial popularity of the Cédras military dictatorship among the dominant class and the middle sectors indicates clearly that their opposition to predatory regimes tends to be tenuous as the costs of sacrificing relatively affluent lifestyles and of rejecting individual prebends mount with the passage of time. While the middle sectors may support the idea of a minimal liberal state, they may quickly feel threatened by the mobilization of popular society and opt for an easy compromise with an emerging dictatorship. Given their ideological individualism and their fear of subordinate classes, the middle sectors are prone to all sorts of opportunistic defections from the democratizing coalition and personal accommodations with authoritarian forces.

Structure, Choice, and Political "Crafting"

Thus, the Haitian process of democratization rests on a precarious foundation. It is debilitated further by an environment of acute material scarcity that severely limits the capacity of the political system to deliver resources with which to co-opt and integrate social actors into a more accountable public realm. This is not to argue that liberal democracy is impossible in poor countries, but rather that wealth, insofar as it provides rulers with expansive material means, facilitates their difficult passage to democratization.[62] Thus, poverty is a formidable constraint on democratic governance but not an absolute obstacle. In fact, as Doh Chull Shin has pointed out,

> The establishment of a viable democracy in a nation is no longer seen as the product of higher levels of modernization, illustrated by its wealth, bourgeois class structure, tolerant cultural values, and economic independence from external actors. Instead, it is seen more as a product of strategic interactions and arrangements among political elites, conscious choices among various types of democratic constitutions, and electoral and party system.[63]

To this extent, the implantation and consolidation of democracy is increasingly perceived as a matter of political "crafting" and constitutional engineering.[64] For instance, in the Haitian case, Dupuy has argued that the "prophetic," presidential style of Jean-Bertrand Aristide was partially responsible for his overthrow in 1991. Aristide, he suggests, ruled as if he had never been elected president of the Republic; instead, he governed as a "leader of the opposition," with a wild and unnecessarily antagonistic rhetoric. He lacked the attributes that would have brought his opponents into his own orbit and situated them within his programmatic strategy of social change. He was a prophet who had yet to acquire the agility and cunning of a "prince."[65] Aristide's incapacity to transcend his political base precipitated his own downfall as he decided to limit his already bounded horizon of options.

In this reading of Aristide's journey to exile, structural constraints and the obdurate opposition of classes are not seen as determinant of the outcome:

[Instead, they merely] narrow the possible courses of action in a given situation but always leave available more than one alternative to the actors involved. Although the actors face difficult economic and political problems, they in principle have the choice to act in ways that can prevent the breakdown of democratic institutions. This breakdown is therefore far from inevitable.[66]

While it is true that politics can be protean, the structure of power and the balance of class forces can nullify choices that really do matter and represent historical alternatives. It is one thing to argue that political leaders have multiple choices; it is another to assume that those choices constitute fundamental and plausible options. In the conjuncture of 1991, where the class power of the dominant classes still rested on brute military force and that of the subordinates on rhetorical exhortations, Aristide had little choice. At the time, the options were just too narrow to assume that in the process of crafting Haitian democracy "the realm of the possible, the plausible, indeed, the probable, [could] be expanded."[67] In reality, Aristide's behavior was immaterial; the coup was bound to happen.

Similarly, it is highly unlikely that a different constitutional system would have prevented the coup. Whether Aristide headed a presidentialist or parliamentarist regime was irrelevant; the balance of class forces and the Lavalasian program blocked the type of "deadlock-breaking" compromises that parliamentarism entails, and debilitated the effective "imperial" rule of presidentialism.[68] At any rate, the semipresidentialist regime of Aristide acquired only the vices of both presidentialism and parliamentarism. The pesident sought to bypass the national assembly by imposing his program through popular mass mobilization, while parliament sunk into political immobilism under the paralyzing divisions of class, ideology, and personality. In short, the design of institutions could play only a very marginal role in the making of a Haitian democracy, given the balance of class forces and the praetorian role of the military as the last trench of the dominant classes' power. Institutions have never prevented, nor will they prevent, dominant classes from violating and destroying whatever constitutional framework they had adhered to once they perceive that their fundamental interest is endangered. This, at least, is the hard lesson of the recent Haitian experience to whose political history we now turn our attention.

Notes

1. See Alex Dupuy, *Haiti in the World Economy* (Boulder: Westview Press, 1989); Michel-Rolph Trouillot, *Haiti: State Against Nation* (New York: Monthly Review Press, 1990); and "Haiti's Nightmare and the Lessons of History," *NACLA* 27, no. 4 (January-February 1994): 46–51.

2. Douglass North, *Structure and Change in Economic History* (New York: Norton, 1981), pp. 22–28; see also Peter Evans, *Embedded Autonomy* (Princeton: Princeton University Press, 1995), p. 12; Robert Fatton Jr., *Predatory Rule* (Boulder: Lynne Rienner, 1992).

3. James C. Scott, *Domination and the Arts of Resistance* (New Haven: Yale University Press, 1990).

4. Ibid., pp. 183–200.

5. Ibid., p. xiii.

6. The *moun andeyo* is Creole for outsiders, those who are not part of the nation and are excluded from its benefits and recognition. See Gérard Barthélémy, *Le Pays en Dehors* (Port-au-Prince: Éditions Henri Deschamps, 1989).

7. Alain Turnier documents well these "moments of madness" and retribution that have marked Haiti's history since it became an independent nation. See Turnier, *Quand la Nation Demande des Comptes*, 2d ed. (Port-au-Prince: Éditions Le Natal, 1990).

8. Jean-Bertrand Aristide, *Tout Moun Se Moun, Tout Homme Est un Homme* (Paris: Seuil, 1992).

9. Franklin Midy, "Changement et Transition," in Gérard Barthélémy and Christian Girault, eds., *La Republique Haïtienne* (Paris: Karthala, 1993), p. 206. Translated from the original French by Carrol Coates:

> En recouvrant la faculté de la parole politique et le droit de réplique, les exclus d'Haïti ont recouvré leur humanité et leur citoyenneté, ils sont devenus acteurs historiques, sujets de l'Histoire. De plus, ils ont cassé le monopole de la parole, jusque-là detenu par "l'élite," et celui du pouvoir sur le pouvoir de la parole, monopole qui faisait que la parole du "chef" ou des "autorités" était sans réplique possible, donc qui garantissait leur monopole du pouvoir. Il y a eu subversion du rapport de communication unilatérale et unidirectionnelle qui était un rapport de pouvoir, un rapport d'assujettissement.

10. *Déchoukaj* is the Creole word for uprooting; it became the slogan of the popular Lavalasian forces in their attempt to eradicate Duvalierism and punish Duvalierists.

11. Fatton, *Predatory Rule*, pp. 105–106.

12. The program of Lavalas is contained in Opération Lavalas (OL), *La Chance qui Passe* (Port-au-Prince: Opération Lavalas, 1990); and *La Chance à Prendre* (Port-au-Prince: Opération Lavalas, 1990). See also Alex Dupuy, "The Prophet Armed: Jean-Bertrand Aristide's Liberation-Theology and Politics," unpublished manuscript, 1995.

13. In the following pages I expand on my use of the concept of class; an excellent survey of the Haitian class structure is Etzer Charles, *Le Pouvoir Politique en Haïti de 1957 à Nos Jours* (Paris: Karthala, 1994), pp. 13–176; see also Robert Malval, *L'Année de Toutes les Duperies* (Port-au-Prince: Éditions Regain, 1996), pp. 97–102.

14. Arthur Mahon, "Haïti: Une Dictature Rampante," *Rouge*, December 7, 2000. See also Gilles Danroc, "Imbroglio, Précarités et Démocratie," *Diffusion de l'Information sur l'Amérique Latine*, Dossier 2358, March 1–15, 2000, pp. 1–2.

15. The Creole *Tonton Macoute* means "the bogeyman" in Haitian popular folktales; Tontons Macoutes was the name given to the brutal paramilitary force created by Duvalier. *Macoutisme* refers to the system of terror imposed by François Duvalier. For a fuller discussion of the term, see Gérard Barthélémy, *Les Duvaliéristes Après Duvalier* (Paris: L'Harmattan, 1992), pp. 44–46; see also

Michel S. Laguerre, *The Military and Society in Haiti* (Knoxville: University of Tennessee Press, 1993), pp. 114–117; and Michel-Rolf Trouillot, *Haiti: State Against Nation* (New York: Monthly Review Press, 1990), pp. 152–156.

16. Laguerre, *The Military and Society in Haiti,* pp. 171–172.

17. Haitian Information Bureau, "Chronology," in James Ridgeway, ed., *The Haiti Files: Decoding the Crisis* (Washington, D.C.: Essential Books, 1994), pp. 206–207, 212.

18. Robert Putnam, *Making Democracy Work* (Princeton: Princeton University Press, 1993), pp. 15–88.

19. See Opération Lavalas, *La Chance qui Passe;* Opération Lavalas, *La Chance à Prendre;* Dupuy, "The Prophet Armed."

20. Luiz Carlos Bresser Pereira, José María Maravall, and Adam Przeworski, *Economic Reforms in New Democracies* (Cambridge: Cambridge University Press, 1993), pp. 200–201.

21. T. H. Marshall, *Class, Citizenship and Social Development* (Westport, Conn.: Greenwood Press, 1973), pp. 71–72.

22. Ibid.

23. See note 15.

24. Amy Wilentz, *The Rainy Season* (New York: Touchstone, 1989), pp. 128, 224.

25. Ibid., p. 128.

26. See Chapter 3 in this volume.

27. Wilentz, *The Rainy Season,* reports the following comments by Aristide (p. 234):

> One good thing about all the assassination attempts is that I survived them. I know that sounds silly, or obvious, but think about it this way: Here you have a man, everyone is against him, the Macoutes, the hierarchy of the Church, the government, the Army. They go after him, with guns, machetes, stones. What happens? He survives. How do you think this makes people feel? I'll tell you. They think I'm protected. That I can't be hurt. That Jesus or the spirits are protecting me. That I am indestructible. This is great protection for me, because it makes a hired killer a little reluctant to take me on. Who wants to have on his hands the blood of someone the spirits protect? Worse, if he comes to kill me, the odds are, he thinks, that I will survive, and he will be punished. He thinks a powerful force is keeping me safe.

28. See William Smarth, "Une Page de l'Église des Pauvres: Le Père Jean-Bertrand Aristide, Président d'Haïti," in Gérard Barthélémy and Christian Girault, eds., *La Republique Haïtienne* (Paris: Karthala, 1993), pp. 55–62.

29. Jean-Claude Jean and Marc Maesschalck, *Transition Politique en Haïti* (Paris: L'Harmattan, 1999), pp. 47–48, 92. Translated from the original French by Carrol Coates:

> Même si "Lavalas" est un phénomène populaire, la "source" du courant réside dans une initiative personnelle fondée sur un leadership "charismatico-religieux." Malgré sa complexité et ses contradictions, tout le mouvement repose sur une seule personne, la seule capable de lui donner une impulsion et éventuellement de le relancer. Il y a donc une relation de dépendance complète à l'égard du leader. Or celui-ci a une pratique anti-organisationnelle déjà reconnue: aucun groupe n'a pu, dans son entourage, prendre un statut autonome et se développer librement. Spontanément, ce leader s'oppose à toute forme de contrôle de son pou-

voir. Son action est stimulante pour les individus et peut produire des effets de masse, mais elle est destructurante pour un groupe qui cherche a se constituer et à s'organiser sur une base objective. . . .

Le rapport religeux au leader a plutôt favorisé l'attentisme, les relations fondées sur la confiance, à l'intérieur desquelles l'interpellation des dirigeants, l'autonomie des acteurs et la conscience critique, sont perçues comme étant de la trahison. Le prêtre-président a neutralisé chez les masses le développement d'un jugement politique éclairé. Il a transformé un peuple revendicatif en une masse assagie, confiante dans la venue du miracle.

30. Ellen Meiksins Wood, *Democracy Against Capitalism* (Cambridge: Cambridge University Press, 1995); see also her *Retreat from Class* (London: Verso, 1986).

31. Dietrich Rueschemeyer, Evelyne Huber Stephens, and John D. Stephens, *Capitalist Development and Democracy* (Chicago: University of Chicago Press, 1992).

32. World Bank, *World Development Report 1997: The State in a Changing World* (Oxford: Oxford University Press, 1997), p. 220; World Bank, *World Development Report 1999/2000: Entering the 21st Century* (Oxford: Oxford University Press, 2000), p. 234; see also Charles, *Le Pouvoir Politique en Haïti*, pp. 44–47.

33. Haïti Solidarité Internationale, *Haïti Elections 1990: Quelle Démocratie?* (Port-au-Prince: Jean-Yves Urfie, 1990), pp. 217–227.

34. Samuel Huntington, *The Third Wave* (Norman: University of Oklahoma Press, 1991), p. 9.

35. Ibid.

36. Guillermo O'Donnell and Philippe C. Schmitter, *Transitions from Authoritarian Rule: Tentative Conclusions About Uncertain Democracies* (Baltimore: Johns Hopkins University Press, 1986); and Adam Przeworski, *Democracy and the Market* (Cambridge: Cambridge University Press, 1991), pp. 54–66, explain well the relationship between liberalization and the extension of individual and group rights. O'Donnell and Schmitter contend (p. 7):

> The process of redefining and extending rights we have labeled "liberalization." It is indicative of the beginning of the [democratic] transition that its emergence triggers a number of (often unintended) consequences which play an important role in ultimately determining the scope and extension of that process. By liberalization we mean the process of making effective certain rights that protect both individuals and social groups from arbitrary or illegal acts committed by the state or third parties.

37. "Extrication" entails antiauthoritarian forces uniting in a bloc powerful enough to effect a negotiated transition to democracy. This process should not be confused with the lasting constitution of a democratic system, for the two phenomena are not necessarily mutually reinforcing: while extrication requires the unity of the protodemocratic bloc, it does not necessarily generate agreement on fundamental constitutional and institutional issues. Moreover, the founding of democracy leads eventually to a competitive division of the bloc itself and hence to potential instability. In *Democracy and the Market,* Przeworski explains this dilemma well (pp. xi–67):

> [To] bring about democracy, anti-authoritarian forces must unite against authoritarianism, but to be victorious under democracy, they must compete with each other.

Hence, the struggle for democracy always takes place on two fronts: against the authoritarian regime for democracy and against one's allies for the best place under democracy.

Thus, even if they sometimes coincide temporally, it is useful to focus separately on the two different aspects of democratization: extrication from the authoritarian regime and the constitution of a democratic one.

38. The concept of "satisficing" is developed in O'Donnell and Schmitter, *Transitions from Authoritarian Rule*, p. 70. It indicates that to achieve a successful democratizing pact all political players must feel that they have "[obtained in the process] some important satisfactions and [avoided] the worst possible dissatisfactions."

The fear of mutually assured destruction may also contribute to a "satisficing" solution as a relative balance of power between authoritarian and democratic blocs forces them into a compromise. As Huntington argues in *The Third Wave* (p. 161),

> The risks of confrontation and of losing thus impel government and opposition to negotiate with each other; and guarantees that neither will lose everything become the basis for agreement. Both get the opportunity to share in power or to compete for power. Opposition leaders know they will not be sent back to prison, government leaders know they will not have to flee into exile. Mutual reduction in risk prompts reformers and moderates to cooperate in establishing democracy.

39. Alex Dupuy, *Haiti in the New World Order* (Boulder: Westview Press, 1997), pp. 103–104.

40. My conception of the Haitian class structure is similar to Charles's; see his *Pouvoir Politique en Haïti*. Our terminology is different, however. Charles calls the "possessing" class a *bourgeoisie d'affaires* and the ruling class a *bourgeoisie politico-administrative*.

41. Charles, *Le Pouvoir Politique en Haïti*, p. 20. Translated from the original French by Carrol Coates:

> [La classe possédante] est en grande partie une bourgeoisie d'origine étrangère issue d'horizons différents, en particulier des USA, d'Italie, du Liban, de Syrie, etc. Nombre de bourgeois actuels—presque tous d'ailleurs—ont débarqué dans le pays sans fortune et sont parvenus à accumuler leurs capitaux et constituer du même coup une classe dominante, grâce à leur dynamisme.

42. The concept of "protection" is well developed by Diego Gambetta, *The Sicilian Mafia* (Cambridge: Harvard University Press, 1993).

43. James Ridgeway, ed., *The Haiti Files: Decoding the Crisis* (Washington, D.C.: Essential Books, 1994), pp. 29–39.

44. Charles, *Le Pouvoir Politique en Haïti*, p. 100. Translated from the original French by Carrol Coates:

> Ce qui a surtout marqué la situation de la bourgeoisie d'affaires par rapport aux gouvernants, c'est le silence ou l'impuissance politique qui s'en dégage, expression d'une réelle soumission au groupe au pouvoir. Durant (presque) toute la période [Duvalier], elle a subi diverses mesures fiscales sans manifester la moindre opposition. Le chantage à la persécution et d'autres moyens de pression sont souvent utilisés par les autorités pour soutirer de l'argent aux membres de la bourgeoisie. Ceux-ci connaissent donc un état de domination qui, tout en nuisant à leurs intérêts directs, les conduit par la même à rechercher la protection des dirigeants.

45. Ibid., p. 23. Translated from the original French by Carrol Coates:

> En fait, leur pouvoir et leur richesse reposent non pas sur la possession de moyens de production, mais sur leur position et leurs pratiques à l'intérieur du champ politique. Aussi leur maintien ou non au sein de la classe dominante dépend-il de l'évolution du jeu ou de la lutte politique.

46. Malval, *L'Année de Toutes les Duperies,* pp. 97–102.

47. For a military perspective on the events leading to the coup against Aristide, see Prosper Avril, *Vérités et Révélations: L'Armée d'Haïti, Bourreau ou Victime?* (Port-au-Prince: Le Natal, 1997), pp. 256–266.

48. As J. P. Slavin explained in his article "The Elite's Revenge: The Military Coup of 1991," in NACLA, ed., *Haiti: Dangerous Crossroads* (Boston: South End Press, 1995), p. 59,

> The exact size of SSP is unknown, but estimates range from 30 to 300. Furious army officers likened the SSP to Duvalier's ferocious Tontons Macoutes . . . which some have numbered at 300,000, that was loyal to the president and effectively blocked the army from the political arena. "We had a presidential militia in 1957," said a Haitian colonel, referring to the Macoutes. "It started with ten people. Then it became fifteen. Then it became 100, then 1,000, then 10,000, then 300,000. . . . The army cannot tolerate something like that again."

49. Przeworski, *Democracy and the Market,* p. 13.

50. Rueschemeyer, Huber Stephens, and Stephens, *Capitalist Development and Democracy,* p. 5.

51. William Robinson, *Promoting Polyarchy* (Cambridge: Cambridge University Press, 1996).

52. For instance, most foreign observers and nongovernmental organizations described the first round of the parliamentary and municipal elections of June 1995 as a "step in the consolidation of democracy," but the total organizational chaos in which they unfolded weakened their legitimacy. The Carter Center found these elections wanting and called the Aristide government and the opposition to engage in negotiations in order to settle their differences. Robert Pastor, director of the center's Latin American and Caribbean Program, declared, "Of the 13 elections that I have observed, the June 25 Haitian elections were the most disastrous technically with the most insecure count. . . . I personally witnessed the tainting of about one-third of all ballots in Port-au-Prince." The quotation is taken from "Haiti-Election-Carter," C-Reuters@clarinet, July 20, 1995. A similar assessment was made by the Organization of American States, whose secretary-general, César Gaviria, declared, "It is very difficult for us to say that [the election] was free and fair," but he added that the vote was "a contribution to democracy." The citation is taken from C-Reuters@clarinet, July 21, 1995. Most observers do not dispute the fact that the overwhelming victory of Aristide's supporters would have materialized even in absolutely perfect elections; see "Haitian Parties Threaten to Boycott Run-off Polls," C-Reuters@clarinet, July 23, 1995.

53. The minimal liberal democracy, as Richard Sandbrook (*The Politics of Africa's Economic Recovery* [Cambridge: Cambridge University Press, 1993], p. 18) has pointed out, is one that strictly limits statist intrusion into politics and economics and whose determining function is "to maintain the conditions for private capital accumulation."

54. Alfred Stepan, *Rethinking Military Politics* (Princeton: Princeton University Press, 1988), p. 4.

55. Ibid.

56. "Background and Analysis on the May 28th Confrontation at Champ de Mars," *Haïti Progrès*, July 21–27, 1999, pp. 9–20.

57. Robert Fatton Jr., "The Impairments of Democratization: Haiti in Comparative Perspective," *Comparative Politics* 21, no. 2 (1999): 209–229.

58. Rueschemeyer, Huber Stephens, and Stephens, *Capitalist Development and Democracy.*

59. As quoted in Alex Dupuy, "1986–1990: The Struggle for a Democratic Alternative," unpublished manuscript, 1995, p. 14.

60. Rueschemeyer, Huber Stephens, and Stephens, *Capitalist Development and Democracy,* pp. 168–287.

61. On the democratic limitations of liberal democracy, see Ralph Miliband, *Marxism and Politics* (New York: Oxford University Press, 1977); see also Meiksins Wood, *Democracy Against Capitalism.*

62. Seymour Martin Lipset emphasized a long time ago the correlation between wealth and democracy, arguing essentially that without material abundance brought about by bourgeois industrial development, democracy was impossible; see his "Some Social Requisites of Democracy: Economic Development and Political Legitimacy," *American Political Science Review* 53, no. 1 (1959): 69–106.

63. Doh Chull Shin, "On the Third Wave of Democratization: A Synthesis and Evaluation of Recent Theory and Research," *World Politics* 47, no. 1 (October 1994): 138–139.

64. Guiseppe Di Palma, *To Craft Democracies* (Berkeley: University of California Press, 1990).

65. Dupuy, "The Prophet Armed." See also Franklin Midy, "Qui Êtes-Vous, Père Aristide?" *Haïti en Marche,* October 26–November 2, 1988; and Midy, "Aristide: Entre le Prophète et le Prince," *Haïti en Marche,* December 26, 1990–January 1, 1991.

66. Youssef Cohen, *Radicals, Reformers, and Reactionaries* (Chicago: University of Chicago Press, 1994), pp. 119–120.

67. Di Palma, *To Craft Democracies,* p. 6.

68. Alfred Stepan and Cindy Skach, "Constitutional Frameworks and Democratic Consolidation," *World Politics* 46, no. 1 (1993): 1–22.

3

The Fall of Duvalier and the Contradictions of Democratization

The Antinomies of Liberalization Under
Jean–Claude Duvalier's Authoritarianism

Haiti's political history, from the revolutionary period through independence in 1804 to the contemporary post-Duvalier era, reflects the predatory nature of the dominant class that has persistently refused to ground its rule in a meaningful system of accountability. The dominant class has controlled the state for its exclusive benefit, using it to extract resources from the poor majority. The predatory character of that class derives more from its own class interests and rationality[1] than from some inherent Haitian cultural norm.[2] The violence of the dominant class reflects its determination to prevent the subordinate groups from redistributing or expropriating its power, wealth, and privilege. It is a naked class struggle that has little to do with a special Haitian attraction to brutality or despotism.

While it is true that the authoritarian tradition has colored Haitian history, its rise and persistence can hardly be attributed to some indigenous trait. Cultural explanations of Haiti's dictatorial heritage verge on racism and ignore completely the simple reality that this heritage is rooted in the predatory interests of the dominant class.[3] The 1804 revolution against slavery and the persistent open and "hidden" forms of popular resistance against the repressive reach of the state indicate clearly that Haitians do not have a particular affinity for, and attachment to, dictatorial rule. Indeed, the old practice of *marronnage*, of exiting first the spaces of slavery and then the regimented arena of a predatory state to create communities of freedom and cooperation, has demonstrated the remarkable capacity of the poor peasant and urban majorities to revolt against, and withstand, the most severe forms of exploitation and domination.[4] The history of *marronnage* is the history of the constant quest for liberty and solidarity by the abused Haitian masses. It is this tradition, rather than the imaginary democratic

51

propensity of an elusive political center dominated by privileged classes, that can generate the basis of an accountable system of governance.

In addition, the old practice of *kombit* (a Creole word meaning "working together"), which inspired cooperative work and transcended the pursuit of self-interest, has resurfaced with the rise of the new "democratic movements." These movements originating from the grassroots and comprising trade unions, peasant associations, religious groups, and diverse professional organizations are the very foundation on which democratization can plant its seeds and flourish. This is not to espouse an easy triumphalism. On the contrary, the democratic movements face huge difficulties; they lack resources and organization, and many of their leaders have become fatigued and demoralized by years of struggles and apparent failures, and some have even degenerated into opportunistic *grands mangeurs*.[5] To this extent, members and cadres of the movements can easily lapse into irresponsible, unaccountable, and self-seeking behavior. They can become the new patrons as they use their position to acquire illicit wealth and power, and followers can revert to being clients seeking modest prebends to survive in an environment of utter scarcity.

The island's predicament is rooted in this pervasive scarcity. The intensity of the great majority's struggle to escape from its devastating consequences is matched only by the utter determination of most members of the dominant class to avoid at all costs any slippage in their privileged status. These two opposite strategies have contributed to the huge divide separating the dominant class from the masses and have transformed Haiti into two worlds.[6] The first world, comprising the wealthy, French-speaking, and cosmopolitan minority, displays an utter disdain for the masses and sees politics as a win-or-die proposition. Most mulatto or light-skinned individuals belong to this world. It is antidemocratic and completely excludes the second world from its privileges. The second world comprises *le peuple* and represents the vast majority of the population. It is overwhelmingly peasant, illiterate, poor, and black. It comprises also the large population living in the squalor of ever expanding urban slums. The destitution of this second world is pervasive: according to UN estimates, 65 percent of Haiti's population lives below the poverty line, and in rural areas the number rises to an alarming 81 percent. Life expectancy at birth is fifty-one years for men and fifty-six years for women, and the mortality rate for infants under the age of five is 125 per thousand.[7] Not surprisingly, Haitians have dubbed the second world as the world consisting of those *san non,* those who have no name.

It would be wrong, however, to assume that these two worlds exist in mutual isolation. In fact, first and second worlds are relational; they are the opposite sides of the same coin. The second world is defined in relation to the dominant class; it is dependent on it and subject to it. At the same time, the first world's wealth and status derive from its control and taxation of the poor majority.[8] First and second worlds are thus bound together in unequal but interdependent relationships that have generated an enormous gap between the haves and the have-nots. According to conservative estimates, the richest 1 percent of the population monopolizes 46 percent of the national revenue.

The dichotomic structure of Haitian society is also reflected in acute color consciousness.[9] The conflict of color, or the rift between "brown" and "black," exacerbates further social tensions. The line that divides Haitians most, however, is not color but class. The line of class expresses the fact that while first and second worlds are thoroughly intertwined in an exploitative material web, the dominant class has always sought a total moral and psychological dissociation from *le peuple,* whom it has dehumanized into meek and servile creatures. Armed with an acute sense of cultural superiority, the dominant class is conscious of its privileged status in the social order and is bent on defending it. It has an adversary position toward subordinate classes, whom it regards with scorn and fear. By dissociating itself from *le peuple* through its language, religion, education, and etiquette, the dominant class has tried to validate its elevated position and its claims to a natural right of governance.

Cultural differences are important in Haiti. They separate the French-speaking, wealthy, Catholic minority from the Creole-speaking majority of poor *vodouisants* and Protestant fundamentalists. They accentuate racial distinctions dividing mulatto from black. But if there are differences, there are also deep common cultural qualities. Paradoxically, these commonalities may have been the unintended result of the U.S. occupation from 1915 to 1934. As Amy Wilentz has correctly argued,

> The U.S. occupation, and national resentment over the Americans' racist behavior and imperialist goals, fertilized the intellectual soil for the new, proto–Black power movement. The occupation taught the elite that despite their best efforts, they were still unregenerate Negroes in the eyes of the civilized world . . . hardly better than their coal-black brothers in the fields, and often equally unfit to enter the Americans' houses through the front door. Unwittingly, William Jennings Bryan, then Secretary of State, summed up American attitudes about the Haitian elite: . . . "Dear me! Think of it!" he said. "Niggers speaking French!"[10]

Thus, the occupiers' racism shortened somewhat the cultural distance between the dominant class and the masses. Albeit slowly and piecemeal, the dominant class incorporated into its Europeanized worldview the peasants' indigenized African heritage. A common culture began to crystallize, however much it was divided by class. Expressed in the universal use of Creole and in music, food, dance, and artistic taste, it helped bridge the gap separating rulers from subordinates. In fact, all Haitians have amalgamated European and U.S. contributions to their distinctively African civilization.

Nothing illustrates better this amalgamation than *Vodou*.[11] In Vodou, Catholicism is joined with Haitianized African religions to form an integrated system of beliefs and rituals. As one peasant put it, "One has to be a Catholic to serve the *loa* (vodou spirits)." For most Haitians, Vodou is a way of life that provides them a haven from the harsh realities of poverty and powerlessness.[12]

Moreover, in the profoundly hierarchical world of Haitian society, Vodou offers, in the words of Wade Davis, a "quintessentially democratic faith," open to all irrespective of age, class, or gender.[13] Male priests—*houngans*—and female priestesses—*mambos*—are mediators between the faithful and the spirits and function as heads of "autonomous sects or cult-groups, rather than members of a clerical hierarchy."[14] This lack of hierarchy should not mask, however, the exploitative side of Vodou. *Houngans* and *mambos* can request sacrifices in money and food from their disciples and use their spiritual authority to legitimate a repressive social order. Vodou became so closely associated with the Duvalier regime that once Duvalier fled, many *houngans* and *mambos* were killed in the ensuing popular uprising.[15] On the other hand, Vodou can be a liberating force; it clearly played an essential role in the war of independence by uniting the slaves in a viable army that eventually defeated the master classes. Thus, Vodou is a complex and contradictory system of belief whose plasticity is evidenced in its secular functions as well as in its continuously evolving pantheon of *loas*.[16] Interweaving indigenous beliefs with Christian eschatology, Vodou creates a sense of national identity and solidarity by cultivating communities of shared values and aspirations.[17]

Moreover, Vodou's role in Haiti's successful war of independence enhanced the sense of *haïtièneté*—Haitian-ness. While Jean Price-Mars, one of the most important Haitian intellectuals of the twentieth century, may have exaggerated its significance when he declared "1804 est issu du Vodou" [Vodou is responsible for the revolution of 1804],[18] it would be wrong to minimize its contribution to the slaves' sense of grievance and identity. As Carolyn Fick has pointed out,

> Despite rigid prohibitions, voodoo was indeed one of the few areas of totally autonomous activity for the African slaves. As a religion and a vital spiritual force, it was a source of psychological liberation in that it enabled them to express and reaffirm that self-existence they objectively recognized through their own labor. . . . Voodoo further enabled the slaves to break away psychologically from the very real and concrete chains of slavery and to see themselves as independent beings; in short, it gave them a sense of human dignity and enabled them to survive. Indeed the sheer tenacity and vigor with which slaves worshipped their gods and

danced in their honor . . . eloquently attest to voodoo as a driving force of resistance in the daily lives of the slaves.[19]

Thus, by instilling a profound sense of pride, Vodou contributed to the first successful black revolution against white colonialism. While belief in Vodou has always been a function of class appurtenance, it nonetheless fueled a deep nationalism and a strong sense of identity among rich and poor alike. Indeed, Haitians can be relaxed to the point of arrogance in assuming their nation's place in history, in feeling the dignity of their race and culture, and in knowing that Haiti in spite of its huge problems belongs to Haitians. Sidney Mintz has insightfully suggested that such arrogance is possible "largely because hardly anyone in [Haiti] is white."[20]

What truly divides Haitians is thus neither culture nor color. However much weight is assigned to cultural and color differences within Haiti, the reality is that those differences correspond generally to relations of power and class and seldom transcend class considerations. As Mintz has pointed out,

> The linkage between color and power in Haitian history is real and specific; but color means perceived color, and perception of "race" in a society such as Haiti's is profoundly influenced by factors (such as class, education, one's own perceived color, and speech) that do not logically precede the perception of color but accompany it. Color, in other words, is not salient in Haiti in the way it is in a truly racist society. . . . Haitian social distinctions do not rest solely on considerations of physical type; a black skin does not "doom" an individual if his attainments make him otherwise the equal of his lighter-skinned fellow citizens.[21]

To this extent, class appurtenance goes a long way in determining one's color. This fact is well captured in the Haitian Creole proverb "Neg rich sé mulat, mulat pov sé noua" [a rich black is a mulatto, a poor mulatto is a black].

It is true, nevertheless, that the issue of color has played a significant role in Haitian politics. Politicians in search of power have manipulated it, and it has helped to hide the reality that both mulatto and black elites have behaved with similar contempt for the poor black majority.[22] In fact, *noirisme*, which hails the occupation of the highest political offices by blacks as the inevitable conquest of power by the poor masses, is nothing more than the ideology of a black petite bourgeoisie in search of hegemony. For instance, the "darkening," as it were, of the upper sectors that occurred under François Duvalier's regime did not translate into any meaningful improvement in the life of the second world. "Black power" in this instance was a cover that masked the ascendancy of a black bourgeoisie, who lorded it over the poor majority. As Etzer Charles put it,

> If, in principle, noiriste philosophy can be summarized as wanting to give power to the blacks, that means giving power to its defenders—that is, to a few of the upper black bourgeois and a significant part of the petty black bourgeoisie—and defending their class interests or personal ambitions. That petty bourgeoisie, by its situation in the fields of social activity, is simply dreaming of power and opulence. The color question then becomes a politico-ideological weapon used by [Duvalier] with the goal of garnering the support of the dominated classes (black in the majority).[23]

Moreover, the growth of a black bourgeoisie under François Duvalier's brutal rule did not lead to the direct disempowerment of the mulatto elite. While it was forced to relinquish its political subjugation of the black majority, the mulatto minority managed to keep a firm hold on the economy. In fact, an uneasy compromise materialized whereby the brown minority continued to dominate the private sector while the black bourgeoisie took control of the state as a means to enrich itself. To paraphrase Robert Malval, the achievement of the Duvaliers consisted in sharing power within the framework of a great historical compromise: the black middle classes monopolized political power through their command of the public sector; the mulatto bourgeoisie had economic power vested in its control of the private sector; and both benefited from the protection of the repressive machine against popular demands. Finally, at the very top, the Duvaliers established their presidential monarchism and took advantage of the powerful and active friendships of the mulatto oligarchy in the world of international high finance.[24]

That historic compromise found its ultimate expression when Jean-Claude Duvalier abandoned his father's *noiriste* policies and married Michèle Bennett, a mulatto woman. The Duvalierist old guard, which was increasingly marginalized from power and replaced by technocratic cadres and Bennett family cronies, resented this union between mulatto and black elites.[25] The new configuration of the regime contributed to the erosion of Jean-Claude Duvalier's political base.[26] As James Ferguson explained,

> The desertion or expulsion of former old guard Duvalierists thus marked a crucial trend in political developments and further underlined the internal contradictions that were gradually destabilizing Baby Doc's rule. While the son had inherited from his father a state apparatus rooted in the black middle class and the more prosperous peasantry, he had slowly moved away from these sectors of support, favoring the mulatto "technocrats" and businessmen who shared the background and outlook of his wife and father-in-law. The 1985 sacking of [the powerful hard-liner, minister of the interior, Roger] Lafontant was another step in this direction, and, as such, it alienated the supporters of traditional anti-mulatto Duvalierism, who suspected the machinations of the elite to be behind a seemingly erratic governmental policy.[27]

The internal political tensions besieging the regime were compounded by the growing economic crisis of the early 1980s that further undermined Jean-Claude Duvalier's vanishing popularity. The relatively "open" techno-cratic project of *Jean-Claudisme* exhausted itself as liberalization terminated in repression and as economic growth came to a halt due to massive corruption and state predation. Yet, this liberalization of the mid- and late 1970s had contributed to the resurgence of civil society.[28] When Jean-Claude Duvalier ascended to the presidency in 1971, he promised that he would lead an "economic revolution" in the wake of the "political revolution" he inherited from his father. He set out to modernize the infrastructure, take advantage of ultracheap labor, and open up the country to foreign investments. His goal was to transform the country through the creation of an export-oriented economy,[29] which in turn required significant political transformations. Thus began Jean-Claude Duvalier's hesitant, contradictory, and ultimately ill-fated process of liberalization. In spite of its failure, it brought about the birth of what was to become an increasingly assertive civil society.

It was the press that instigated the first wave of public censure of the Duvalierist regime The radio, in particular, and more specifically Jean Dominique's Radio Haïti Inter, and later on Radio Soleil, seized the opportunity to break the fear that silenced Haitians during François Duvalier's reign of terror. While Jean-Claude Duvalier was rarely if ever targeted for criticism, the media condemned in increasingly severe terms the authoritarianism of his government. In reality, the media was pushing for a full liberalization that would eventually culminate in a real democracy. The press was liberating *la parole*—the word—and reaching a receptive mass audience. Creole that had seldom been used on the airwaves became the hegemonic means of communication and greatly enhanced popular participation. It integrated *le peuple* in the national discourse and gave it the right to be heard and to voice its grievances. Radio stations were not the only thorn in the side of the government; newspapers like *Le Petit Samedi Soir* were also vehicles critical of the regime.

Under pressure from an increasingly vocal media and from U.S. president Jimmy Carter's new policy of human rights, Jean-Claude Duvalier accepted hesitantly the idea of deepening liberalization. He introduced some degree of political pluralism and tolerated the 1979 "election" of Alexandre Lerouge as an independent deputy from Cap-Haïtien. In addition, in the same year, Grégoire Eugène and Sylvio Claude were allowed to create two non-Duvalierist political parties, respectively the Parti Démocrate Chrétien, which would eventually become the Parti Social Chrétien d'Haïti (PSCH), and the Parti Démocrate Chrétien Haïtien (PDCH). Both parties condemned the dictatorial system in place, questioned the legitimacy of the presidency-for-life, and called for free elections. Moreover, human rights movements as well as popular organizations like trade unions and students' associations began to resurface and challenge authoritarian rule. The countryside was also mobilizing in the form of peasant cooperatives known as *gwoupmans* to resist repression and rural exploitation.[30]

The government's relaxation of authoritarianism generated autonomous centers of power that began to articulate an alternative future. Instead of strengthening Duvalierism and co-opting opponents, relaxation widened the gap between rulers and ruled and fomented political uncertainties and vacillations. Nongovernmental organizations challenged state corruption and predation and offered material as well as moral and political assistance to a battered population that had received precious little from the oppressive *macoutiste* regime. Civil society was on the verge of outflanking the government; it was opening new possibilities that had hitherto been suppressed.

The Emperor Has No Clothes: The Fall of Duvalier

Thus, Jean-Claude Duvalier faced the typical dilemma confronting dictators embarked on liberalization: the process unleashes powerful forces and demands for change that go beyond the constraining limits set by the interests of the dictatorial coalition. While the coalition initiates liberalization to enlarge its base of support, it dreads that a resurgent civil society will undermine its vital interests. As Guillermo O'Donnell emphasizes,

> The first steps of political liberalization usher in the resurrection, the intense repoliticization, of society—a process that soon outpaces liberalization itself. . . . [People] suddenly lose their paralyzing fear of the coercive capacity of the state apparatus. Recently feared figures are now publicly ridiculed. After years of censorship, avid readers find themselves swamped in a flood of publications that . . . antagonize the existing powers. Various artistic expressions distill long-festering grievances and demands. In other words, civil society, until lately flat, fearful, and "apolitical," reemerges with extraordinary energy.[31]

Thus, while the liberalization of the 1970s contributed to the resurrection of civil society, it opened a Pandora's box with so many uncertainties and dangers for the continued survival of the regime that it felt compelled to resort once again to repressive measures. Ronald Reagan's election to the U.S. presidency in 1980 spelled the end of Jimmy Carter's human rights policy and facilitated Haiti's authoritarian turn. Barely three weeks after

Reagan's victory, liberalization came to an abrupt halt on November 28. On that day, the regime launched a wave of arrests in a brutal effort to decapitate the nascent democratic movement. Over 130 political dissidents, journalists, lawyers, and leaders of civil society were jailed and sent into exile. The press was silenced again and a tense sense of dictatorial normalcy was reestablished. Liberalization, however, had implanted seeds of contestation that would prove impossible to kill.

The Catholic Church soon filled the vacuum left by the removal of civil society's leaders and organizations.[32] It challenged the abuses of *duvalierisme* and called for social justice and human rights. Regrouping the most active and committed sisters, priests, and religious people, the Conférence Haïtienne des Religieux (CHR)[33] condemned immediately the repressive measures of November 28. It called on the government to cease the deportations and arrests of its critics and asserted that the church "cannot remain silent, for her duty is to make life more humane and people more conscious so all the values of their lives really correspond to true human dignity."[34] The CHR espoused the cause of the suffering masses and was part of a growing prophetic movement bent on eradicating "evil" and bringing justice to the poor. At the head of the movement was the radical wing of the Catholic Church, known as Ti Légliz (little church), which articulated within a theology of liberation a devastating public critique of *macoutisme*.[35] *Macoutisme* came to symbolize everything that was wrong with Haiti: class exploitation, arbitrary political rule, corruption, and state violence. At the Eucharistic and Marial Congress held in Port-au-Prince in December 1982, 120 religious authorities committed themselves and the church to the struggle against injustice and the "preferential option for the poor." "Légliz sé nou, nou sé Légliz" [the church is us, we are the church], they proclaimed.[36] The slogan of the congress—"something has to change here"—echoed the demands of Ti Légliz and the vast majority of Haitians for a massive social, political, and economic transformation.

The prophetic movement found in Pope John Paul II a sympathetic and powerful ally. Visiting Haiti on March 9, 1983, the pope echoed the theme of the Eucharistic and Marial Congress and proclaimed, "Things have got to change." With Jean-Claude Duvalier at his side, the pope made a forceful plea for fundamental human rights and dignity:

> Christians have attested to divisions, injustice, excessive inequality, degradation of the quality of life, misery, hunger, fear by many, of peasants unable to live on their own land, crowded conditions, people without work, families cast out and separated in cities, victims of other frustrations. Yet, they are persuaded that the solution is in solidarity. The poor have to regain hope. The Church has a prophetic mission, inseparable from its religious mission, which demands liberty to be accomplished.[37]

John Paul II's homily shocked and angered an embarrassed Jean-Claude Duvalier, who had sought a few months earlier to reverse the authoritarian turn taken in November 1980.[38] In April 1982, the president-for-life rekindled hopes of liberalization by calling for the institutionalization of democracy, promising municipal elections, and appealing for a political dialogue with the diaspora. But Duvalier's initiative found few takers; in fact, no sooner had he voiced his democratic intentions than a new wave of repression fell on the country. The leader of the Parti Démocrate Chrétien Haïtien, Sylvio Claude, and his daughter, Marie-France, were jailed again. Moreover, the Gérard Duclerville affair put an end to whatever reformist illusions may have existed. In December 1982, the police arrested and tortured Duclerville, director of the Catholic Volunteers, generating unprecedented antigovernmental activities. Civil society and particularly religious organizations openly challenged the dictatorial methods of the Duvalier regime. In a forceful pastoral letter read in all churches, the Conference of Haitian Bishops argued that the difficult period confronting the country "rather than dividing us . . . should unify us. Today it is Gérard and those whose names we don't know. Tomorrow, it's us, you, me. Everyone's a victim. Wherever a man is humiliated and tortured, the whole of humanity is."[39] Radio Soleil filled the airwaves with a song proclaiming, "The flag of violence has been raised," and for the first time the Duvalier regime was publicly likened to "assassins."[40] The power of the word had finally been liberated and everything was now possible. Neither the release of Duclerville a month before the pope's visit, nor the legalization of certain political parties could halt the revolt of civil society that would ultimately overturn almost three decades of Duvalierist domination.

Duvalier's liberalization was ensnared in contradictions: it promised democratic rule but it never went beyond the constraining parameters of Duvalierism and the presidency-for-life. Initially, it engendered cautious optimism, then increasing frustrations, and finally rage and rebellion. "Liberalization is inherently unstable," as Adam Przeworski has explained,

What normally happens is . . . "the thaw": a melting of the iceberg of civil society that overflows the dams of the authoritarian regime. Once repression lessens, for whatever reason, the first reaction is an outburst of autonomous organization in the civil society. Student associations, unions, and proto-parties are formed almost overnight. . . . Thus, on the one hand, autonomous organizations emerge in the civil society; on the other hand, there are no institutions where these organizations can present their views and negotiate their interests. Because of this *décalage* between the autonomous organization of the civil society and the closed character of state institutions, the only place where the newly organized groups can eventually struggle for their values and interests is the streets. Inevitably, the struggle assumes a mass character.[41]

This is the moment when politics becomes "contentious" and the "opportunity structure" widens, providing resources that had been previously inaccessible or nonexistent to people who had hitherto been passive. The social movement crystallizes and confronts with sustained popular challenges rulers and officeholders.[42] The outcome is generally a change of regime and in a few rare cases a genuine revolution. The point here is that marginalized and repressed masses organize in unprecedented ways to change their existence. Divisions and vacillations within the ruling bloc offer opportunities for outbreaks of rebellion, which in turn generate further incentives for collective action. What I shall call the structure of obedience and silence falls. In other words, the system of state repression, the patterns of individual and collective behavior, and the moral authority of power no longer hold. The victims of injustice simply stop putting up with their condition; they know now that their sufferings are neither inevitable nor permanent. They have conquered the "sense of inevitability" that had kept them passive for so long; ultimately, they rebuff the routine of obedience.[43]

In May 1984, the slum dwellers and the youth of Raboteau, the largest shanty in the city of Gonaïves, set in motion this rebuff. By 1985 their cycle of protests had intensified and spread nationwide to eventually culminate in the departure of Jean-Claude Duvalier in 1986. Initially the protests condemned the regime's corruption and authoritarianism and deplored the deteriorating economic conditions that compelled most Haitians to live in dire poverty or exit as boat people to the United States. Resorting again to its traditional repressive methods, an insecure and divided government alienated further an increasingly outraged population. The immediate cause of this outrage was the shooting of three teenagers on November 28, 1985, and the ensuing wave of arrests and beatings of Gonaïves dissidents. Jean-Robert Cius, Mackenson Michel, and Daniel Israel, the three students murdered by Duvalier's security forces, became martyrs to the struggle for dignity and freedom. Their deaths unleashed a new symbolic repertoire of contestation and a determined popular resistance. Indeed, for the first time, during these Gonaïves demonstrations Jean-Claude Duvalier himself was personally, directly, and openly attacked as an "assassin" who had to go.[44] Shouting "Aba Jan Klod, Aba la Konstitusyon, Aba la Diktati, Viv Lamé,"[45] protesters called for the overthrow of Duvalierism and implicitly for a military takeover of the government.

The emperor, as it were, was totally naked, and now nothing could protect him from popular scorn and a flood of demonizing and ridiculing words. Jean-Claude Duvalier was no longer above the fray; he was thoroughly implicated in the murders, repression, and corruption of his regime. The population challenged the legitimacy of the presidency-for-life, likening it to a satanic sin because "only Jesus Christ deserved the title of chief for life."[46] The question, however, was how would Duvalier be ousted? How could he be convinced or compelled to abandon the National Palace? This dilemma is why a large number of protesters chanted slogans extolling the army, hoping that the military would intervene and force the issue. The army itself had shown serious signs of discontent with Duvalier: a clandestine group of soldiers—Mouvman Solda Dayiti—called for his arrest, accusing him of leading Haiti into the abyss.[47] The military were thus at the center of the political chessboard; few conceived of overthrowing the regime without their critical assistance.

In fact, when it became clear that Duvalierism was collapsing under the powerful wave of a popular rebellion spreading from the provinces to Port-au-Prince, key organized foes of the dictatorship turned to the army for a temporary solution. In the eyes of many, the vacuum that Duvalier's departure would create necessitated the incorporation of the military in any postdictatorial dispensation, lest the country be engulfed in utter chaos and bloodshed. As Martin-Luc Bonnardot and Gilles Danroc explained,

> In this period of vacillating power in which Jean-Claude Duvalier is losing his support, the role of the army seems preponderant to everybody. But nowhere does any document appear reflecting on the organization of the army, its role, and its power. Instead of establishing strategic options, the tactical choices are discussed and rediscussed, along with that persistent topic bandied about among progressive milieus, the church, and the bourgeoisie: "What honest military, what enlightened military could be integrated into a transitional government?"[48]

Finding an "untainted" military leader would ultimately prove impossible. Three decades of Duvalierism had inevitably transformed the army into a corrupt, brutal, and incompetent institution. As the dominant coercive apparatus, it played and would play, however, a critical role in the demise of the dictatorship and the future of Haitian politics. Moreover, it had its own distinctive interests that did not necessarily coincide with the continued rule of Jean-Claude Duvalier. While it was a Duvalierist organization, it had hopes of surviving and indeed thriving without Duvalier. Elizabeth Abbott contends that her brother-in-law, General Henri Namphy, chief of staff of the army and eventual head of state, started conspiring against "Baby Doc" in the fall of 1985.[49] Initially the conspiracy included a handful of people, such as Colonel Williams Régala and the powerful lawyer Gérard Noël, but as the rebellion intensified, senior Macoutes and civilian officials joined in. Old Duvalierists like Clovis Désinor, Alix Cinéas, Prosper Avril, and Commandant Madame Max Adolphe were enlisted in the scheme to force the peaceful exit of the president.[50] Namphy knew that without the support of the Macoutes, the army could not by itself fulfill the aims of the conspiracy. His task was greatly facilitated by the simple reality that the conspirators were bent on preserving the basic structure of the old regime and ridding themselves of its increasingly unpopular head.

Thus, in spite of their differences, the army and the Macoutes had a common interest in seeking to establish a Duvalierist system without Duvalier in which they would not merely avoid the wrath of the population but continue to control political power. As Abbott put it, the conspirators desired "a Duvalierist housecleaning" and certainly not a revolution.[51] Moreover, in her view, "An integral part of the plan was for the post-Duvalier government to protect the Macoutes in return for their cooperation, exempting them from judicial prosecution for crimes committed under Duvalier and guarding their physical safety as much as possible."[52]

While it is difficult to ascertain the complete accuracy of Abbott's conspiratorial rendition, it is clear that the popular rebellion that engulfed Haiti in late 1985 and early 1986 fragmented the Duvalierists and prompted them to imagine the future without their president. When the rebellion finally reached Port-au-Prince, Jean-Claude Duvalier found himself completely alone: he had been abandoned by the dominant classes, repudiated by the masses, condemned by the churches, and criticized in his own palace by *mambos* and *houngans*.[53] He was depicted now as a criminal, an "outlaw," a "dangerous individual" who had alienated and marginalized the people because of the "endemic corruption" of his regime.[54] By January 1986, the *déchoukaj* of Jean-Claude Duvalier took on a sense of inevitability. He was the target of all protests, and calls for his departure became public and incessant. Facing economic paralysis and increasing waves of strikes and dissent, the regime opted for repression and imposed a state of siege on January 31, 1986.

This decision, however, squelched neither popular opposition nor persistent and informed rumors of Jean-Claude Duvalier's impending political demise and departure from the country. The very day when martial law was declared, Larry Speakes, spokesman for President Reagan's White House, announced erroneously to Haitians listening to shortwave radio that their "former" president and his family and entourage had left the country. It appears that during a meeting held on January 30, Clayton McManaway, the U.S. ambassador, had assumed that he had convinced the president-for-life to leave the island. At the last moment, however, Duvalier changed his mind and decided to try one last time to regain control of the situation.[55] To dissipate rumors about his exit, he went on national radio and announced, "The President is here, stronger than ever, as strong as a monkey's tail."[56] In spite of his efforts, Duvalier was unable to put the genie back in the bottle; the false news of his departure had raised popular expectations and provoked celebrations that quickly turned into the *déchoukaj*. Violence against powerful Macoutes, looting and destruction of Duvalierists' property, and unstoppable and virulent anti-Jean-Claude *télédjol* (rumors) clearly announced that the dictatorship was nearing the end.[57] Moreover, Larry Speakes's broadcast that incorrectly had the Duvaliers already in exile confirmed that the regime had been deserted by its foreign allies. It was now clear that the United States and France were encouraging Jean-Claude to leave the country peacefully. And this he finally did on February 7, 1986, acknowledging that he could no longer contain mounting popular discontent and protest and increasing international isolation.

Duvalierism Without Duvalier

Duvalier's departure, however, should not be confused with a revolution.[58] Duvalier himself personally chose the members of the Conseil National de Gouvernement (CNG), the new ruling body that succeeded him. Headed by Lieutenant General Henri Namphy, chief of staff of the army, the CNG reflected, with the exception of Human Rights League founder Gérard Gourgue, a thoroughly Duvalierist composition. Along with Namphy and Gourgue, Alix Cinéas, Colonel William Régala, and Colonel Max Vallès, all closely associated with the dictatorship, composed the five-man junta entrusted with Haiti's future and promised transition to democracy. Moreover, Duvalier's long-time confidant, Colonel Prosper Avril, was appointed as the official adviser of the new government. Power thus remained overwhelmingly in authoritarian and repressive hands. Whatever democratic steps Haiti took in the aftermath of Duvalier's flight into exile, they were always in spite of, and indeed against, the CNG.

While the army initially enjoyed significant support, its brutal reflexes and dictatorial instincts soon alienated the vast majority of Haitians. It is true that the Tontons Macoutes were disbanded, that the press was free, that political activities flourished, and that political prisoners were released from the despicable dungeons of the Duvalier tyranny; but these democratic achievements were fragile and always in danger of being eroded if not altogether shattered by the CNG's military men. The army was bent on recapturing the privileged position of political arbiter that it occupied before the ascendancy of François Duvalier in 1957. It sanctioned the dissolution of the Macoutes to eliminate a competitor and regain the monopoly of the forces of coercion. At the same time, however, the army integrated key Macoutes into its own command structure and protected many of them from popular revenge. The complicity between the Macoutes and the military reached its most brutal stage with the vicious abortion of the elections of November 29, 1987.

The period between the flight of Duvalier and these elections was marked by a gradual deterioration of the political climate. Opération Déchoukaj had forced the resignation of some of the Duvalierists in the

CNG, including Colonel Vallès, Alix Cinéas, and Colonel Prosper Avril. It led also to the trial and court martial of several of the well-known Macoutes who had engaged in criminal activities. In addition, there were many symbolic gestures of de-Duvalierization, such as the adoption of a new flag and the removal of the Duvalier name from all public buildings and places. Most importantly, the CNG promised to organize free and fair elections, and on March 29, 1987, an overwhelming majority of Haitians voted for a new liberal and democratic constitution. Among other things, Article 291 of the constitution banned Duvalierists from running for office for ten years and entrusted an independent civilian organ, the Conseil Électoral Provisoire (CEP), with the responsibility of running and supervising the electoral process. Composed of nine members recruited from the main associations and institutions of civil society, the CEP represented a fundamental obstacle to the dictatorial pretensions of the military. From its inception, it engaged in permanent guerrilla warfare with Namphy and his cronies, who, in turn, resisted any encroachment on their growing authoritarianism. The CNG simply could not tolerate an alternative, legitimate source of power.

Not surprisingly, on June 22, in a desperate attempt to impose its complete political supremacy, the CNG rescinded the CEP's constitutional authority and granted itself sole control over the organization of the promised elections. In the same breath, the CNG decreed the dissolution of CATH, the country's dominant trade union, which had called for a general strike against the government. This, however, was a gross miscalculation. Rather than intimidating the opposition, the CNG's actions reactivated it and prompted a resurgence of popular protests. A movement regrouping fifty-seven organizations and associations crystallized to challenge the government, and massive strikes paralyzed the country. Facing such unexpected resistance, the CNG backed down: CATH was again free to operate, and General Namphy proposed to discuss the modalities of a compromise to create an effective and legitimate CEP. The concessions, however, came too late; civil society in its entirety now requested the resignation of the CNG. On June 30, a defiant Archbishop Romélus attacked the government and pronounced the famous words "Raché Manyok ou" [government get out of the way].[59]

In an effort to coordinate and mobilize popular protest, the group of fifty-seven organizations decided to create the Front National de Concertation (FNC). Realizing, however, that popular pressures would not dislodge Namphy from power, the FNC embarked on a strategy of "electoral *déchoukaj*." It decided that the electoral road would grant it the legitimacy of a democratic victory that would finally sweep away the vestiges of Duvalierism. Most major political parties and politicians followed the FNC's lead; all were determined to participate in the presidential elections scheduled for November 29, 1987. Thirty-four candidates entered the race, but most observers estimated that only four had a chance of winning the presidency. The Big Four—Gérard Gourgue of the FNC, Sylvio Claude of the PDCH, Marc Bazin of the Mouvement pour l'Instauration de la Démocratie en Haïti (MIDH), and Louis Déjoie of the Parti Agricole Industriel National (PAIN)—dominated the political chessboard; they accounted for 82 percent of likely voters, according to a widely cited poll.[60]

All did not share in the electoral euphoria. Father Jean-Bertrand Aristide, leader of Ti Légliz, warned that any elections supervised by the junta would end up in disaster: "Many many people will perish and disappear and all over Haiti people will die like flies."[61] Having no confidence whatsoever in Namphy's CNG, Aristide believed that democracy could come about only through the revolutionary seizure of power. Only then would Duvalierism without Duvalier end, and only then would liberation arrive. Otherwise, the daily violence of hunger and military repression would persist and the lethal dance of roaming death squads and Zinglendos would intensify. Elections were not a solution; they were an invitation to a funeral procession.[62] Aristide had good reason to fear the CNG's violence. In July, a massacre of over 300 peasants occurred in Jean-Rabel, and he himself had been the target of assassination attempts and brutal intimidation.[63] Moreover, had it not been for determined popular resistance, the prevaricated attempts of Namphy and his junta to violate Article 291 and allow old Macoutes and Duvalierists to participate in the electoral process would have succeeded.[64]

Indeed, just as Aristide feared, the CNG struck back with a vengeance because it faced defeat and a total loss of power. On election day, it orchestrated with the Macoutes a savage murderous spree on innocent voters. Armed with Uzi submachine guns and machetes, the Macoutes shot and hacked to death defenseless citizens who had lined up in a schoolyard to vote in the early hours of Sunday, November 29, 1987. "Bloody Sunday" aborted in terror Haiti's hesitant march to democracy.[65] The massacre ended with at least seventeen dead and the inevitable cancellation of the electoral process.[66] In a cynical boast, General Namphy declared, "Haiti has only one voter. The army. Ha ha."[67] As Ferguson explains, the junta had good reasons for its drastic actions:

> The motivation for destroying the electoral process was partly fear that a civilian administration led by Sylvio Claude or Gérard Gourgue was likely to initiate legal action against Duvalierists and weaken the army. It was also partly sheer reluctance to hand over unconditional political power to an elected government. But, most importantly, it was a deliberate decision to obstruct the slightest shift of wealth and privilege away from a small military-dominated clique which saw itself as natural successor to Baby

Doc. Fuelled by this mixture of apprehension and ambition, the views of the more extremist military faction prevailed, and together with the banned Duvalierist candidates and their paid henchmen, this faction succeeded in undermining the elections at the eleventh hour.[68]

The junta's victory, however, generated a series of legitimizing problems that would prove difficult and indeed impossible to resolve. The immediate issue was how to appease domestic and international outrage at the CNG-inspired electoral violence and how to divide and conquer the democratic movement. General Namphy opted for a mixture of repression and halfhearted concessions. He decided to organize new, CNG-run elections to be held on January 17, 1988. The government promulgated an election law that violated constitutional provisions and gave ultimate control of the whole process to the military.[69] The Big Four (Bazin, Claude, Déjoie, and Gourgue) refused to participate in the "army's election," calling instead for the creation of an autonomous electoral council that would supervise a new ballot independent of the army. The political class, however, was not unanimous in its opposition to the army's stage-managed elections. Bent on an opportunistic quest for power, lesser political figures accepted Namphy's deal. Knowing full well that the boycott of the Big Four would automatically grant them the status of front-runners, Grégoire Eugène, Hubert Deronceray, Leslie Manigat, and Gérard Philippe-Auguste declared their candidacy for the presidency. Their anti-Duvalierist status and conservative ideological tendencies convinced the junta that it had found "respectable" contenders from whom it had nothing to fear.[70]

In fact, General Namphy and his colleagues felt so secure in assuming that any victor in *their* elections would be their man that they tolerated the supreme court's ban of Duvalierist candidates. The ban was also a means of demonstrating to public opinion at home and abroad that they were not prisoners of the old regime and that they could uphold some elements of the constitution. The military and their Duvalierist and Macoute allies, however, did not want to take any chances; they struck a preelection bargain with Leslie Manigat that guaranteed his election. For Manigat the army was, as he put it, "an inevitable fact of life." Not only did he promise that his administration would not retaliate against them, he also pledged to appoint some of their key officers to important cabinet positions.[71] Armed with such opportunistic realism, Manigat became president in a farcical election that Haitians dubbed a "selection."[72]

Manigat, however, had some serious credentials and attributes that could not be easily dismissed. As Ferguson explains,

Acceptable to the US and chosen by the military, the new president took office among accusations of fraud, corruption and opportunism, but also amidst personal compliments. Newspapers and politicians around the world condemned the result as a charade, as the second stage in the military *coup,* yet stressed that Manigat himself was a proven democrat and, in any other circumstances, a worthy president. In this respect, it was possible that the junta's choice had been the right one, since for many, Manigat's much vaunted respectability and personal integrity seemingly almost compensated for the manner of his election.[73]

Whatever merits Manigat may have had were soon lost when he sought to liberate himself from his masters in the army. Believing that he could create a winning alliance with the ambitious "narco-officer" Colonel Paul, whom he had just promoted to brigadier general, Manigat retired General Namphy, placed him under house arrest, and demoted Avril. Manigat's attempt to outmaneuver the military was, however, doomed. The former professor and political scientist had simply forgotten an old Creole adage, "Si lamé fé, sé lamé kap défé" [if the army makes you, it is the army that will destroy you]. On June 19, 1988, after barely four months in office, Manigat was overthrown in a bloodless coup. His predecessor, General Namphy, became his inevitable successor. Duvalierism without Duvalier had again regained the upper hand.[74]

The military's return to power signaled a recrudescence of violence and a descent into terror. The democratic facade they had previously maintained soon collapsed under the menacing weight of a new dictatorship. Old Duvalierists and Macoutes such as Paul Véricain, Frank Romain, Claude Raymond, and Prosper Avril occupied important political offices or played influential roles behind the scenes. General Namphy's behavior, however, grew increasingly pathological as he tolerated and indeed encouraged the most brutal repression, ranging from harassment to assassination. He finally overstepped the mark when, on September 11, armed thugs linked to the army and Frank Romain penetrated and attacked St. Jean Bosco, Father Aristide's church, killing innocent parishioners. Aristide, who was preaching that day, survived the massacre and miraculously escaped the assassins' bullets.[75]

The assault on St. Jean Bosco consecrated Aristide as the embodiment of poor people's hopes and struggles and invested him with mythical and mystical powers.[76] From that moment on, he became the pivotal figure of Haitian politics and history. Adored by the masses and reviled by the dominant class, he continuously exposed the ugliness of the immense chasm dividing the destitute majority from the wealthy minority. He did so in a prophetic, apocalyptic, and menacing way; in a sermon following the disarmament of a Macoute who had come to threaten him during mass, he voiced his outrage and warned of revolutionary days:

We are telling you today that we have anger in our veins, in our guts, but one day—we don't know when that day will arrive—one day we will put that anger into action. From one moment to the next, anything can happen, because when the winds of vicissitude blow, when the winds of hunger blow, when the storm of injustice is raging, one fine day a people weighed down by all this human and inhuman suffering—this people will become a people marching toward justice. One day, they will establish their own tribunals.[77]

While Aristide's continuous denunciations of the government transformed him into a logical target of the military, the massacre at St. Jean Bosco went beyond acceptable bounds; it transgressed what civil society and even the army itself could tolerate. Barely a week later, it provoked the revolt of the *ti soldat* (literally, little soldier) who could no longer identify with the increasing savagery of the top brass.[78] Enraged by General Namphy's collaboration in the massacre and by their horrible material and corporate situation, the *ti soldats* fomented another coup d'état. Led by Sergeant Joseph Hébreux, they called for the prosecution of all those involved in criminal activities, the restoration of the 1987 constitution, and the political marginalization and exclusion of individuals who had collaborated with the Duvalier, Manigat, and Namphy regimes. Their demands seemed to have corresponded with those of the popular and democratic movement, but General Prosper Avril, who had been chosen as the new provisional president by the *ti soldats* themselves, soon undermined them.

Outmaneuvering Sergeant Hébreux, Avril sought to reestablish army discipline and impose his own political solution to the crisis while simultaneously trying to satisfy a multiplicity of conflicting constituencies.[79] Ultimately, his attempt failed miserably; he was incapable of reempowering the Duvalierists, impotent in the face of the demands of the democratic movement, and unable to unify an increasingly fragmented army. In fact, Avril survived an attempted coup but never recovered fully from it. Finally, on March 10, 1990, he was forced to resign under the combined weight of popular resistance and U.S. pressure.[80]

Several organizations—such as the Assemblée de Concertation (AC), which was a regrouping of many political parties, and the group Honneur Respect Constitution (HRC), headed by Father Antoine Adrien—led the fight against Avril. While they declared themselves ready to assume the reins of government, they ultimately accepted the nomination of Judge Ertha Pascal-Trouillot as the new provisional president. Pascal-Trouillot, who was entrusted with the organization of elections, had to share power, however, with a council of state chaired by Dr. Louis Roy. Relations between the president, the council, and the HRC and other popular movements soon deteriorated. Pascal-Trouillot proved incapable of gaining the trust of the democratic sectors; her authority derived from her links to the army and Haiti's international patrons. In addition, her rather soft approach toward Duvalierists, and particularly toward Roger Lafontant, who remained free upon his return to the country in spite of an arrest warrant, generated strong doubts and suspicions about her democratic commitment.[81]

In fact, certain leaders of popular groups and Ti Légliz thought that little had changed with Pascal-Trouillot's advent and that elections could easily terminate in another bloodbath or farce. Moreover, they believed that elections, even free and fair, could lead to the victory of conservative forces and might well be a trap that would bury any revolutionary hope.[82] While they acknowledged that that some Macoutes had been uprooted and that the 1987 constitution minimized chances of dictatorial temptations, they had serious misgivings about the virtues of "bourgeois" legality and norms. They feared that by calling for a dramatic expansion of parliamentary authority and imposing severe limitations on presidential prerogatives, the constitution might well block fundamental reforms and disenfranchise the poor majority.[83] According to the constitution, the president was to share some of his power with a prime minister, who in turn had to be chosen from the ranks of the majority party of the national assembly. Moreover, the president could no longer manipulate the command structures of the military; the chief of the army now had to win the approval of the national assembly.

Thus, Haiti's new constitution was designed to block the rise of any form of personal rule,[84] but it could also prove a formidable obstacle to the radical restructuring of society—a situation the future Aristide administration would soon confront. The constitution, with all its checks and balances, tended to produce a stultifying immobilism that favored the status quo of the dominant classes. Instead of generating compromise, it created deadlock; instead of facilitating civil debates, it exacerbated antagonisms; and instead of enhancing peaceful patterns of governance, it spawned popular mobilization that easily degenerated into "mob rule." Paradoxically, the constitution blocked any effective form of governance. It was to become a thorn in the side of the future Aristide administration and a serious obstacle to any fundamental reform.

Notes

1. See Michel-Rolph Trouillot, *Haiti: State Against Nation* (New York: Monthly Review Press, 1990); and Trouillot, "Haiti's Nightmare and the Lessons of History," in NACLA, ed., *Haiti: Dangerous Crossroads* (Boston: South End Press, 1995), pp. 121–132.

2. For an extreme instance of the cultural explanation of Haiti's underdevelopment, see Lawrence E. Harrison, "Voodoo Politics," *Atlantic Monthly,* June 1993, pp. 101–107. Harrison, a former director of the USAID mission in Haiti, contends (pp. 105–107):

> I believe that culture is the only possible explanation for Haiti's unending tragedy: the values and attitudes of the average Haitian are profoundly influenced by traditional African culture, particularly the voodoo religion, and by slavery under the French. . . . The Haitian people see themselves, their neighbors, their country, and the world in ways that foster autocratic and corrupt politics, extreme social injustice, and economic stagnation. . . . [Haitian society] is characterized by a limited radius of trust and identification, usually confined to the family. . . . The imprint of African culture, particularly Vodun, and slavery on Haiti, sustained by long years of isolation from progressive ideas, open political systems, and economic dynamism, is, I believe, the only possible explanation for the continuing Haitian tragedy.

Harrison's argument leads him to endorse the idea of a U.S. Baptist missionary who contended that since Haitians are not part of the Judeo-Christian tradition, they externalize their guilt and are thus not responsible for their destiny. Allegedly, they can even steal without shame. In Harrison's view, Haitians are different from "modern," "rational" individuals, and they are possessed of "anti-progress values" (pp. 106–107). But this is not all. According to him, Haitian childrearing practices generate an irresponsible, immoral, and helpless individual who is condemned to live in a thoroughly "uncivil" culture (p. 107).

As Trouillot has argued in "Haiti's Nightmare," p. 46, racist comments of this kind reflect the "dangerous and resilient . . . idea that the Haitian political quagmire is due to some congenital disease of the Haitian mind. Such a conclusion makes Haiti's political dilemma immune to rational explanation and therefore to solutions that could be both just and practical."

3. Trouillot, *Haiti: State Against Nation;* Trouillot, "Haiti's Nightmare."

4. Jean Fouchard, *Les Marrons de la Liberté* (Port-au-Prince: Éditions Henry Deschamps, 1988); Carolyn E. Fick, *The Making of Haiti* (Knoxville: University of Tennessee Press, 1990). Robert Maguire, *Bootstrap Politics: Elections and Haiti's New Public Officials* (Baltimore: Hopkins-Georgetown Haiti Project, February 1996), p. 3, describes *marronnage*—in Creole *mawonaj*—as "a strategy from the country's past and evocative of runaway slaves that boils down to 'resistance through elusiveness.' When threatened, leaders and groups blended into the woodwork until it was safe to reemerge. This practice would serve them well, not just during their early days of organization, but in the future. Using *mawonaj*, Haiti's evolving grassroots movement survived Duvalier and the rapacious military regimes led by Henri Namphy, Prosper Avril, and, finally, Raoul Cédras and his cohorts."

5. See "Carnaval Grands Mangeurs," *Haïti en Marche,* February 12–18, 1997, pp. 1–8; *Haïti en Marche,* February 19–25, 1997, p. 12.

6. See Brian Weinstein and Aaron Segal, *Haiti: The Failure of Politics* (New York: Praeger, 1992).

7. *World Development Report 1999/2000: Entering the 21st Century* (Oxford: Oxford University Press, 2000), pp. 232, 236.

8. Mats Lundahl, *Peasants and Poverty: A Study of Haiti* (London: Croom Helm, 1979).

9. David Nicholls, *From Dessalines to Duvalier: Race, Colour and National Independence in Haiti* (Cambridge: Cambridge University Press, 1979); see also Micheline Labelle, *Idéologie de Couleur et Classes Sociales en Haïti* (Montreal: Les Presses de l'Université de Montréal, 1978).

10. Amy Wilentz, *The Rainy Season* (New York: Touchstone, 1989), p. 205.

11. I use the term *Vodou* because it is close to the Creole spelling; *Vodun* would be appropriate, but it corresponds more to African pronunciation, than to the

Creole, French, or English. I reject the term *voodoo* because it tends to be associated with black magic and sorcery. I am indepted to Carrol Coates for this explanation.

12. Alfred Métraux, *Voodoo in Haiti,* with new introduction by Sidney Mintz (New York: Schocken Books, 1972).

13. Wade Davis, *Passage of Darkness: The Ethnobiology of the Haitian Zombie* (Raleigh: University of North Carolina Press, 1988), pp. 46–47.

14. Métraux, *Voodoo in Haiti,* p. 62.

15. Laennec Hurbon, *Voodoo: Search for the Spirit* (New York: Harry N. Abrams, 1995), pp. 118–123; see also Hurbon, *Comprendre Haïti* (Paris: Karthala, 1987), pp. 115–119, 148–169.

Vodouistes have claimed that about 2,000 *houngans* and *mambos* were killed in what they have called "The Pogrom." Although it is difficult to ascertain the exact number, 500 cases have been confirmed. The violence against Vodou priests and priestesses was not merely an anti-Duvalierist phenomenon, it was also the result of Christian incitement against vodou. As John Merrill pointed out in "Vodou and Political Reform in Haiti: Some Lessons for the International Community," *Fletcher Forum of World Affairs* 20, no. 1 (winter-spring 1996): 46,

> [*Houngans and mambos*] were victims of a zealous Haitian Christian clergy eager to exploit public anger at the *Tontons Macoutes* excesses as an opportunity to resume their long-standing inquisition to eradicate Vodou's power altogether. For while many of those who died were *houngan* or *mambo,* they were not necessarily *Macoute.*

16. See Davis, *Passage of Darkness;* Métraux, *Voodoo in Haiti;* and Michel S. Laguerre, *Voodoo and Politics in Haiti* (London: Macmillan, 1990).

17. Métraux, *Voodoo in Haiti.*

18. As quoted in Hans Schmidt, *The United States Occupation of Haiti, 1915–1934* (New Brunswick, N.J.: Rutgers University Press, 1971), p. 23.

19. Fick, *The Making of Haiti,* pp. 44–45; see also Hurbon, *Comprendre Haïti.*

20. Sidney Mintz, *Caribbean Transformations* (Chicago: Aldine, 1974), p. 301.

21. Ibid., pp. 283–286.

22. See Labelle, *Idéologie de Couleur et Classes Sociales en Haïti.*

23. Etzer Charles, *Le Pouvoir Politique en Haïti de 1957 à Nos Jours* (Paris: Karthala, 1994), pp. 253–254. Translated from the original French by Carrol Coates:

> Si, en principe, l'idéologie noiriste se résume à vouloir donner le pouvoir aux Noirs, il s'agit en fait pour ses defenseurs, c'est-à-dire pour quelques grands bourgeois noirs et une partie importante de la petite bourgeoisie noire, de défendre leurs intérêts de classe ou leurs ambitions personnelles. Celle-ci, par sa position sur le terrain des pratiques sociales, ne rêve que de pouvoir et d'opulence. La question de couleur devient alors une arme politico-idéologique que [Duvalier] utilise dans le but d'acquérir l'appui des classes dominées (à majorité noire).

24. Robert Malval, *L'Année de Toutes les Duperies* (Port-au-Prince: Éditions Regain, 1996), p. 98. According to Malval,

> [L'action] des Duvalier n'a consisté qu'à partager les pouvoirs, dans le cadre d'un large compromis historique: aux classes moyennes noires le pouvoir politique et le secteur public; à la bourgeoisie mulâtre le pouvoir économique et le secteur privé, la machine répressive devant protéger les intérêts de cette dernière contre les reven-

dications populaires et les amitiés puissantes et agissantes de l'oligarchie mulâtre dans le monde de la haute finance internationale s'exerçant au profit du pouvoir en place.

[(The action) of the Duvaliers consisted in sharing power within the framework of a great historical compromise: the black middle classes had political power and the public sector; the mulatto bourgeoisie had economic power and the private sector, and its interests were protected by the repressive machine against popular demands; moreover, the Duvaliers took advantage of the powerful, active friendships of the mulatto oligarchy in the world of international high finance.] (Translated by Carrol Coates)

25. Apart from Duvalier's father-in-law, Ernest Bennett, the new powerful circle of technocrats and elite members with connections to the old mulatto-dominant class comprised Frantz Merceron, Theodore Achille, Jean-Marie Chanoine, Henry Bayard, Pierre Sam, and Jean-Robert Estimé. These men served in different capacities and periods in Duvalier's many cabinets from the 1970s to the very end of the regime.

26. See Michel S. Laguerre, *The Military and Society in Haiti* (Knoxville: University of Tennessee Press, 1993), pp. 120–122; and Martin-Luc Bonnardot and Gilles Danroc, *La Chute de la Maison Duvalier* (Paris: Karthala, 1989).

27. James Ferguson, *Papa Doc, Baby Doc: Haiti and the Duvaliers* (New York: Basil Blackwell, 1987), p. 87.

28. See Laguerre, *The Military and Society in Haiti,* pp. 122–123; Bonnardot and Danroc, *La Chute de la Maison Duvalier,* pp. 11–150; and Claude Moïse and Émile Ollivier, *Repenser Haïti,* (Montreal: CIDIHCA, 1992), pp. 64–87.

29. Alex Dupuy, *Haiti in the New World Order* (Boulder: Westview Press, 1997), pp. 24–35.

30. Among these, the largest and oldest, the Peasant Movement of Papaye (MPP), founded in the early 1970s, remained clandestine until the fall of Jean-Claude Duvalier in 1986. Since then it has become one of the most important popular organizations in the fight for democracy.

31. Guillermo O'Donnell, *Counterpoints* (Notre Dame: University of Notre Dame Press, 1999), p. 122.

32. See Anne Greene, *The Catholic Church in Haiti* (East Lansing: Michigan State University Press, 1993), pp. 129–209; see also Ferguson, *Papa Doc, Baby Doc,* pp. 75–77.

33. Greene describes the CHR as "the collective conscience of the Church during the Jean-Claude presidency. The preponderantly female organization (over 80 percent of its 16,000 members are women), repeatedly took issue with the government against injustices and encouraged and pressured the [Conference of Haitian Bishops] to take a stand" (ibid., p. 141).

34. Ibid., p. 134.

35. See Jean-Bertrand Aristide, *In the Parish of the Poor* (New York: Orbis, 1991).

36. Greene, *The Catholic Church in Haiti,* pp. 134–135.

37. As cited in ibid., p. 138.

38. Ibid. See also Moïse and Ollivier, *Repenser Haïti,* pp. 79–80; and Ferguson, *Papa Doc, Baby Doc,* pp. 75–77.

39. As cited in Greene, *The Catholic Church in Haiti,* p. 144.

40. Ibid.

41. Adam Przeworski, *Democracy and the Market* (Cambridge: Cambridge University Press, 1991), pp. 58–59.

42. Sidney Tarrow, *Power in Movement,* 2d ed. (Cambridge: Cambridge

University Press, 1998).

43. Barrington Moore Jr., *Injustice: The Social Bases of Obedience and Revolt* (White Plains, N.Y.: M. E. Sharpe, 1978).

44. Bonnardot and Danroc, *La Chute de la Maison Duvalier,* p. 22.

45. "Down with Jean Claude, down with the constitution, down with the dictatorship, long live the army." See Ibid.

46. Ibid., p. 57.

47. Ibid., p. 184.

48. Ibid., p. 179. Translated from the original French by Carrol Coates:

Dans cette période où le pouvoir vacille, où Jean-Claude Duvalier perd ses appuis, le rôle de l'armée semble à tous prépondérant. Mais nulle part n'apparaît de document, de réflexion sur l'organisation de l'armée, sur son rôle, sur son pouvoir. Au lieu d'établir des options de stratégie face au pouvoir, on discute et rediscute des choix tactiques, avec cette question lancinante qui traîne dans les milieux progressistes, dans l'Église, dans la bourgeoisie: "Quel militaire honnête, quel militaire progressiste pourrait-on intégrer dans un gouvernement de transition?"

49. Elizabeth Abbott, *Haiti: The Duvaliers and Their Legacy* (New York: McGraw-Hill, 1988), p. 284.

50. Ibid., pp. 301–307.

51. Ibid., pp. 286–287.

52. Ibid., pp. 303–304.

53. Bonnardot and Danroc, *La Chute de la Maison Duvalier,* pp. 213–273.

54. Ibid., pp. 271, 245.

55. Abbott writes that Jean-Claude Duvalier was on his way to the airport to flee into exile when longtime adviser Prosper Avril convinced him that he still could stand firm and fight successfully to keep power. See Abbott, *Haiti,* pp. 312–317.

56. Ibid., p. 314.

57. *Télédjol* is the Creole word for rumors. In the last few days of the Duvalier regime, *télédjol* went wild. Abbott, *Haiti,* writes (p. 319):

The extravagance of rumors spread in place of news inflamed [people] even more. The people of Cap Haitien had cut off their Prefect Auguste Robinson's head and stuck it on a post, the people of Port-au-Prince repeated to each other. In Jacmel every single Macoute in town had been killed, except one wounded man who had made it into Port-au-Prince to tell the tale. Michele was already in France, in New York, in Miami. Jean-Claude was going to divorce her, was mad at her for ruining his government, had only used her to cover up his homosexuality. But Michele didn't care, the rumor-mongers declared, because she was a lesbian, smoked marijuana and had her eyes on buxom Carmine Christophe, owner of the Carmen gambling bank chain and a re-born Christian.

58. As Trouillot put it in his important book *Haiti: State Against Nation* (p. 225),

What Haitians witnessed on February 7, 1986, was not the disorderly escape of an "entire leadership" pushed out by popular resistance, . . . but a transmission of power, orchestrated with absolute order—albeit against the background of a popular uprising.

59. Moïse and Ollivier, *Repenser Haïti,* pp. 104–113; Bonnardot and Danroc, *La Chute de la Maison Duvalier,* pp. 285–288.

60. Abbott, *Haiti,* p. 355.

61. Ibid., p. 349.
62. Paul Farmer, *The Uses of Haiti* (Monroe, Maine: Common Courage Press, 1994), pp. 136–142.
63. Ibid., pp. 136–137.
64. Moïse and Ollivier, *Repenser Haïti*, pp. 114–117.
65. Ibid., pp. 117–118; see also Farmer, *The Uses of Haiti*, pp. 141–142; Wilentz, *The Rainy Season*, pp. 322–324; Bonnardot and Danroc, *La Chute de la Maison Duvalier*, pp. 288–289; and Abbott, *Haiti*, pp. 358–360.
66. In *The Rainy Season*, Wilentz describes the gruesome scene (pp. 323–324):

> The men went chopping and shooting through the panicked crowd, showing no emotion other than enthusiasm. The Ecole Argentine was a good place for a bloodbath, because there was no way out of the enclosed schoolyard except the entrance through which the attackers had come. The voters tried to escape, fleeing into the playground, into empty classrooms, overturning chairs and school benches, hunkering down in the bathroom, trying to scale the compound's back wall, tearing their hands and legs on the cemented broken glass that topped the barrier, a disincentive to trespassers. At least seventeen of the voters were killed, and a television journalist from the Dominican Republic was gunned down after he put his hands up over his head. Under an almond tree in the school's front yard, the attackers hacked a screaming woman to death. Two more women were killed in the bathroom. One family who came to vote, grandmother, daughter and granddaughter, were all killed. Voters who piled up in a corner of a classroom were massacred. . . . Of course neither the police nor the Army attempted to stop the killing.

67. Abbott, *Haiti*, p. xii.
68. Ferguson, *Papa Doc, Baby Doc*, pp. 176–177.
69. Abbott, *Haiti*, pp. 360–361.
70. According to Abbott, *Haiti* (p. 353),

> Grégoire Eugene, Hubert [Deronceray], and Leslie Manigat all argued that the army was a Haitian reality that had to be accommodated, not challenged. Respectable and proven anti-Duvalierists, their candidacies were a bitter pill for the boycotting Group of Four. Their participation cheered the government as much as it discouraged the boycotters. All were moderates, so it was not crucial which of them won.

71. Several key Duvalierist figures—Colonel Williams Régala, Colonel Prosper Avril, and Frank Romain, former chief of the secret police—supported Manigat and convinced Namphy that he had to be the "chosen" president. See Abbott, *Haiti*, p. 363; and Ferguson, *Papa Doc, Baby Doc*, pp. 184–185.
72. Wilentz, *The Rainy Season*, p. 335; see also Abbott, *Haiti*, pp. 363–364; and Ferguson, *Papa Doc, Baby Doc*, pp. 184–187. While writing his book, *The Military and Society in Haiti*, Laguerre interviewed personally key figures of the army who told him that (pp. 171–172)

> three days before the general elections, Manigat was informed of his selection by the army to serve as the new president of Haiti. The following day, the American, Canadian, and French Embassies were informed of the National Council of Government's choice. When the general elections were held on 17 January (with the participation of less than 5 percent of the voting population), General Namphy of course proclaimed Manigat the winner of the contest.
>
> The selection of Leslie F. Manigat as president by the army-run National Council of Government was the result of a "historic compromise." Through this compromise, the popular democratic candidates were not supposed to run for

office, the Duvalierists were similarly constrained, the army was to handpick the members of the electoral council, the ballots on election day were not to be secret, and the army was finally to select the president and all the members of the Chamber of Representatives and the Senate. That was the first package of the compromise.

The second package . . . consisted of the unstated and unwritten understanding that the new president would run the country side-by-side and in collaboration with the army. This [guaranteed that] . . . prominent Duvalierists would not be prosecuted for alleged crimes committed during the previous administrations, Duvalierist army officers would not be dismissed, and the army would have a free hand to reorganize itself and implement its new set of rules.

73. Ferguson, *Papa Doc, Baby Doc*, p. 185.

74. Moïse and Ollivier, *Repenser Haïti*, pp. 120–122; Ferguson, *Papa Doc, Baby Doc*, pp. 185–191; Wilentz, *The Rainy Season*, pp. 334–339; see also Abbott, *Haiti*, pp. 365–366.

75. Jean-Bertrand Aristide, *Aristide: An Autobiography* (Maryknoll, N.Y.: Orbis, 1993), pp. 89–106; Wilentz, *The Rainy Season*, pp. 348–357.

76. Wilentz, *The Rainy Season*, p. 234.

77. Ibid., p. 344.

78. *Ti soldat* is Creole for the nonofficer and lower-ranked military.

79. Moïse and Ollivier, *Repenser Haïti*, pp. 124–130.

80. Ibid., pp. 133–135; Farmer, *The Uses of Haiti*, pp. 150–151.

81. Farmer, *The Uses of Haiti*, pp. 150–151; Greg Chamberlain, "An Interregnum: Haitian History from 1987 to 1990," in NACLA, ed., *Haiti: Dangerous Crossroads* (Boston: South End Press, 1995), pp. 38–39; Moïse and Ollivier, *Repenser Haïti*, pp. 134–145.

82. Aristide's view of the electoral process (*Autobiography*, pp. 116–117) expressed these concerns well:

The winner might be a conservative who was not too badly compromised, supported by Ertha, the privileged, and by Uncle Sam, and international opinion would applaud the conclusion of the crisis and the elimination of one of the most shameful warts in the Americas. . . . Dark forces, relieved of their criminal component, would be able to regain control and perpetuate themselves.

83. Moïse and Ollivier, *Repenser Haïti*, pp. 104–106, 141–145.

84. See Haïti Solidarité Internationale, *Haïti 1990: Quelle Démocratie?* (Port-au-Prince: Jean-Yues Urfie, 1990), pp. 118–119.

4

The Rise, Fall, and Second Coming of Jean–Bertrand Aristide

Lavalas in Power

In the previous chapter, I noted that the constitution of 1987 generated an unanticipated antinomy between the limits it imposed on rapid executive decisionmaking and on the popular clamor for immediate radical change. The constitution halted any drastic social transformation and unintentionally preserved the status quo that an increasingly vibrant civil society sought to challenge.

In the period of the late 1980s, Haitian civil society comprised a multiplicity of private groups bent on curbing the predatory reach of the state. While it continued to encompass conservative, populist, and radical organizations, civil society soon came to be dominated by Lavalas, whose name symbolized the huge power of the nascent and loosely structured mass movement of the destitute. Lavalas carried Father Jean-Bertrand Aristide, the embodiment of the radical voices of Ti Légliz, to the presidency in the free elections of December 16, 1990, with close to 70 percent of the vote. Father Aristide had initially been opposed to the electoral process, which he described as an imperialist U.S. affair bent on emasculating popular forces and reempowering the "reactionary bourgeoisie." In addition, he doubted that Ertha Pascal-Trouillot's transitional government could remain impartial and organize free and fair elections. Finally, he decried presidential candidates for suffering from *la présidentite*—the disease afflicting those who are interested in nothing but the exclusive promotion of their personal ambitions and interests. And yet, while Father Aristide declared his immunity from *la présidentite*, he was ultimately convinced to run for office.[1]

Aristide justified his candidacy as a historical necessity to stop reactionary forces from legitimizing their continued hold on privilege and to empower the marginalized poor majority. In short, he was left with no alternative; he had to lead Lavalas to the elections. As he put it in his autobiography:

> The result of our electoral boycott would be a formal system that would eliminate all the lower classes. We would ultimately concede to the bourgeoisie a limited suffrage that they would not have dared to propose themselves, which would produce an administration without social perspectives, opaque to outside observers, and devoid of justice. . . . It was . . . necessary to achieve unity in the popular movement. And finally, it was necessary to go to the polls. . . .
>
> I expended a lot of energy in fighting against the obstinacy of those opposed to the election, but that did not make the least change in my willingness to have it out with the mafia when the moment came. Let us be as clever as they, let us be aware of the trap, let us respond with unity: how many times did I hammer out these words, all of them summed up in the Creole saying: *"fouchet divizyon pa bwe soup eleksyon"* [you cannot eat the soup of democracy with the fork of division]?[2]

Aristide announced his candidacy on October 18. It materialized at the last minute and generated Opération Lavalas, an uneasy coalition of the popular movement of the poor and progressive anti-Duvalierist parties. The candidacy reflected on the one hand Aristide's partial acknowledgment that he could become the vehicle of an "electoral *déchoukaj*," and on the other hand the desire of reformist forces headed by the FNCD to replace their uninspiring candidate—Victor Benoît—by a more charismatic and popular leader.[3] Moreover, both Aristide and the FNCD were united in their opposition to Marc Bazin, who represented U.S.-supported conservative forces, and the Macoute Roger Lafontant.[4] In fact, the elections, as Claude Moïse and Émile Ollivier explained, became a confrontation between the "forces of evil" and the "forces of God."[5] In this confrontation, Aristide was the ideal candidate;[6] he was the messiah who would overcome all obstacles and triumph over the satanic forces of Duvalierism, privilege, and corruption. The vast majority of Haitians shared Ti Légliz's vision of him as the symbolic figure of the prophet who, inspired by God, would establish justice on earth and save the poor from the predations of the well-off.[7] Gérard Pierre Charles, who in 1990 was a strong ally of Aristide and one of the most important "organic intellectuals" of the popular movement, stated,

> Jean-Bertrand Aristide is not a self-chosen leader. He gradually emerged as he carried out his pastoral and social action. He did not come from the traditional political class. Unlike the principal candidates belonging to the historical class exercising state power (Déjoie, Manigat, Théodore, Bazin), Aristide came from the peasantry. . . . [He benefits] from the religious beliefs of the majority, which adds a messianic note to [his] leadership.
>
> That leadership is based on the resolute and logical anti-*macoutism* of Aristide's character, his historical rejection of the system, his adherence

to protest struggles, his identification with the elements of popular culture.[8]

Thus, in 1990, Aristide embodied the aspirations of the destitute; he was the personification of Lavalas. In turn, Aristide defined Lavalas as not just a "collection of a variety of movements and political parties"; it was "much, much more: a river with many sources, a flood that would sweep away all the dross, all the after-effects of a shameful past."[9] In Aristide's eyes, Lavalas was the united movement of the poor. As he put it in a message delivered in November 1988, "Alone, we are weak. Together, we are strong. Together, we are the flood."[10] Lavalas was the revolutionary flood that would sweep away all the vestiges of *duvalierisme* as well as the parasitic and exploitative bourgeoisie. "Let that flood descend [Aristide declared]! And then God will descend and put down the mighty and send them away, And He will raise up the lowly and place them on high."[11]

Needless to say, all did not share Aristide's prophetic vision. He knew that old Macoutes, the military, and a segment of the bourgeoisie would oppose his call for social solidarity and for an equitable redistribution of wealth. Once in power, Aristide could not help but face these harsh realities.[12] In spite of his multiple condemnations of imperialist and capitalist exploitation, his economic policies remained extremely pragmatic; at most they entailed a commitment to social democracy and the World Bank vision of "basic needs." He was always appealing for the cooperation of what he called the "nationalist bourgeoisie," and he accepted the necessity of dealing with international financial organizations.

Aristide acquiesced to a program of structural adjustment designed by the World Bank and the International Monetary Fund—two institutions he had previously denounced as vile capitalist instruments sucking Haiti's blood.[13] He espoused strict fiscal austerity, an anticorruption drive, and the modernization of public enterprise. These economic reforms achieved significant success and gained massive international support. As Kern Delince explained,

> Through the implementation of the most rigorous fiscal and financial policies, the majority of the reform objectives are reached in a relatively short time: growth of current receipts in the public sector, reduction of state expenditures, better allocation of operating funds, reduction of the budgetary deficit, amelioration of the exchange rate of the gourde, increase in reserve cash, reduction of personnel in public enterprises.
>
> The healthy management of public finances and success in the fight against fiscal fraud, contraband, bribery of officials, and high criminality encouraged confidence among those controlling foreign moneys. Western powers and multilateral institutions decided to reestablish on a large-scale public aid for development that was suspended in 1987. Promises of loans and gifts amounted to more than 500 million U.S. dollars, an exceptional

sum that allows for the planning of a program of public investment for 1991–1992 on the order of 430 million U.S. dollars, 80 percent of which will be financed by external assistance.[14]

Thus, in spite of its radical socialistic rhetoric, Aristide's first administration committed itself to a very moderate economic program. It had few alternatives; moreover, given the utter predatory nature of the Duvalierist inheritance, the urban poor and the peasantry would hardly suffer from the imposition of fiscal restraints and the policy of privatization. The absence of a redistributive welfare state thus facilitated the imposition of a structural adjustment package. The Aristide regime attempted, however, to reform the package by introducing into it some of the policies associated with the "basic-needs" model that had gained a certain popularity in the 1970s.[15] The effort sought to mitigate the most deleterious consequences of structural adjustment without alienating international financial institutions and donors. In this model, as Alex Dupuy has argued, "the state limits its ownership of assets to a minimum of key strategic enterprises and ascribes a much greater role to the private sector and the market. Nonetheless, the state plays a significant regulatory and redistributive role by determining which sectors of the population and economy are in greatest need of support and by redirecting resources to them."[16]

The Aristide administration was thus pursuing privatization with a "human face" while relying on a "social" market to minimize popular disenchantment and disaffection. In fact, only Duvalierist businesspeople who pillaged the national treasury and public sector employees who had benefited from a paltry prebend could oppose such a variant of structural adjustment.[17] At any rate, Haiti's desperate material situation and profound dependence on external economic forces left Aristide with few choices. He was thus fully cognizant that his radical rhetoric had obdurate limits. As he put it, "I never ceased disputing the value of believing in miracles . . . we cannot do everything or provide everything tomorrow; we will simply try to move from destitution to poverty."[18]

Such a modest project constituted, however, a revolutionary vision in a predatory society like Haiti. The vision encompassed three fundamental ideas: "dignity, transparent simplicity, and participation," which were symbolized in Lavalas's main electoral slogan: "Chanjé Leta: ba li koulè revandikasyon pèp-la" [we have to change the state: we will give it the colors of the people's demands].[19] The political implementation of that project was at odds with the constitutional constraints of liberal democracy that limited the executive power of the Lavalasian president and ultimately protected the privilege of the privileged.[20]

I do not wish to suggest that Aristide and the forces he represented were enemies of democracy; on the contrary, Aristide's brief first presidency marked the freest and most hopeful period of Haiti's modern political history. Rather, the Lavalasian conception of democracy departed from the liberal representative democracy that the constitution of 1987 sought to enshrine. Indeed, many in the Lavalas movement regarded the electoral process with ambiguity, if not disdain. It was not merely because of the tragic memory of the violence unleashed against the popular sectors in the aborted ballot of 1987; it was also because elections could be robbed and "bought" by the vast resources at the disposal of privileged groups. In addition, there was the distinct conviction that elections were both a machination engineered by U.S. imperialism and a form of "bourgeois" representation that would leave untouched existing alignments of wealth and power. Finally, radical Lavalasians believed that elections lacked the purity of a popular revolutionary uprising and would abort the desired *déchoukaj* of Duvalierism and its corrupt supporters.[21] Participation in the elections was a means to an end rather than a matter of principle. As Aristide himself put it, "What is important is to know the moment when history calls upon us to forge a tactical unity . . . in order to stop the Macoutes."[22]

The reluctance with which Aristide opted for the electoral road generated, however, a series of contradictions and tensions once he seized and exercised power. He had little patience for the constitutional and parliamentary niceties that constrained his executive governance. What Aristide desired was something else. As he put it, "The democracy to be built should be in the image of Lavalas: participatory, uncomplicated, and in permanent motion."[23] The legislative structures of governance to which Aristide had unintentionally granted legitimacy were paradoxically a constant thorn in Lavalas's populist project.[24] The compromises and gradualism entailed by constitutionalism coexisted uneasily with the Lavalasian desire for a messianic and prophetic transformation of society. As Moïse and Ollivier argued,

> Participation in elections does not mean that radicals, with Aristide as their leader, bow in the face of the virtues of formal democracy. To the extent that they are striving to assume national responsibilities, that they are aspiring to power, they can no longer be satisfied with viewing politics from a religious angle, with spending their time in proclaiming their faith like mystics and contemplative monks. They will have to act by taking into account realities and restraints even as they continue to keep in view objectives of justice and freedom. Their abrupt change of strategy holds a danger of confusion and ambiguity; it produces confusion of revolutionary methods and institutional means that will be the mark of the coming government. It will be bogged down since it does not have the means to carry out its revolutionary intentions. It will dispose only of traditional institutional tools . . . and will feel trapped in a corner. It will roar and lash out even as it is held back by the politics that it does not wish to carry out.[25]

Déchoukaj and parliamentarism remained in serious tension and ultimately proved incompatible. Such incompatibility was accentuated further by Aristide's failure to institutionalize a political society that may have helped mediate conflicts and minimize political deadlock.[26] Aristide's prophetic style of governance blinded him to the "princely" necessity of compromise and undermined his support for political society. In fact, his disdain for the entire political class caused inevitable and immediate divisions within the Lavalas movement. Aristide alienated many of his supporters by failing to give them any important position of power. He excluded the FNCD and other important components of his electoral coalition from his government.[27] Moreover, on February 4, 1991, three days before assuming the presidency, Aristide created his Lavalas Organization in an unambiguous rejection of the FNCD, under whose legal banner he ran his campaign.[28]

Clearly, Aristide was bent on controlling the mass movement. He was not prepared to cede leadership of it to any independent party; his Lavalas Organization embodied the outward structure of a regime of friends who were totally devoted and loyal to his persona.[29] Aristide did not trust "professional politicians" who might quickly turn against him and abandon his transformative agenda. As Dupuy put it,

> Aristide . . . entertained a jaundiced view of the existing political parties, even those on the Left like the FNCD that were close to his political views. He saw them basically as "talk shops" that held congresses, engaged in legitimate but Byzantine discussions . . . and whose proliferation rendered them ineffective. . . . [Aristide's] allegiance was only to the people and to . . . *Opération Lavalas*—cleansing flood—movement, which he believed was more significant than the FNCD (or any other political organization then in place), and of which he was the self-proclaimed leader.[30]

Justifying his policy of marginalizing allied forces, Aristide declared cryptically, "You cannot drink the soup of democracy with a fork of division."[31] His rejection of former allies, however, helped to undermine political consensus and exacerbated unnecessarily his relations with parliament. In fact, many observers have claimed that these divisions weakened Aristide's regime to such an extent that they were a major factor in the coup of September 1991.[32] From this perspective, it was Aristide's confrontational style symbolized in his toleration and indeed incitation of mob rule that was responsible for his own downfall. He never acquired the political skills required to seduce his opponents; he sought to silence them through intimidation rather than cooperation and compromise. Moreover, his loyalty to supporters was always tenuous and dependent on their blind subservience to his own changing agenda.[33] In short, Aristide had neither the presidential stature nor the statecraft that would have empowered him to accomplish his objectives. Robert Malval, who would become Aristide's prime minister during his exile in Washington, summarizes well this view:

> [Aristide] had only short-winded social rhetoric that he had taken from the doctrine of liberation theology and that he used on all occasions in order better to hide the absence of any real political, social, and particularly economic thinking.
>
> Neither before September 30, 1991, nor after October 15, 1994, will he ever manage to make clear for himself the substance and the limits of the immense power that he had received at the polls, and from that stems the vagueness of his speeches, the impropriety of the terms that often slip out automatically and the redundancy that he puts forth as a defense each time that he finds himself lacking in ideas. If his discourse was consequently predictable, his action, on the other hand, disconcerted more than one observer. An idea may be as quickly approved as abandoned, thus giving to his political action a contradictory nature that will continue to prevent him from rising to the level of his incredible destiny.[34]

While it is true that Aristide's prophetic style and enigmatic policies may have deepened the profound alienation existing between the popular forces that he symbolized and the dominant classes, nothing suggests that these classes would have responded positively to a more "princely" demeanor. The dominant classes despised him, they engaged in plotting maneuvers immediately after his election, and they never entertained the idea of compromise.[35] Only surrender would have satisfied them. In reality, whatever may have been Aristide's style of governance, his call for social solidarity and for an equitable redistribution of wealth was bound to incite the opposition of old Macoute leaders, the military, and a segment of the bourgeoisie. Moreover, the dominant classes' hatred of Aristide stemmed not from what he ultimately did, but rather from what he symbolized. They abhorred the president who came to embody everything they feared from the "populace"; their visceral revulsion toward him stemmed, however, more from emotional than rational motivations. As David Nicholls has pointed out,

> Aristide's presence in the presidential palace reflected and reinforced a new confidence among the poor people of Haiti. Servants refused to do what they were told, and were even heard to say that their master's luxurious house and cars would soon be theirs. The rich became worried that their privileged position was being threatened. The prospect of a social revolution appeared on the horizon.[36]

The dominant classes' fears of a revolution and a world turned "upside down" prompted their mobilization and support for the coup of September 1991. Moral appeals to share wealth and opportunities more equally, and

Aristide's hugely popular slogan that *tout moun se moun* had very little impact on the dominant classes' behavior. Clearly, the time for a Haitian "deliberative" democracy had yet to arrive;[37] brute force would settle the issue and Aristide could not help but face this harsh reality.

The failure of constitutionalism was largely caused by the unequal balance of power between the contending political blocs. The countervailing force of a popular civil society was still too weak, unorganized, and defenseless to prevent the military coup; and while the Haitian authoritarian habitus facilitated Aristide's overthrow, it was of very secondary significance. In reality, a democratic consensus for a radical transformation of Haitian society was impossible given that the stark demarcation of class had historically generated a politics of ferocious struggles rather than civil compromises. The question really was, and still is, Would the Haitian dominant class be prepared to accept electoral defeat and relinquish its power to radical populist forces without resorting to a preemptive coup?

The overthrow of President Aristide on the night of September 29, 1991, clearly demonstrated that the ruling class contemplated nothing of the sort. It is clear that the military and the bourgeoisie felt increasingly threatened by Aristide's appeals for popular justice. They feared a social explosion that would end their domination. The coup symbolized not their alleged defense of the constitution, but rather their determined resistance to any fundamental change. When Aristide made his famous "Père Lebrun" speech on September 27, the speech in which he rhetorically extolled in front of a huge crowd the virtues of necklacing his Macoute enemies, he had already lost the battle.[38] The speech was a desperate attempt to prevent the army and the bourgeoisie from striking down Lavalas.

Rather than articulating a clear strategy of revolutionary violence,[39] Aristide's wild rhetoric represented a last-ditch attempt to intimidate those who had been busy planning his overthrow. As he later explained, "I was using words to answer bullets."[40] His words, however, symbolized and underlined his preference for a radical discourse that masked Lavalas's inherent organizational and political weaknesses and incapacity to implement a revolutionary program. While such words electrified his mass followings, they betrayed impotence rather than strength and contributed to the inevitable fury of the dominant class and the military. The Lavalasian movement convinced itself that the combined power of both its huge following and its revolutionary discourse was sufficient to change Haiti and defeat reactionary forces. The aborted coup of Roger Lafontant greatly nurtured these illusions. Aristide and his supporters believed that the massive opposition of the masses—by itself alone—not only prevented Lafontant and his Macoute allies from regaining power, but also emasculated the army.[41] This was a terrible mistake: while the role of the mobilized masses should not be underestimated, it was only one, albeit important, factor in squashing the coup. Indeed, at this juncture what mattered was that the military was not yet prepared to massacre people, and decided—for its own corporate reasons—to withhold its support for Lafontant when it became clear that neither the United States nor France would tolerate the return to power of an old hard-line Duvalierist.[42]

Aristide drew from that crisis the rather naïve and ultimately erroneous lesson that an essentially demilitarized form of "people's power" coupled with wild rhetorical flourishes and the threat of more "Père Lebruns" could frighten the dominant classes into silence and submission. That interpretation of the Lafontant coup generated a Lavalasian illusion about Aristide's power and capacity to rule. In fact, the first Aristide regime lacked the means to carry out its words and policies. Intoxicated by its utter voluntarism and disdain for programmatic action, it governed through radical theological incantations.[43] Moïse and Ollivier describe the behavior of Aristide's administration during its short-lived seven months in office:

> What dominates during this period is the voluntarism of the new leaders, their fascination with radical methods that, according to them, should allow them to check corruption, to short-circuit slow, faulty procedures of which delinquents take advantage in order to escape justice; it is also, without speaking of theory, an absence of thought corresponding to the specificity of the circumstances. Transposed to the field of political struggles and targeting not only enemies and concrete adversaries but also those who are neutral, skeptical or uneasy, the discourse of government partisans, who are touchy, unanimists, fanatics, sinks into fiction, distortion of fact, Manichaeism, demonization, attribution of guilt, intellectual terrorism, sacred language, absolute certainties, demeaning of adversaries—everything needed to bulldoze the hesitant and annihilate the opposition.[44]

While Lavalas's discourse was truly antagonistic and menacing to the privileged sectors of society, how could it have been otherwise? How could we be surprised? To a large degree the discourse corresponded to the public explosion of the majority's "hidden transcripts."[45] In *Daniel Deronda,* George Eliot expresses well the feelings of detestation that must have taken over Haiti's majority: "The intensest hatred is that rooted in fear, which compels to silence and drives vehemence into constructive vindictiveness, an imaginary annihilation of the detested object, something like the hidden rites of vengeance with which the persecuted have a dark vent for their rage."[46] There was thus hatred in Lavalas's discourse, because for too long it had been violently forced underground. Democratization and elections allowed virulent attitudes to rise and flourish. Such attitudes were the logical response to the dominant class's utterly reactionary contempt for the masses. In their private as well as public utterances, members of the dominant class held *le peuple* in nothing but disdain, scorn, and ridicule. The intensity of their detestation expressed their conviction that the majority of their compatriots lacked the full attributes of the human species and embodied a gesticulating, savage, and animalistic mass, incapable of civilized and rational behavior. In the 1992 documentary film *Killing the Dream*, Aubelin Jolicoeur, a journalist and celebrity of Haiti's "higher circles," betrayed their fascist tendencies:

> The people made a choice that is at the root of all our problems. Aristide was elected by 67 percent of the vote, maybe 70 percent. But that is an erroneous way of seeing democracy and perhaps a terrible error because people who cannot read cannot possibly make a valid choice.[47]

Simply put, the dominant class could not countenance the transformation of the *moun andeyo* into citizens;[48] it could not allow the world to "turn upside down." The new citizens, however, armed with the knowledge that *tout moun se moun*[49] would no longer put up with being silent victims, they would no longer tolerate being ordered to "pa fouré bouch ou nan afè moun" [mind their own business]. Thus, the political discourse of the time betrayed the ugly realities of a naked political confrontation in a society deeply fissured between dominant and subordinate classes.

In fact, there was a new geography of class power that forced members of the dominant class into erecting walls of armed security to separate themselves from the *moun andeyo* who were increasingly "invading their territory."[50] Wealthy Haitians feared being overwhelmed by a vengeful, violent, and criminal mass of poor people who had trespassed the boundaries of private property to settle on land that had hitherto been the exclusive space of the rich. As Simon Fass explained, the collapse of the Duvalier dictatorship created a relative "breakdown of control permitting one significant act that for 30 years had proven impossible: land invasion and squatting."[51] Panic seized the dominant class; it dreaded living in close proximity to *la populace* and barricaded itself against Lavalas. As a wealthy Haitian told me in an alarming tone, "Ils sont partout, ils nous entourent, ils sont parmi nous!" [the masses are everywhere, they surround us, they are among us].[52]

Instead of bringing the classes together, the sense of social proximity generated a new impetus and energy to enlarge and consolidate the huge fissure dividing Haitians.[53] The fissure was indeed a chasm that conciliatory words could neither mask nor bridge. It is this chasm and not Lavalas's rhetoric that explains Aristide's overthrow. A decade later, Aristide himself reached the same conclusion:

> The human power in my country is the huge majority of the poor. The economic power is that 1% that controls 45% of the wealth.
> The *coup d'état* of 1991 showed how terribly afraid the 1% is of the

mobilization of the poor. They are afraid of those under the table—afraid they will see what is on the table. Afraid of those in *Cité Soleil*, that they will become impatient with their own misery. Afraid of the peasants, that they will not be *"moun andeyo"* anymore. They are afraid that those who cannot read will learn how to read. They are afraid that those who speak Creole will learn French, and no longer feel inferior. They are afraid of the poor entering the palace, of the street children swimming in the pool. They are not afraid of me. They are afraid that what I say may help the poor to see.[54]

Thus, there was a structural inevitability to the tragedy of September 29, 1991.[55] Indeed, rumors of an impending coup, and the preparations for the coup itself, long preceded Aristide's "Père Lebrun" speech.[56]

Hence, while the speech came to haunt Aristide's three long years of exile, it had little to do with the coup itself. It provided the dominant classes, however, with a useful pretext for ushering in military rule and for the constitutionality of class privilege and abuse. The coup demonstrated beyond doubt that the old structures of power remained resilient: the army resisted civilian control, old Macoutes and Duvalierists were still influential, and the elites maintained their utter contempt for *le peuple*. What was striking about the post-Duvalier era even after Aristide was restored to the presidency and even after his chosen heir, René Préval, succeeded him peacefully was not the *déchoukaj* of the old state, but rather its persistence under new forms. The regime may have changed, but the ancient structures of class power have endured in spite of the emergence of new Lavalasian political rulers.

In fact, Lavalasian rulers have been increasingly accused of imposing a system of governance rooted in the despotism that had characterized Haiti's past. While there might well be an authoritarian momentum, it differs in significant ways from old dictatorial structures. Clearly, despite the Chimères and the wild rhetoric, the level of political repression is nowhere close to what it used to be under the military or Duvalier tyrannies. The press and the opposition, constrained as they may feel, operate freely. Civil society can still publicly challenge executive power and organize against the Lavalasian state. These realities should not mask, however, the emergence and consolidation of what I have called a predatory democracy—a form of democracy that shares the plebiscitary presidentialism of a "delegative democracy."[57] As Guillermo O'Donnell explains,

Delegative democracies rest on the premise that whoever wins election to the presidency is thereby entitled to govern as he or she sees fit, constrained only by the hard facts of existing power relations and by a constitutionally limited term of office. The president is taken to be the embodiment of the nation and the main custodian and definer of its interests. . . . Since this paternalistic figure is supposed to take care of the whole nation, his political base must be a movement, the supposedly vibrant overcoming of the factionalism and conflicts associated with parties. . . . In this view, other institutions—courts and legislatures, for instance—are nuisances that come attached to the domestic and international advantages of being a democratically elected president. Accountability to such institutions appears as a mere impediment to the full authority that the president has been delegated to exercise.[58]

Both Aristide and his successor, Préval, have ruled with acute disdain for the legislative branch, emasculated the autonomy of the judiciary, and diluted the independence of the electoral council. Once elected, they governed as providential leaders, giving free rein to their executive powers. Their presidential monarchism has failed, however, to transform Haitian society. In fact, many of the old patterns of corruption, nepotism, and incompetence have resurfaced at all governmental levels. In addition, the emergence of a new Lavalasian political elite benefiting from unencumbered access to state resources has done precious little to shake the old balance of class power and the constellation of external forces that confines the country to utter dependence. The question, then, was and still is whether, given entrenched class divisions and the constraints imposed by external sources of power, the promised Lavalasian transformation is at all realizable. Ironically, the conditions surrounding Aristide's U.S.-engineered return to the presidency in October 1994 have probably spelled the end of the Lavalasian illusion that had captured the hearts and minds of most Haitians.

Exile and Return

While the coup of September 1991 interrupted abruptly the "utopian moment," it failed miserably to gain domestic and international support. The United States and its key allies decided that the military had to return to the barracks and that Aristide's presidency had to be restored. These two objectives generated a frustrating and long series of international negotiations culminating in several ill-fated agreements. While the failure of diplomacy ultimately engendered the reluctant U.S. military intervention of October 1994, it debilitated Aristide's populist and nationalist credentials.

Aristide's gradual emasculation began with the vicissitudes of exile, intensified with the Governors Island Accord that was to have returned him to power on October 30, 1993, and truly crystallized with the Port-au-Prince agreement that did in fact result in his restoration a year later. It is readily apparent that these different pacts compromised significantly much of Lavalas's original program and vision. They eventually forced Aristide to accept the inclusion of old opponents in his new "enlarged" government of national reconciliation. At Governors Island, Aristide, rather than General Raoul Cédras and the other perpetrators of the coup, made the major concessions.[59] It is true that the Haitian junta signed the agreement on July 3, 1993, in response to growing international pressures and particularly the arms and oil embargo imposed by the UN Security Council a few days earlier.[60] However, as Mark Danner correctly pointed out,

> [The accord] made no provision for justice: those responsible for the coup [would] simply retire . . . or be transferred to other posts. The Haitian army would not have to endure a "housecleaning." . . . In one way or another, under the . . . accord, Aristide would be expected to work with many of the same officers that had overthrown him and murdered his followers.[61]

Thus, as Ian Martin, former director for human rights of the Organization of American States (OAS)/UN International Mission in Haiti, put it, "Regrettably, the Governors Island Agreement made no reference to respect for human rights."[62] Moreover, the accord entailed the suspension of sanctions and the dilution of the Lavalasian component of Aristide's new government. The fact that in spite of these concessions Aristide's restoration failed to occur was ample proof that the military and the elites would not surrender easily.

The dramatis personae were locked in a dangerous equilibrium. Neither the populist democratizing bloc nor the neo-Duvalierist, authoritarian coalition was capable of imposing its respective agenda on the other. This impasse also reflected—until the shift in U.S. policy in May 1994—the military's conviction that the external forces advocating the reinstatement of Aristide had neither the will nor the power to impose his return.[63] Their conviction was further strengthened when the U.S. warship *Harlan County*, sent in accordance with the Governors Island Accord, failed to dock in Haiti in October 1993. Fearing a violent confrontation with army-backed thugs, the *Harlan County*, carrying nearly 200 U.S. troops on a non-combat mission to prepare the island for Aristide's return, pulled out of Haitian waters.[64]

Having successfully engineered the retreat of U.S. forces and thus the collapse of the Governors Island Accord, the Haitian military and elite believed that the international community and the United States in particular had grown tired of supporting Aristide and would eventually accept an "internal solution" that excluded Aristide and might lead to new elections.[65] Alternatively, the coup leaders were prepared to wait for new negotiations and more concessions, so that should Aristide return he would be totally *déplumé*—that is, totally fleeced.

The reading of the situation by the Haitian elites was reinforced by the collusion between the CIA and the Haitian military[66] as well as by the indecisive, confusing policies of the Clinton administration.[67] In fact, the

United States had always been ambivalent about the power shift that Aristide's election symbolized and had traditionally supported the elite and the army.[68] Haitian politicians of very distinct ideological tendencies, and friends as well as foes of Aristide, have maintained that the United States had such a difficult time countenancing his 1990 victory that a delegation headed by Jimmy Carter asked him to desist in favor of Marc Bazin the very night of his electoral triumph.[69] The legacy of a strong U.S. undercurrent against Aristide inevitably impinged on the policies of the Clinton administration and paralyzed any decisive action.

Until May 1994, the United States had been unwilling to contemplate the use of military force and had been hesitant about imposing a total embargo. The U.S. objective at the time was to force Aristide into accepting the integration of an anti-Lavalasian front into his government. Ambassador Lawrence Pezzullo, the State Department's envoy to Haiti at the time, contended that the involvement of allegedly "moderate" forces would have offered Aristide a "broader constituency" and thus facilitated his return to the presidency.[70] It is in this light that one must understand U.S. support for former prime minister Robert Malval's planned initiative to convene a national conference in December 1994.

As Ambassador Pezzullo explained, the conference was to have been an effort at "reconstructing . . . a political coalition in the center."[71] The goal was thus to blunt Aristide's radicalism and force him into political cooperation with the neo-Duvalierist and bourgeois blocs. This was a price that Aristide was not yet prepared to pay. Facing Aristide's rejection, the humiliation of the retreat of the *Harlan County*, intense domestic criticisms, and a growing number of boat people, President Clinton was forced into a major shift of policy.

By late April, the shift was formalized: William Gray, a former African-American congressman who had been very influential in the Congressional Black Caucus, replaced Ambassador Pezzullo as special envoy to Haiti. The change in personnel symbolized a new determination to restore Aristide to the presidency. The Clinton administration then moved quickly to impose a total economic embargo on the island. It froze U.S.-held assets of wealthy Haitians and banned U.S. commercial flights to Haiti. In addition, Washington indicated clearly that it was prepared to use force if sanctions failed to dislodge the coup leaders. At its urging, on July 31, 1994, the United Nations adopted Resolution 940, which authorized a multinational military force "to use all necessary means" to oust the military junta and restore Aristide to the presidency.[72]

While a U.S. invasion was becoming increasingly likely given the intransigence[73] of the Haitian military and growing waves of boat people,[74] it constituted an alternative that neither Clinton nor Aristide necessarily welcomed. Intervention was potentially costly for both men; it could become a quagmire for the United States and it could undermine Aristide's nationalistic credentials. The killing of eighteen U.S. Rangers in Mogadishu, Somalia, on October 3, 1993, had convinced many Washington policymakers that the loss of U.S. lives in the pursuit of vague international objectives in situations of minor strategic significance was intolerable. In this view, armed intervention was justified only when matters of vital "national interest" were at stake. Moreover, U.S. policymakers feared that in the absence of a clear timetable for an exit, any intervention might well degenerate into "mission creep." In other words, U.S. troops might find themselves shifting from the initial goals of peacekeeping, to peacemaking, and ultimately "nation building." In the eyes of many members of the U.S. foreign policy elite, this was a dangerous, counterproductive, and wasteful use of U.S. power. Haiti, with its extremely limited strategic value, was thus a very dubious place for U.S. military involvement.

On the other hand, intervention had the potential of becoming a very cheap triumph for President Clinton; it might well have enabled him to assert decisive leadership and eradicate the "Somalia syndrome" that had temporarily immobilized U.S. power.[75] As David Malone has argued,

> Military intervention in Haiti derived in part from a need by the Clinton administration to demonstrate domestically that the USA retained the will and capacity to act decisively on the international level, in the wake of the USA's withdrawal from Somalia and at a time when the USA was frustrated over the nature of the UN's involvement in the Former Yugoslavia.[76]

Moreover, an intervention would inevitably deradicalize Aristide, transforming him from an anticapitalist prophet into a staunch U.S. ally committed to the virtues of the market. A U.S.-led restoration of Aristide's presidency was thus likely to dampen his populist appeal, erode his nationalist credentials, and emasculate whatever radical project he may have favored. It was the fear of such a fate that explained Aristide's ambivalence and ever changing attitude toward a U.S. military intervention. In the end, however, Aristide had no choice.[77] Indeed, his return was totally dependent on the exercise of U.S. power, over which he had no control.

The question, then, was whether after months of hesitation President Clinton would ultimately resort to military force. By September 1994, it became clear that diplomacy was exhausted and that U.S. credibility was at stake.[78] Public condemnations, economic sanctions, an international embargo, and veiled threats of armed intervention had all failed to dislodge the coup leaders. Moreover, by reluctantly drifting toward elevating Haiti to the foremost position in its national security agenda, the Clinton administration boxed itself into an inevitable intervention.

The ascendancy of Haiti in Clinton's agenda of priorities was not without some logic. Failure to intervene would have further diminished

Clinton's already dwindling international prestige. At the domestic level, the African-American community—one of the president's most important constituencies—accused him of conducting a racist foreign policy. The well-publicized hunger strike of TransAfrica's director, Randall Robinson, and the Congressional Black Caucus's calls for military action clearly contributed to transform Haiti into a critical national security issue. Moreover, the political problems caused by the flood of Haitian refugees fleeing political persecution and material deprivation gave the United States added incentives to end the island's crisis promptly.

Malone summarizes well how domestic political concerns influenced U.S. policy toward Haiti:

> Aristide and his advisers ambushed the White House through channels it could not afford to ignore with Congressional elections looming in November 1994. They managed to unite the Congressional Black Caucus, representing a bedrock component of Clinton's electoral coalition, into vocal opposition to the US President's Haiti policy. Much of the media and certain liberal constituencies, including some highly visible entertainment-industry figures, joined in. The last straw was Randall Robinson's highly mediagenic hunger strike against the Administration's Haitian refugee policy. In April and May 1994, the Administration reassessed its policy and, rising above inter-Agency disagreements, opted to restore Aristide before November (thereby, it was hoped, putting an end to the flow of refugees). Domestic political factors drove the reappraisal of policy, not concern over the credibility of the OAS and the UN. Had these domestic factors not emerged, it seems unlikely that Clinton would have mobilized the full range of diplomatic and military instruments he did to resolve the crisis.[79]

Significant domestic considerations therefore contributed to the eventual decision to take military action against Haiti's ruling junta and launch Operation Uphold Democracy.

It is unlikely, however, that domestic interests represented a sufficiently powerful constellation of constituencies to force the issue. The Clinton administration had shown repeatedly that it could ignore and even alienate its allies in the African-American community at no real cost. Furthermore, while the Haitian refugees posed a political and moral dilemma for the president, they could be—and indeed were—rerouted to shores far away from Florida. Finally, with more than two-thirds of the U.S. public opposed to any military intervention, the Clinton administration had little to gain from invading Haiti and risking the loss of American lives. In fact, President Clinton himself thought a military strike against the "de factos" might well "ruin everything he had worked all his life to build."[80] He is reported to have confided to historian Taylor Branch

[that] his closest friends in the U.S. Senate advised him in person that his contemplated military intervention was worse than misguided or foolish—it was insane. As if it weren't bad enough to send Democratic candidates against the GOP Contract with America on weak political standing and a freshly failed health-reform crusade, now, they said, six weeks before the election, Clinton wanted to invade a country that nobody in America cared about. "They were furious!" said Clinton. "They said no political leader in his right mind would consider it for a second." The Haiti venture violated the whole political canon on leadership and support for choosing which battles to fight. In the event of minor trouble, he could count on no more than eight Senate votes against censure, they warned, and with major casualties there would be talk of impeachment.

[Moreover, President Clinton acknowledged] that public fervor for him to do something about Haiti evaporated as soon as the refugees stopped washing ashore. "I had racism working for me," he fumed, "but now it's working against me."[81]

Why then the intervention? Laennec Hurbon, a prominent Haitian intellectual, has suggested that the intervention signaled a "new age" in international relations—an age in which the "Kantian idea of a human universal has begun to emerge as a concrete reality in the geopolitical sphere."[82] In Hurbon's view, this is the age when military force becomes the agent of democratic liberation rather than authoritarian repression. If this were not the case, asks Hurbon, how can we explain that American lives were put at risk "solely in order to assist a people in danger and to restore democracy to a country that has no such tradition [?]"[83]

While Operation Uphold Democracy cannot be fully accounted for without paying attention to the ideological power of a democratic aspiration, it would be exceedingly naïve to fall into Hurbon's Kantian elation. The determining but not exclusive answer lies in the vicissitudes of U.S. foreign policy toward Haiti. It is clear that, whatever may have been its role in the coup of September 1991, the U.S. government had very little sympathy for Aristide. In fact, Aristide's prophetic messianism and left-leaning tendencies made him an enemy of Washington's Cold Warriors. In the presidential elections of December 1990, the Bush administration opposed his candidacy and supported Marc Bazin, a former World Bank executive and minister of finance under Jean-Claude Duvalier. The CIA and the Pentagon, along with the Haitian elite, never accepted Aristide's victory—Raoul Cédras, Philippe Biamby, and many other key figures in the coup of 1991 were, after all, on the CIA payroll. In the de factos era, the CIA was involved in the creation of the violent paramilitary organization Front for the Advancement and Progress of Haiti (FRAPH), which was supposed to constitute a political force counterbalancing the Aristide movement.

It is not surprising that the support the de factos received from Washington convinced them that the external forces advocating the reinstatement of Aristide were prevaricated and had neither the will nor the power to impose his return. The *Harlan County* episode further reinforced this conviction. The U.S. retreat was emblematic of an incoherent foreign policy that vacillated between two contradictory goals: an accommodation with the de factos at Aristide's expense, and a determined commitment to return Aristide to the presidency. While this commitment crystallized in the massive military occupation of Haiti in October 1994, it responded more to the vagaries of U.S. domestic politics than to international norms of the UN or the OAS.

It is true that the "Santiago declaration" approved by the OAS in June 1991 guaranteed that the organization would respond decisively to any undemocratic transfer of power in any member state. Haiti was thereby catapulted onto the international agenda, which led to Security Council Resolution 940, the unprecedented UN endorsement of military intervention to remove power holders and replace them with the regime that they had previously overthrown. It is also true that the end of the Cold War generated a short-lived liberal euphoria about an "emerging right to democratic governance,"[84] superceding entrenched notions of national sovereignty. In short, while the international climate conspired against Haitian coup makers and facilitated Aristide's restoration, it cannot fully explain U.S. behavior.

Instead, I would argue that if we are to understand the U.S. decision to invade, we must analyze it in the context of the emerging new international order. With the end of the Cold War and in the aftermath of the Somalian fiasco, the United States was bent on reasserting its credibility as the only remaining superpower. To do so it had to engineer a triumphant display of strength. Haiti, with its brutal, small, ill-trained, undisciplined, and unpopular army, provided an irresistible opportunity. At little cost the United States could exhibit a renewed determination to use force when necessary in order to defend and protect human rights and democracy. Haiti was the ideal place to demonstrate that armed intervention and high moral principles could be mutually supportive. As Malone pointed out,

> [The] ability of the USA to mobilize international political and military coalitions in support of key priorities can be cast as an important national interest, which was both served and exemplified by Operation Uphold Democracy at a time when, following the retreat from Mogadishu and the *Harlan County* incident, the USA was increasingly seen by some as a toothless tiger.[85]

This was precisely Clinton's message when he announced on September 15, 1994, that the United States had "exhausted diplomacy" and would "force from power" the murderous and tyrannical coup leaders unless they departed immediately. The president indicated clearly that an invasion of more than 20,000 U.S. troops was imminent.

Clinton wanted, however, to have his cake and eat it too. He wanted a forceful display of military power and resolve without the risk of U.S. casualties and the appearance of imperialism. Therefore, while he secretly set the invasion for the night of September 18, President Clinton sent a delegation to Haiti on September 17, headed by Jimmy Carter, in a last-ditch effort to stave off armed conflict.[86] The delegation comprised two other major figures of U.S. politics: Senator Sam Nunn and General Colin Powell. After long hours of tense negotiations with the coup leaders, the delegation reached the so-called Port-au-Prince Agreement, which averted the U.S. invasion while allowing U.S. forces to enter Haiti peacefully. It is clear that this agreement was a consequence of the use of force rather than the outcome of a diplomatic triumph. The Haitian military rulers acquiesced to step down from power only when they learned during the last moments of their negotiations with the Carter mission that the invasion was under way, as U.S. warplanes were actually in the air. The junta leaders would never have signed on to the agreement had they only faced the rather gentle and understanding Carter. The agreement made possible the peaceful entry of U.S. troops into Haiti, but it symbolized appeasement rather than justice.

The agreement mentioned neither President Aristide nor his government and provided no date for the reinstallment of either; it legitimized the military-imposed regime of Émile Jonassaint and promised to the coup leaders who were no longer required to leave the country an "early and honorable retirement" by October 15, 1994. In fact, Carter went out of his way to praise Jonassaint and the Haitian junta while simultaneously condemning Clinton's foreign policy, of which he was "ashamed."[87] Not surprisingly, the Port-au-Prince Agreement stipulated that the "economic embargo and the economic sanctions" would be "lifted without delay" and that Haiti's "military and police forces [would] work in close cooperation with the US Military Mission." Suddenly, the men described by President Clinton as thugs and murderers became honorable people whom the United States would treat as partners.

The moral flip-flop of the Clinton administration raises the question whether there was a viable alternative between the appeasement of the Port-au-Prince Agreement, which left the junta's tyrants unpunished, and a U.S. intervention that might have caused thousands of unnecessary deaths. Paradoxically, the flawed Carter compromise accidentally generated a more viable alternative. After a series of violent incidents in which the Haitian police and the neo-Macoute paramilitary group FRAPH opened fire on pro-Aristide marchers, U.S. troops began to curb their cooperation with the junta.[88] The murderous behavior of Haiti's repressive forces obliged Washington to renege on its commitment to the Port-au-Prince Agreement. The United States was reluctantly forced into weakening the Haitian military, which it had already partially disarmed. In addition, under strong U.S. pressure the coup leaders were compelled to leave the country on October 13. Finally, the promise of an immediate lifting of the embargo was not kept; the UN Security Council decided not to end its crippling economic sanctions until October 16, a few hours after Aristide's safe return to Haiti.

While the fall of the military dictatorship and Aristide's "second coming" did away with the most vicious aspects of political repression, authoritarian tendencies persisted. In fact, Lavalas gradually began to establish the structures of a predatory democracy. Rooted in the Haitian habitus, the old patterns of messianic rule and presidential absolutism resurfaced and heralded times of dangerous uncertainties.

Notes

1. Claude Moïse and Émile Ollivier, *Repenser Haïti* (Montreal: CIDICHA, 1992), p. 142; see also Jean-Bertrand Aristide, *Aristide: An Autobiography* (New York: Orbis, 1993), p. 118.

2. Aristide, *Autobiography,* pp. 116–117.

3. Benoît condemned his party's choice of Aristide as "political adventurism," a dangerous descent into the unknown. See Marx V. Aristide and Laurie Richardson, "Haiti's Popular Resistance," in James Ridgeway, ed., *The Haiti Files: Decoding the Crisis* (Washington, D.C.: Essential Books, 1994), pp. 67–68.

4. Ibid., pp. 145–150. Lafontant was ultimately banned from participating in the elections. The constitution of 1987 had provided for the exclusion of major Duvalierist figures from the electoral process for ten years.

5. Ibid., p. 148.

6. Moïse and Ollivier, *Repenser Haïti,* pp. 146–153, explain well the Aristide "phenomenon":

> La percée électorale d'Aristide . . . s'explique sans doute par la personnalité de l'homme: mélange de mysticisme, de martyre, de théâtralité, symbole de l'anti macoutisme populaire, mais aussi par la volonté des animateurs du secteur populaire de contrer le macoutisme par un coup d'éclat et par la même occasion de ruiner la candidature de celui que l'on donnait pour être l'homme des Américains, Marc Bazin, celui dont on redoutait qu'il finirait par l'emporter par défaut sous le parapluie de l'ANDP. . . .
>
> Contre la bourgeoisie spoliatrice, contre l'impérialisme infâme, notamment l'Américain blanc raciste et bouffeur de peuples, contre les criminels Macoutes et leurs complices et associés dans toutes les sphères de la haute société, le petit prêtre chétif, l'incorruptible, celui qui ne connaît pas la peur, qui a déjà miraculeusement échappé à plusieurs tentatives d'assassinat, incarne le sauveur, le rédempteur. C'est l'envoyé de Dieu.
>
> [Aristide's electoral victory can doubtless be explained by the man's personality—a mixture of mysticism, of martyrdom, of theatricality, a popular symbol of anti-*macoutisme*—but also by the will of those monitors of the popular sector who wanted to counter *macoutisme* by means of a brilliant coup and, at the same time,

to ruin the candidacy of the man who was being presented as the puppet of the Americans, Marc Bazin, the man they feared might eventually win by default under the umbrella of the ANDP. . . .

Against bourgeois despoilers and infamous imperialists, in particular the racist white American and the devourer of peoples, against the Macoute criminals and their accomplices and associates in all spheres of upper society, the puny, incorruptible little priest, the one who knows no fear and who has already escaped several assassination attempts miraculously, incarnates the savior, the redeemer. God has sent him.] (Translated by Carrol Coates)

7. Ti Légliz's representatives put it in these words (as cited in ibid., p. 152):

A travers la figure symbolique du prophète, le peuple des pauvres fait une expérience d'Église. . . . Le grand prophète de l'Eglise haïtienne, c'est le père Aristide. . . . Aujourd'hui, le père Aristide est un symbole du peuple haïtien en lutte et personne n'a le droit de voler ce don de l'Esprit à tous les pauvres et à tous les jeunes qui se sont mobilisés autour de lui.

[By means of the symbolic figure of the prophet, poor people enjoy a Church experience. The great prophet of the Haitian Church is Father Aristide. . . . Today, Father Aristide is a symbol of the struggling Haitian people and nobody has the right to steal this gift of the Spirit from all the poor and all the youth who have mobilized around him.] (Translated by Carrol Coates)

8. Gérard Pierre-Charles, "Fondements Sociologiques de la Victoire Electorale de Jean-Bertrand Aristide," in Gérard Barthélémy and Christian Girault, eds., *La République Haïtienne: État des Lieux et Perspective* (Paris: Karthala, 1993), pp. 223–224. Translated from the original French by Carrol Coates:

Jean-Bertrand Aristide n'est pas un leader choisi par lui-même. Il a émergé au fur et à mesure de son action pastorale et sociale. Il n'est pas issu de la classe politique traditonnelle. À la différence des principaux candidats, qui appartiennent à la classe historique du pouvoir d'État (Déjoie, Manigat, Théodore, Bazin), Aristide est issu de la paysannerie. . . .

[Il a bénéficié] des croyances religieuses des majorités, ce qui ajoute une note méssianique à [son] leadership.

Ce leadership se fonde sur l'anti-macoutisme résolu et conséquent du personnage, son rejet historique du système, son adhésion aux luttes revendicatives, son identification au populaire-culturel.

9. Aristide, *Autobiography,* p. 126.
10. Ibid., p. 104.
11. Ibid.
12. See Moïse and Ollivier, *Repenser Haïti,* pp. 137–192.
13. Aristide used the French acronym FMI to call the IMF "Fonds des Malfaiteurs Internationaux" (Funds of International Criminals) and "Front de Misère Internationale" (Front for International Misery).
14. Kern Delince, *Les Forces Politiques en Haïti* (Paris: Karthala, 1993), p. 300. Translated from the original French by Carrol Coates:

S'appuyant sur une politique fiscale et financière des plus rigoureuses, la plupart des objectifs de la réforme sont atteints en un temps relativement court: accroissement des recettes courantes du secteur public, compression des dépenses de l'État, meilleure affectation des crédits de fonctionnement, diminution du déficit budgétaire, amelioration du taux de change de la gourde, augmentation des réserves en devises, compression des effectifs des enterprises publiques.

La saine gestion des finances publiques et le succès de la lutte contre la fraude fiscale, la contrebande, la corruption des fonctionnaires et la grande criminalité suscitent la confiance des bailleurs de fonds étrangers. Les puissances occidentales et les institutions multilatérales décident de rétablir, sur une grande échelle, l'aide publique au développement suspendue fin 1987. Les engagements de prêts ou de dons portent alors sur plus de 500 millions de US $, montant exceptionnel qui met la planification nationale en mesure de prévoir, pour l'exercice 1991–1992, un programme d'investissements publics de l'ordre 430 millions de US $, financé par l'assistance externe à concurrence de 80%.

See also Greg Chamberlain, "Haiti's 'Second Independence': Aristide Seven Months in Office," in NACLA, ed., *Haiti: Dangerous Crossroads* (Boston: South End Press, 1995), pp. 53–54; Moïse and Ollivier, *Repenser Haïti,* pp. 172–174.

15. Alex Dupuy, *Haiti in the New World Order* (Boulder: Westview Press, 1997), pp. 93–113.

16. Ibid., p. 96.

17. Alex Dupuy, "A Neo-Liberal Model for Post-Duvalier Haiti," unpublished manuscript, 1995, p. 21. See also Leslie Delatour, *Propositions pour le Progrès* (Port-au-Prince: Fondation des Industries d'Haïti, 1990).

18. Aristide, *Autobiography,* p. 128.

19. Ibid.

20. See Moïse and Ollivier, *Repenser Haïti,* pp. 149–174.

21. Amy Wilentz, *The Rainy Season* (New York: Touchstone, 1989), pp. 131–132, 330–331. Wilentz reports that Aristide opposed the vote for the new constitution of 1987 (pp. 131–132); he also condemned the elections of 1987, which he had predicted—accurately—would generate right-wing violence against innocent voters. That violence led him to explode in "an anger he reserved for crimes against humanity." Aristide declared (p. 330):

> The people of Ruelle Vaillant were sent to die a brutal, criminal death. . . . Who is responsible? First and foremost, the butchers who came with their machine guns and machetes. But not only these Macoutes. No, not only. The candidates too must accept their share of the blame. Who encouraged these people, these poor, innocent victims, to believe in false prophets, false elections? The candidates, the CEP [Conseil Electoral Provisoire], the Americans. We have said all along that there is no possibility for free elections under this criminal, Namphy. The Haitian people should never have been led into this trap, this electoral trap from which there was finally no exit but a bloody death. No election can be held until the people have thrown off the yoke of the Macoutes and the military. Haitian history will never happen the way the U.S. envisions it.

See also Moïse and Ollivier, *Repenser Haïti,* pp. 104–105.

22. As cited in Aristide and Richardson, "Haiti's Popular Resistance," p. 67. See also Aristide, *Autobiography,* pp. 114–121.

23. Aristide, *Autobiography,* p. 126.

24. See Kim Ives, "The Lavalas Alliance Propels Aristide to Power," *NACLA* 27, no. 4 (January-February 1994): 18–19; and Aristide and Richardson, "Haiti's Popular Resistance," pp. 34–35.

25. Moïse and Ollivier, *Repenser Haïti,* p. 149. Translated from the original French by Carrol Coates:

> La participation aux élections ne signifie pas que les radicaux dont Aristide est le chef de file s'inclinent devant les vertus de la démocratie formelle. Dans la mesure où ils cherchent à assumer des responsabilités nationales, où ils aspirent au pouvoir, ils ne peuvent plus se contenter de voir la politique d'un angle religieux, de passer

leur temps à proclamer leur foi tels des mystiques et des contemplatifs. Ils devront agir en tenant compte des réalités et des contraintes tout en gardant les yeux fixés sur les objectifs de justice et de liberté. Leur brusque changement de stratégie comporte un danger de confusion et d'ambiguïté. Confusion des methodes révolutionnaires et des moyens institutionnels dont le future gouvernement portera la marque. Il en sera empêtrée n'ayant pas les moyens de ses intentions révolutionnaires. Il ne disposera que des instruments institutionnels traditionnels, . . . il se sentira coincé. Il rugira, ruera dans les brancards alors qu'il est ligoté par la politique qu'il ne veut pas faire.

26. See Jean-Claude Jean and Marc Maesschalck, *Transition Politique en Haïti* (Paris: L'Harmaltan, 1999).

27. See Chamberlain, "Haiti's 'Second Independence'," pp. 52–53; Delince, *Les Forces Politiques en Haïti*, pp. 299–300; Etzer Charles, *Le Pouvoir Politique en Haïti de 1957 à Nos Jours* (Paris: Karthala, 1994), p. 403; Robert Malval, *L'Année de Toutes les Duperies* (Port-au-Prince: Éditions Regain, 1996), pp. 43, 53–56.

28. According to Aristide and Richardson, "Haiti's Popular Resistance," p. 68, Aristide's motive in creating his Lavalas Organization was obvious:

> to build an independent political structure around the mass mobilization of the people. This signified a divorce from the FNCD, which became threatened by the prospect of a rival party that would inherit Lavalas' glory. Because the FNCD reformists could not control the alliance, they became Aristide's most bitter enemies, and many actively participated in destabilizing his government.

While this may indeed be true, it is equally clear that Aristide did not want any other leader to emerge from the popular movement. He wanted to monopolize the site of power and did everything to have an entourage that was not only loyal but also subservient to him. The marginalization of Evans Paul responded to a large degree to that logic.

29. Greg Chamberlain, "Le Héros et le Pouvoir," in Gerard Barthélémy and Christian Girault, eds., *La République Haïtienne* (Paris: Karthala, 1993), p. 227.

30. Alex Dupuy, "The Prophet Armed: Jean-Bertrand Aristide's Liberation-Theology and Politics," unpublished manuscript, p. 25. See also, Aristide, *Autobiography,* p. 126.

31. As cited in Chamberlain, "Haiti's 'Second Independence'," pp. 52–53.

32. Charles argues in his *Pouvoir Politique en Haïti* (p. 403):

> Dès la formation du gouvernement, un malaise est apparu au sein du Mouvman Lavalas du fait qu'il n'existe aucun ministre venant du FNCD. Alors que ce dernier réclame sa présence au gouvernement comme condition au renforcement de l'alliance, le gouvernement, de son côté, explique sa composition par la necessité de constituer une équipe très unifiée et solide, capable de prendre les décisions urgentes qui s'imposent. Pour autant, l'alliance n'éclate pas. Cependant, en dépit des contacts permanents entre les différentes composantes, elle ne sera jamais au beau fixe. Cette situation n'est pas sans conséquences sur les relations entre l'exécutif et le législatif où les parlementaires du FNCD ne font pas toujours preuve d'un ferme soutien au gouvernement. Ainsi, certains d'entre eux, en août 1991, n'hesitent pas à s'allier à l'opposition pour essayer de renverser—mais en vain—ce dernier.
>
> Dans ce climat de tensions, l'alliance est pratiquement rompue; climat affaiblissant le siège du pouvoir et dont ne manquent certainement pas de tenir compte ceux qui, dans l'ombre, pensent au coup d'Etat (p. 403).
>
> [Since the moment of the government's formation, a malaise has appeared at the heart of the Lavalas movement because there is no minister who comes from

the FNCD. Since the latter demands its presence in the government as a condition for reinforcing the alliance, the government explains its composition by the necessity of constituting a very unified and solid team, capable of making the urgent decisions that are necessary. Because of this, the alliance does not fall apart. Nevertheless, despite ongoing contacts between the different member parties, it will never be the right time. This situation has consequences for the relationship between the executive and the legislature, in which the FNCD parliamentarians do not always firmly support the government. Thus, in August 1991, some of them do not hesitate to join the opposition in order to attempt, but in vain, to overthrow the government.

In that climate of tension, the alliance is virtually broken apart; a climate weakening the seat of power and in which there are not lacking those who, in the shadows, are thinking of a coup d'état.] (Translated by Carrol Coates)

See also Delince, *Les Forces Politiques en Haïti,* p. 299; Moïse and Ollivier, *Repenser Haïti,* pp. 168–170.

33. Anthony Maingot, "Haiti and Aristide: The Legacy of History," *Current History,* February 1992, pp. 65–69, has argued (pp. 67–68),

Aristide's political problem had been evident from the start. Surrounded by ideologues and idealists, all political amateurs, Aristide never seemed able to distinguish friend from foe. Worse, he never seemed interested in the profane art of political maneuvering. In fact, he seemed to excel at turning allies into opponents.

34. Malval, *L'Année de Toutes les Duperies,* p. 51. Translated from the original French by Carrol Coates:

[Aristide] n'avait q'une rhétorique sociale, au souffle court, puisée dans la doctrine de la théologie de la libération et qu'il brandissait à tous les coups pour mieux occulter l'absence de toute véritable pensée politique, sociale et surtout économique.

Il ne parviendra jamais, ni avant le 30 Septembre 1991 ni après le 15 Octobre 1994, à se préciser à lui même la substance et les limites de l'immense pouvoir qu'il avait reçu des urnes, d'où le vague de ses discours, l'impropriété des termes qui lui échapperont souvent comme par automatisme et les redondances qui lui servent de défense avancée toutes les fois où il sera à court d'idées. Si la parole était ainsi prévisible chez lui, ses actes, par contre, deconcerteront plus d'un observateur. Une idée peut être aussi vite approuvée qu'abandonnée, donnant ainsi à son action politique un caractère contradictoire qui l'empêchera toujours de se hisser à la hauteur de son incroyable destin.

35. In an attempt to prevent Aristide from becoming president, Roger Lafontant, a notorious Duvalierist and Macoute, launched a coup on January 6, 1991, against the provisional government of Pascal-Trouillot. The coup failed when thousands of Aristide's supporters overwhelmed the streets of Port-au-Prince and forced the army to abort the coup. The mass mobilization of Lavalas supporters was not the only important factor contributing to the failure of the coup; Malval explains well that had it not been for the diplomatic intervention of the United States and France, such mass mobilization might well have failed to squash Lafontant's putsch (Marval, *L'Année de Toutes les Duperies,* p. 47). Aristide eventually became president on February 7, 1991.

36. David Nicholls, *From Dessalines to Duvalier,* rev. ed. (New Brunswick, N.J.: Rutgers University Press, 1996), p. xxx.

37. Irwin P. Stotzky, *Silencing the Guns in Haiti* (Chicago: University of Chicago Press, 1997).

38. The expression "Père Lebrun" originated from a tire commercial in which the salesman, Père Lebrun, would put his head through the tires. It became the Creole expression for the ghastly practice of "necklacing." Victims of "Père Lebrun" are forced into tires that are set afire with gas. Aristide's speech was at once surprisingly conciliatory and wildly threatening. Aristide began his address by imploring the bourgeoisie to

> cooperate by using [its] money . . . to create work opportunities . . . so more people can get jobs. If you do not do so [he added], I feel sorry for you. Really I do. It will not be my fault because this money you have is not really yours. You acquired it through criminal activity. You made it by plundering, by embezzling. . . . You made it under oppressive regimes . . . under a corrupt system. . . . Today, seven months after 7 February[*], on a day ending in seven, I give one last chance. I ask you to take this chance, because you will not have two or three more chances, only one. Otherwise, it will not be good for you. [*February 7 has a symbolic quality in Haitian politics. It marks the date of Jean-Claude Duvalier's departure in 1986 and of Aristide's installation as president in 1991.]

Aristide then proceeded to make a plea to legislators to "work together with the people," and he reminded civil servants that "diverting state money is stealing, and thieves do not deserve to stay in public administration." Soon after, however, Aristide, encouraged by the loud cheers of the Lavalasian crowd, called metaphorically for the unleashing of "Père Lebrun" against all Macoutes. To tens of thousands of supporters he declared,

> You are watching all Macoute activities throughout the country. We are watching and praying. If we catch one, do not fail to give him what he deserves. What a nice tool! What a nice instrument! What a nice device! It is a pretty one. It is elegant, attractive, splendorous, graceful, and dazzling. It smells good. Wherever you go, you feel like smelling it. It is provided by the Constitution, which bans Macoutes from the political scene.

The quotations are taken from Mark Danner, "The Fall of the Prophet," *New York Review of Books,* December 2, 1993, p. 52.

39. See Moïse and Ollivier, *Repenser Haïti,* pp. 157–160.

40. See Joel Attinger and Michael Kramer's interview of Aristide, "It's Not If I Go Back, but When," *Time,* November 1, 1993, p. 28.

41. Aristide, *Autobiography,* pp. 132–133.

42. Malval's analysis of the Lafontant crisis seems more appropriate (*L'Année de Toutes les Duperies,* p. 47):

> Les événements du 7 Janvier revêtent une importance capitale . . . pour éclairer la psychologie du Président Aristide et les erreurs d'appréciation qu'ils suscitèrent chez lui. Je sais, pour avoir été un témoin involontaire des pressions exercées par les ambassades étrangères sur l'armée, le rôle déterminant joué par les représentants diplomatiques dans l'heureuse solution de la crise née du coup d'État. La population y avait, certes, contribué aussi mais il est permis de douter qu'elle aurait, seule, triomphé contre les forces qui, encore indécises, attendaient de connaître l'attitude des États-Unis et de la France, pour livrer bataille à Lafontant ou pour se rallier à lui. Aristide, de son antre, ignorait tout des tractations de cette nuit. Il sortira de son refuge, convaincu que seul le peuple avait sauvé son pouvoir et que, dorénavant, il pouvait compter sur lui pour le defendre à l'avenir. A ses yeux, l'armée était devenue une coquille vide qu'il n'aurait aucun mal à domestiquer.
>
> [The events of January 7 take on major importance . . . in clarifying President

Aristide's psychology and the errors in judgment that they have created in him. Because I was an involuntary witness of the pressures exerted by foreign embassies on the army, I know the determining role played by the diplomatic representatives in the fortunate solution of the crisis that arose from the coup d'état. The population had also contributed to that, of course, but we can doubt that the people alone would have triumphed against the still indecisive forces that were waiting to find out the attitude of the United States and France before fighting against or rallying for Lafontant. In his lair, Aristide knew nothing of the negotiations of that night. He comes out of his refuge, convinced that the people alone had saved his power and that, henceforward, he could count on them to defend him in the future. In his eyes, the army had become an empty shell that he would have no problem in taming. (Translated by Carrol Coates)

See also Moïse and Ollivier, *Repenser Haïti,* pp. 155–160.

43. In his *Autobiography* (pp. 127–128), Aristide justified his programmatic escapism:

I have often been criticized for lacking a program, or at least for imprecision in that regard. Was it for lack of time?—a poor excuse. "La chance qui passe" ("the opportunity that is getting away") and "La chance à prendre" ("the opportunity to be seized") are two basic texts, long, interesting, but often indigestible and inaccessible to 90 percent of Haitians. In fact, the people had their own program. It did not require a wizard to formalize it after years of struggle against neo-Duvalierism. It was a simple program: dignity, transparent simplicity, participation. Those three ideas could be equally well applied in the political and economic sphere in the moral realm.

At the risk of annoying certain technocrats, I have always avoided the jargon of the social sciences. One does not set oneself to listen to the people in order to reply to them in incomprehensible terms. Is this populism or demagoguery? It is neither one! Rarely did a candidate promise so little. Moral values? Yes. Commercial values? Very few.

Both La Chance Qui Passe and La Chance à Prendre were the programs of Lavalas; the documents, however, were written in French and accessible only to the progressive intellectual elites and to the top cadres of the popular movement (see Jean and Maesschalck, *Transition Politique en Haïti,* pp. 40–42).

44. Moïse and Ollivier, *Repenser Haïti,* p. 163. Translated from the original French by Carrol Coates:

Ce qui domine au cours de cette période, c'est le volontarisme des nouveaux dirigeants, leur fascination pour les méthodes radicales qui, selon eux, devraient leur permettre de faire échec à la corruption, de court-circuiter des procédures lentes et poreuses dont abusent les delinquents pour échapper à la justice; c'est aussi, pour ne pas parler de théorie, une absence de pensée correspondant à la spécificité de la conjoncture. Transposé sur le plan des luttes politiques et ciblant non seulement des ennemis, des adversaires concrets mais aussi des neutres, des sceptiques et des inquiets, le discours des partisans du gouvernement, chatouilleux, unanimistes, fanatisés, s'est dégradé en fabulation, distorsion des faits, manichéisme, satanisation, culpabilisation, terrorisme intellectuel, langage sacré, certitudes absolues, dénigrement de l'adversaire; tout ce qu'il faut pour bulldozer les hésitants et anéantir les opposants.

45. James C. Scott, *Domination and the Arts of Resistance* (New Haven: Yale University Press, 1990).

46. As cited in ibid., p. 1.

47. Interview in the documentary film *Haiti: Killing the Dream*, Crowing Rooster Productions, 1992.

48. Gérard Barthélémy, *Le Pays en Dehors* (Port-au-Prince: Éditions Henry Deschamps, 1989).

49. The slogan "*tout moun se moun*" was the title of the French edition of Aristide's autobiography. It became a plea for equality and equity among Haitians.

50. Personal interview with an individual who asked not to be identified.

51. Simon Fass, *Political Economy in Haiti* (New Brunswick, N.J.: Transaction, 1990, p. xxix. Fass adds (p. 231),

> Invasion expanded very quickly in 1986. Unorganized squatting, a process that landlords found difficulty opposing without Macoute help, finally gained a foothold. But because disbanding of the Macoutes did not alter the basic structure of the party, because erstwhile rival factions were cooperating in mutual defense, because the army was not only preoccupied with maintaining order on the streets but also still composed of party loyalists, and because many landowners had aligned themselves with the provisional government and "progressive" parties and therefore represented a political opposition worthy of attack, much of the growth in squatting remained of an organized variety.

52. These impressions derive from personal observation, conversations, and interviews with members of Haiti's dominant class.

53. In his book *Eyes of the Heart* (Monroe, Maine: Common Courage Press, 2000), Aristide defends the fact that his house in Tabarre has a large swimming pool by pointing out that poor children use it on weekends. While this may be a convoluted justification, it does nonetheless illustrate the distressing reality of Haiti's social apartheid. Aristide writes (p. 44):

> The kids swim with us, with their teachers, with a group of agronomists who work with them on Saturdays, and with American friends and volunteers working at *Lafanmi Selavi*. A mix of races and social classes in the same water. Sometimes these images have appeared on television. Shortly after we began this experience we started hearing reports from friends among the upper classes of rumors that I was preparing these "*vagabon*," these street children, to invade their swimming pools. Were it not tragic it would be comic. Perhaps the real root of the fear is this: If a maid in a wealthy home sees children from *Cité Soleil* swimming in a swimming pool on television, she may begin to ask why her child cannot swim in the pool of her boss.
>
> So it is a system of social apartheid that we are questioning.

54. Ibid., pp. 49–50.

55. Malval, in his *L'Année de Toutes les Duperies*, writes that he was convinced that Aristide would not last more than six months as president. In his view, Aristide's politics and style were bound to lead to his overthrow (p. 47).

56. Aristide, *Autobiography,* pp. 155–158; Malval, *L'Année de Toutes les Duperies,* pp. 61–75.

57. Guillermo O'Donnell, *Counterpoints* (Notre Dame: University of Notre Dame Press, 1999), pp. 159–173.

58. Ibid., p. 164.

59. Kate Doyle, "Hollow Diplomacy in Haiti," *World Policy Journal* 11, no. 1 (spring 1994): 53–55.

60. Ian Martin, "Haiti: Mangled Multilateralism," *Foreign Policy,* no. 95 (summer 1994): 80–85.

61. Danner, "The Fall of the Prophet," p. 53. See Kim Ives, "The Unmaking of a President," *NACLA* 27, no. 4 (January-February 1994): 16–29.
62. Martin, "Haiti," p. 81.
63. Malval, *L'Année de Toutes les Duperies,* p. 475.
64. Ibid., pp. 72–73. The incident represented a humiliation of U.S. power since the warship pulled out of Haitian waters because of a dozen agitated and threatening thugs of the Front for the Advancement and Progress of Haiti (FRAPH).
65. Emmanuel Constant, the leader of the paramilitary group FRAPH and main organizer of the *Harlan County* episode, declared,

> My people kept wanting to run away. But I took the gamble and urged them to stay. Then the Americans pulled out! We were astonished. That was the day FRAPH was actually born. Before, everyone said we were crazy, suicidal, that we would all be burned if Aristide returned. But now we know he is never going to return.

The quotation is cited from Martin, "Haiti," pp. 72–73. Constant's sentiment reflected the convictions of the Haitian elite. A member of the old mulatto bourgeoisie told me, "The U.S. would never send the marines to restore that little communist nigger [Aristide]."
66. A most obvious example of CIA support for the military, and opposition to Aristide, is Brian Latell's 1992 memorandum "Impressions of Haiti" to the agency's former director, Robert Gates. Declaring that "the Haitian regime barely resembles Latin American dictatorships I have known," Latell, the CIA's senior analyst for Latin America, went on to contend that he "saw no evidence of oppressive rule" during his July 1992 visit to Port-au-Prince. In fact, Latell described the coup leader and army chief, Raoul Cédras, as "a conscientious military leader who genuinely wishes to minimize his role in politics, professionalize the armed services, and develop a separate and competent civilian police force." On the other hand, Latell portrayed Aristide as an erratic and even demented individual bent on fomenting mob violence against his opponents. Latell's view of the situation closely resembled that of the Haitian military and privileged classes who favored "an elite-dominated leadership to stabilize Haiti and begin a process of economic development." As cited in Doyle, "Hollow Diplomacy in Haiti," p. 52; see also *New York Times,* November 1, 1993, pp. A1–A8.

The CIA was also involved in the creation of the violent paramilitary organization FRAPH. In the eyes of the CIA, FRAPH would constitute a political front that "could balance the Aristide movement [and do] intelligence against it." For a comprehensive report on the linkage between the CIA and FRAPH, see Alan Nairn, "Our Man in FRAPH," *The Nation,* October 24, 1994, pp. 458–461; and Nairn, "He's Our S.O.B.," *The Nation,* October 31, 1994, pp. 481–482.

The ambiguities of U.S. foreign policy toward Haiti are well summarized in Jane Regan, "A.I.D.ing U.S. Interests in Haiti," *Covert Action,* no. 51 (winter 1994–1995): 7–58. See also Nicolas Jallot and Laurent Lesage, *Haïti: Dix Ans d'Histoire Secrète* (Paris: Éditions du Félin, 1995).
67. Doyle, "Hollow Diplomacy in Haiti," pp. 52–57; Martin, "Haiti," p. 86.
68. Martin, "Haiti," p. 86.
69. Robert Malval, in his *L'Année de Toutes les Duperies,* confirms and describes the story (pp. 42–43):

> Président Carter et sa délégation se rendirent au quartier général électoral d'Aristide. . . . Après avoir congratulé l'heureux élu, même s'il ne l'était pas

encore officiellement, Jimmy Carter laissa a son adjoint Andrew Young le soin d'entamer l'étrange marchandage proposé au vainqueur des urnes. Sans trop brusquer le prêtre-candidat, connu pour sa ténacité, Young lui demanda de reconsidérer sagement la situation. Il invoqua le long cheminement des Noirs américains et le mit en parallèle avec celui des masses haïtiennes qui ne pouvaient, selon lui, en un seul jour, renverser deux siècles d'histoire. Il craignait qu'entraînées par l'élan de la victoire, elles ne finissent par la compromettre. Avec un aplomb imperturbable, il proposa, rien de moins, que le prêtre renonçât a son succès au profit de celui qu'il distançait de plus de 50%, à savoir Bazin. Dans son esprit, une telle marge justement dispensait Aristide du moindre scrupule à l'égard de l'écrasante majorité qu'il avait derrière lui. Nul n'a jamais bien compris l'esprit de cette démarche et la logique anti-démocratique qui la soutenait.

[President Carter and his delegation went to Aristide's electoral headquarters. . . . After congratulating the happy candidate, even if the election was not yet official, Jimmy Carter left to his assistant, Andrew Young, the duty of carrying out the strange bargaining proposed for the winner of the balloting. Not wanting to jostle too much the priest candidate, who was known for his tenacity, Young asked him to reconsider the situation seriously. He noted the long route of black Americans and pointed out a parallel between it and that of the Haitian masses who could not overturn in one day, according to him, two centuries of history. He was afraid that, carried along by the heat of victory, they would end up compromising it. With imperturbable equanimity, he proposed nothing less than that the priest renounce his success in favor of the candidate that he had beat by more than 50 percent, that is, Bazin. To his mind, such a margin would free Aristide from whatever scruples he might have for the crushing majority he had behind him. Nobody has ever quite understood the spirit of this proposal and the antidemocratic logic that promoted it.] (Translated by Carrol Coates)

70. As cited in the *Washington Post,* December 8, 1993, p. A11.

71. Ibid.

72. See C-Reuters@clarinet, July 31, 1994.

73. The military's intransigence reached its climax when in May 1994 they illegally installed a new president, the octogenarian Émile Jonassaint.

74. Doyle, "Hollow Diplomacy in Haiti."

75. On May 13, 1994, Richard Haass, who served in the National Security Council in the Bush administration, joined former Democratic congressman Stephen Solarz in publishing an influential editorial in the *Washington Post* calling for a U.S.-led intervention in Haiti. They argued (as cited in Roland I. Perusse, *Haitian Democracy Restored: 1991–1995* [New York: University Press of America, 1995], pp. 88–89):

U.S. policy toward Haiti is not working. As a consequence, both Haitian democracy and American credibility are on the line. . . . Defeating the small, lightly armed and poorly trained Haitian military would not be hard. If Desert Storm took six weeks, "Caribbean Hurricane" would take six hours.

76. David Malone, *Decision-Making in the UN Security Council: The Case of Haiti* (Oxford: Oxford University Press, 1998), p. 162.

77. In a letter to Boutros Boutros-Ghali, UN secretary-general, Aristide ultimately acquiesced to a U.S.-led military intervention by calling for "swift and determined action" to restore him to power. The letter supported UN Resolution 940, which authorized "the use of all necessary means" to topple the military junta. See AP@clarinet, July 29, 1994.

78. As Martin put it ("Haiti," pp. 88–89),

> It may indeed have been possible in 1993, had key errors not been made, to dislodge the Haitian military from power without the use of force, although the credible threat of force would have made it more likely to accomplish that aim without its actual use. But the international failure has rendered the military's peaceful removal from power in 1994 extremely unlikely.

79. Malone, *Decision-Making in the UN Security Council,* pp. 115–116.
80. Taylor Branch, "Clinton Without Apologies," *Esquire,* September 1996, p. 110. "De factos" is the term used to describe the military regime and its political allies.
81. Ibid.
82. Laennec Hurbon, "The Hope for Democracy," *New York Review of Books,* November 3, 1994, p. 38.
83. Ibid.
84. Thomas Franck, "The Emerging Right to Democratic Governance," *American Journal of International Law* 86 (1992): 46–91. Franck argues (p. 50),

> We are witnessing a sea change in international law, as a result of which the legitimacy of each government someday will be measured definitively by international rules and processes. We are not quite there, but we can see the outlines of this new world in which citizens of each state will look to international law and organization to guarantee their democratic entitlement.

85. Malone, *Decision-Making in the UN Security Council,* p. 180.
86. It is clear that Clinton was nervous about Carter's mission; in the phone conversation during which he asked General Powell to join the delegation, Clinton expressed his misgivings and said, "Carter is sometimes a wild card . . . and the next thing you know, I'm expected to call off the invasion because he's negotiating a deal." This quote is taken from Colin Powell, *My American Journey* (New York: Ballantine Books, 1995), p. 581.
87. Carter invited Cédras to teach Sunday school with him in Plains, Georgia, and called for "mutual respect between American commanders and the Haitian military commanders." Moreover, he equated the demand for the junta's departure from Haiti to "a serious violation of inherent human rights." See *New York Times,* September 20, 1994, p. A10.
88. John Ballard, *Upholding Democracy: The United States Military Campaign in Haiti, 1994–1997* (Westport, Conn.: Praeger, 1998), pp. 105–128.

5

The Vicissitudes of Lavalasian Power

The U.S.-led restoration of Aristide as president clearly weakened his prophetic populist appeal and emptied his project of whatever social democratic elements it might have contained.[1] He was compelled to include old opponents in his new "enlarged" government of national reconciliation. Aristide's apprehension that such a government would prevent him from introducing fundamental reforms explained his ambivalence and ever changing attitude toward any U.S. military intervention. In the end, however, he had little choice.[2] Indeed, only the exercise of U.S. power could have restored him to the presidency. Paradoxically, Aristide, who had always condemned U.S. militarism, was compelled to rely on it for his own survival. He was thus at the mercy of a force over which he had no control and with whom he entertained relations of mutual hostility.[3]

In spite of its huge ambiguities and contradictions, the U.S. intervention was the only means capable of ending the military dictatorship. Without it, the long agony of a permeable system of sanctions would have continued, devastating an already dilapidated economy. Sanctions alone would never have succeeded in reaching their goal of restoring democracy to Haiti. The embargo was porous and largely ineffective in forcing General Raoul Cédras and the other coup leaders from power. In fact, sanctions had the opposite effect: they disempowered the population, destroyed an already fragile economy, and further impoverished the vast Haitian majority, while enriching the "de factos" (military regime and its allies). As Elizabeth Gibbons put it, "The 'preponderance of evidence' points unmistakably to sanctions' disastrous impact on the Haitian economy and welfare of ordinary, innocent citizens, even as they left their military target virtually unscathed."[4]

Moreover, sanctions emasculated both the state and whatever democratic institutions may have existed in the country. The sanctions regime was thus a catastrophe, not only because it created severe economic hardship but also because it devastated the debilitated Haitian state. In Gibbons's words, upon Aristide's return, "the institutions of state had become disjointed and their capacity for governance crippled as much by the consequences of the sanctions as by the de factos' pillage."[5]

In the end, however, the lesson from Haiti is that sanctions and, for that matter, any sanctions regime—no matter how carefully conceived—will be unlikely to dislodge brutal tyrants from power unless they are confronted with an immediate and credible threat of force. In spite of its ineffectiveness, the sanctions regime imposed on Haiti was a necessary step in mustering international, and especially U.S., support for any military intervention. As David Malone explains, "Even though the threat of force, actively supported by the USA, would doubtless have led to the collapse of the *de facto* regime within forty-eight hours of its putsch, sanctions were originally the only form of coercion likely to benefit from broad international support."[6]

One may wonder, however, whether a less porous sanctions regime—that is, the imposition from the very start of the crisis of a total embargo supported by the Dominican Republic, supplemented by a naval blockade and targeted sanctions against the coup leaders and their allies—might have succeeded in returning Aristide to power quickly. The Washington Protocol of 1992 as well as the Governors Island Accord of 1993 demonstrated clearly that whenever the actual imposition or even the threat of more severe sanctions materialized, the "de factos" showed willingness to negotiate and make major concessions. However, whenever the threat was removed, the junta reverted to an intransigent posture. Thus, the U.S. occupation with its exercise of overwhelming force was necessary to restore Aristide and force the exit of the military.

Paradoxically, the intervention tilted *politically* the balance of class forces toward Lavalas. It facilitated the total emasculation of the army and compelled the Haitian elites into accepting Aristide as president of the Republic. Neither new institutions nor drastic changes of heart could have led to such an outcome. The decisive and determinant moment in Haitian politics remained the brute force of arms, even if on this occasion it originated from without.

While the U.S. intervention strengthened Lavalas politically, it diluted completely its social-democratic economic platform. The intervention inevitably deradicalized Aristide, transforming him from an anticapitalist prophet into a staunch U.S. ally committed to the virtues of the market. He became the prince, but a prince partially *déplumé*. His failure to win opposition support of his initial populist project compelled him into considering a more conservative structural adjustment program under U.S. tutelage. The major contradiction facing Haitian society was and continues to be the coexistence of left-wing rhetoric, populist politics, and right-wing economics. It is a contradiction that is not likely to survive for long, however; if the experiences of other "revolutionary" regimes are taken seriously, then it seems clear that economics will eventually prevail and establish the harsh realities of market rationality.[7]

While both Aristide and Préval had limited room to maneuver, they managed to prevaricate and stall reforms. Putting off hard decisions and fearful of the social and political consequences of embarking on a program of structural adjustment, they delayed its forceful implementation. However, with the reelection of Aristide in November 2000, the time for ambiguities may be over; it is unlikely that his new administration will have the option of postponing difficult economic decisions indefinitely. In fact, adopting a structural adjustment program may not be as costly as Aristide fears.[8] At least initially, rather than generating massive opposition, such a program may enjoy widespread popular support since the urban poor and the peasantry have never enjoyed the profligate prebends of the state.[9] Privatization of public enterprises, "rationalization" of the state bureaucracy, and balanced budgets are policies that are unlikely to alienate Aristide's prime constituencies, especially if foreign assistance is forthcoming.

It would be quite wrong, however, to minimize the social and political consequences of economic rationalization. "Downsizing" the state would have devastating consequences for an estimated 45,000 public servants, who would have to confront the vicissitudes of unemployment in an economy that generates few jobs and opportunities in the private sector. In addition, a large section of the population that has grown financially dependent on the civil servants would suffer serious deprivations from the corresponding loss of income. Downsizing would also have a dangerous political impact, particularly in the metropolitan area of Port-au-Prince, where the vast majority of the state bureaucracy resides. It would inevitably generate discontent among the educated middle sectors and erode significantly Lavalas's urban base of support. Aristide and his supporters are not likely to take this risk, especially now that current political conditions are extremely unsteady and volatile. Government spending cuts and the accompanying reduction in the number of civil servants are thus fraught with dangers. They rarely foster the sense of economic fairness and efficiency required for self-sustained and coherent developmental policies.

On the contrary, by promoting market rationality and simultaneously transforming property relations, structural adjustment may well generate urban discontent and plunge society into the uncertainties of polarized instability. In such conditions, the new Aristide government is likely to retreat from the process of economic reform altogether. Confronted with renewed challenges from "above" and "below," it may be forced, like its Lavalasian predecessors, to choose between either abandoning structural adjustment or relapsing into authoritarianism in order to impose it. The consequences of structural adjustment are thus likely to have gravely desta-bilizing effects on the consolidation of Haitian democracy.[10] Adjustment could ultimately unbalance the government, generating more unstable coalitions that would begin their own economic reforms only to arrest them later in a conceivably never-ending cycle.[11] The vacillations of the econo-my could thus compound the vicissitudes of democratic consolidation and stimulate transitions to new dictatorships. The authoritarian temptation and/or the descent into chaos are dangerous alternatives always lurking behind the curtain of the democratic debut.

Rather than challenging the roots of dominant class power, Aristide's return in 1994 managed only to raise momentarily the hopes of the poor. Overburdened, exhausted, and disenchanted, subordinate classes have become increasingly cynical about the future and Lavalas itself. While it is unlikely that they will tolerate the return of a new Duvalierism, they are no longer mesmerized by the appeals of democracy and the electoral process. The hopes of *déchoukaj,* of uprooting the evils of tyranny and implanting a just social order, are gradually fading.

Significant signs of discontent are increasingly visible. *Gran Manjers* became the unofficial song of the 1997 carnival, symbolizing massive pop-ular alienation from the Préval government and its economic program.[12] Huge masses of people chanted accusatory hymns of corruption, incompe-tence, and exploitation against the powers-that-be and the Préval adminis-tration. Such widespread discontent reemerged in the bungled legislative elections of April 1997, in which barely 5 percent of registered voters par-ticipated, and in the continuous waves of students' protests and workers' strikes.[13] Similarly, Aristide's overwhelming victory in the presidential elections of 2000 could not mask profound signs of disenchantment. While he won close to 92 percent of the vote, he faced no real competition, remained in utter seclusion, and virtually never campaigned. In addition, it is highly improbable that more than 60 percent of eligible voters participat-ed in these elections as official results suggested; most impartial observers estimated that participation did not exceed 20 percent but was not as low as the 5 percent bandied about by the opposition.[14] Whatever may have been the exact turnout, it is clear that Aristide's triumph in 2000 lacked the legit-imacy and the euphoria that characterized his first election in 1990. Rejected and indeed despised by an opposition composed of a majority of former supporters, Aristide now has the unenviable task of extricating Haiti from the abyss of a precipitous fall into chaos. At the moment, the country suffers from a general and profound malaise that can easily turn into a fun-damental systemic crisis with unpredictable consequences.

Haitian constitutionalism is thus resting on a precarious political foun-dation that is further undermined by conditions of acute material scarcity. The incapacity of the political system to deliver resources with which to change the situation and integrate social actors into a more accountable public realm has generated a growing sense of generalized discontent. This is not to argue that liberal democracy is impossible in Haiti, but rather that the utter lack of resources hinders further the complicated process of democratization. Indeed, it is clear that a democratic society cannot and will never be erected on the sole basis of a democratic will and consciousness. In the absence of advanced forces of production, a democracy, however hegemonic and popular its idea may be, is condemned to manifold distortions and regressions. In fact, it cannot even pretend to be a democracy; it embodies at best a crude or primitive form of polyarchical rule. As Marx warned long ago,

> [The] conditions of life, which different generations find in existence, decide also whether or not the periodically recurring revolutionary convulsion will be strong enough to overthrow the basis of all existing forms. And if these material elements of a complete revolution are not present (namely, on the one hand the existence of productive forces, on the other the formation of a revolutionary mass, . . .) then, as far as practical development is concerned, *it is absolutely immaterial whether the "idea" of this revolution has been expressed a hundred times already.*[15] (Emphasis added)

Thus, according to Marx, the development of the productive forces is absolutely necessary as a practical premise of democracy, for "without it only want is made general, and with want *the struggle for necessities and all the old filthy business would necessarily be reproduced*" (emphasis added).[16] Indeed, the struggle for material well-being in a situation of generalized scarcity is likely to lead to processes of intense class formation and differentiation *within* the emerging democratic-revolutionary bloc. In the Haitian context, this means that the Lavalas leadership issued from the lower middle classes and the petite bourgeoisie could easily abandon its radical transformative agenda and come to use its newly found state power to accumulate resources and gradually integrate into the existing economic elite.[17]

Moreover, the historical trajectory of the Haitian petite bourgeoisie indicates very short-lived revolutionary proclivities and more enduring long-term aspirations to integrate into the dominant class. The Lavalas cadres could thus easily fall into the most opportunistic type of behavior, faced as they were, and still are, with the vicissitudes of the democratic process, the generalized fatigue caused by difficult and permanent political combats, the acute material hardships of their social class, and their aspirations for upward social mobility. Their attempt to bring *bo tab la* (to the dinner table) the poor who have always been *en ba tab la* (under the table) can, as it were, degenerate into an exclusive supper for the leaders and cronies of Lavalas.[18] These leaders may just join the small circle of *gran manjers* and abandon their destitute followers to the harsh realities of survival in a heartless and hungry world.

Thus, by circumscribing drastically the space for class "climbing," poverty generates a zero-sum game in which wealth is acquired almost exclusively through the monopolization of state power and resources. In these conditions, the capture and continuous control of political offices become an absolute premium that imperils democratic governance as the electoral process loses its civility and turns into a matter of life or death. It is from this perspective that the explosion of the Lavalas movement into competing blocs engaged in a naked struggle for power must be understood.

While the Lavalas movement has always been fragmented, it maintained a certain degree of political unity to ensure both the election of Jean-Bertrand Aristide and his eventual restoration after his overthrow in 1991. Things began to fall apart, however, when Aristide did little to stop a popular campaign that sought to extend his presidential term by the three "stolen" years that he had spent in exile. Although he ultimately consented to step down under international and domestic pressures, he did so reluctantly and thereby alienated the OPL and significant sectors of the old Lavalas alliance. Aristide's desire to stay in power alarmed friends and foes who saw in his behavior a dangerous *dérive totalitaire*.[19] Resorting to the Haitian political habitus, Aristide inadvertently banalized his leadership and came to resemble the opportunist politician who has defined much of the country's history. Kern Delince describes him well:

> The fundamental objective of the one aspiring to power is obviously the accession to the presidency of the Republic. In order to attain this goal, he gathers his group of partisans into a small structure for collective political action—generally of an informal nature—which is charged with the organization of the electoral campaign and carrying out the most diverse political tasks. In fact, it is not the real political parties that compete for the conquest and exercise of power, but political leaders who enjoy the support of a restricted personal clientele. The principal force driving this political activity consists of personal interests more or less successfully camouflaged behind the apparent efforts to serve the general interest of the nation.[20]

When Aristide created Fanmi Lavalas (FL) in 1995, he departed little from these traditional objectives. FL became the machine that would execute his will, regroup his followers, prepare his reelection, and incarcerate his chosen successor, René Préval, into his own orbit. The circumstances surrounding Préval's ascendancy to the presidency in 1995, however, deepened serious cracks in Lavalas's unity.

By 1996 the internal dissent increased, and two years later the fissures within the Lavalas movement completely ruptured when Gérard Pierre-Charles's Organisation Politique Lavalas (OPL), which partially controlled parliament, decided to change its name to Organisation du Peuple en Lutte (OPL). The new name symbolized OPL's profound antagonism to both Aristide and his political party, Fanmi Lavalas. In the eyes of his former allies, Aristide was no longer the embodiment of popular hopes; he had become a dangerous demagogue who tolerated no dissent and was bent on creating a new dictatorship. The progressive cadres who had supported him were now deserting him. From their perspective, Aristide had succumbed to the old Haitian political authoritarian habitus. As Robert White put it,

> As a young priest, Aristide seemed to seek confrontation with Church authority. As a revolutionary, he condemned dictatorship and called for democracy. As president, he visibly chafed under the institutional restraints of the constitution he had fought so effectively to restore. As ex-president and no longer part of the formal decision-making process, his distrust of institutions intensified. With the creation of the new party, Lavalas Family, Aristide appears to have reverted to the ecclesiastical authoritarianism he once condemned. Confronted with a Lavalas movement escaping his personal control, he did not seek to build new coalitions within the party. Instead he excommunicated his longtime friends in the old Lavalas and created a new church, without doctrine or dogma except unquestioning loyalty to its leader.[21]

Aristide's authoritarian tendencies were only one factor in the divorce between Lavalas and its erstwhile followers. Personal rivalries and jealousies nourished by the struggle for power fueled the divorce and threatened any attempt at national reconciliation. The cadres that had supported Aristide saw him as the vehicle that would facilitate their own political ascendancy, fully expecting to control him once he conquered the presidency. Things, however, unfolded very differently; Aristide had such massive popularity that he could ignore, alienate, and break free from these cadres and govern as he saw fit. The intellectuals, who had contributed to his rise and hoped to use him for their own strategic purposes, found themselves excluded from his circles and increasingly powerless. Aristide had proven more astute than they had ever imagined; instead of becoming their puppet, he emerged as the pivotal and dominant figure of Haitian politics. As one of the main leaders of the opposition confessed, "Aristide nous a roulé dans la farine!" [Aristide truly fooled us].[22] This feeling of "being had" has generated among key members of the opposition a visceral personal dislike for Aristide. They resent his cleverness and are busy preparing the moment when they can savor their revenge.

This condition of mutual hostility created an acute political crisis that paralyzed President Préval's vain attempts at governing effectively through executive privilege. The immediate cause of the Lavalas split was the bungled parliamentary elections of April 1997. Poorly organized and with fewer than 10 percent of the electorate participating, the elections were "won" by pro-Aristide candidates and condemned as rigged by former Lavalasian parties, in particular the OPL. The OPL was bent on rejecting and thus blocking the nomination of any prime minister who would not be committed to the annulment of these elections. In addition, the OPL demanded the resignation of the electoral council, which it deemed corrupt and incompetent.

The internecine warfare besieging Lavalas caused a political stalemate and immobilism best illustrated in the incapacity of all political authorities to agree on forming a functioning government.[23] The resignation of Prime Minister Rosny Smarth in June 1997 exacerbated the divisions plaguing the Lavalas movement and impeded compromises on the designation of a successor. The OPL-dominated parliament rejected four nominations,[24] and the twenty-two-month stalemate ended only with Préval's decisive coup de force voiding parliament's term on January 11, 1999. With parliament dismissed, Préval was free to install a new government headed by Jacques-Édouard Alexis "under [what he himself acknowledged to be] abnormal circumstances with regards to the constitution."[25]

The primary mission of the Alexis government was the creation of a climate of peace for the organization of free and fair legislative elections, but the circumstances of its making generated fears of a return to the old patterns of presidential monarchism. The opposition led by the OPL described Préval's January 11 action as a "coup d'état" that would plunge the country into "general anarchy." Haiti, the OPL added, "is no longer under the rule of law," since the president "decided to violate the constitution and destroy institutions."[26]

In spite of these dire predictions, Préval and Alexis nominated a provisional electoral council, which wrote new electoral laws that they eventually supported and signed in July 1999. The laws resolved, albeit ambiguously, the impasse created by the April 1997 elections that had seen the allegedly rigged victory of two senators from Fanmi Lavalas. Although both senators were officially declared winners of their contests at the time, they never took their seats in parliament. Moreover, opposition parties, and the OPL in particular, called for the annulment of the elections and the scheduling of new ones, lest the country fall into utter ungovernability. In the end, the new laws did not directly nullify the 1997 ballot, but they effectively invalidated its results by declaring that nineteen senate seats rather than seventeen would have to be filled in the elections of May 2000. The two senators from Fanmi Lavalas were thus deprived of their controversial victory.[27]

Due to logistical and organizational problems, the elections initially scheduled for November, then December 1999, and then March 2000, were ultimately held on May 21, 2000. The question that dominated the political agenda was under what conditions these elections would occur and whether their results would be acceptable to the main political forces, particularly Fanmi Lavalas and the OPL. While most political parties accepted the necessity of the numerous postponements, opponents of Fanmi Lavalas and especially the OPL had feared that these delays might have been intentional and that the Préval administration was really bent on organizing a November 2000 ballot where both president and parliament would be simultaneously chosen. Most Haitian observers believed that if this were to happen, Aristide's electoral coattails would carry Fanmi Lavalas to an overwhelming majority and thus seal the total supremacy of his political bloc. This possibility alarmed anti-Aristide forces and poisoned an already tense political climate. Instances of violent confrontations at political rallies between supporters and opponents of Fanmi Lavalas[28] undermined the likelihood of a compromise that might lead to the coming to power of an effective and legitimate government. Moreover, a few weeks before the elections, the brutal assassination of Jean Dominique, director and owner of Radio Haïti-Inter and the "conscience of Haitian journalism," exacerbated the situation and generated fears of a slide into anarchy.[29]

Ultimately, however, election day arrived on May 21, 2000, and unfolded peacefully and with a high participation rate, estimated at 60 percent of the eligible population. In spite of some serious logistical problems, most impartial observers believed initially that the elections had been "free, fair, and flawed."[30] International monitors discarded charges by opposition parties that the event was tainted by extensive fraud and should be annulled.[31] While they acknowledged that the elections were plagued by numerous cases of administrative and logistical inadequacies as well as by some violence, these problems, they contended, would not ultimately affect the outcome. Lavalas, it seemed, was headed for a substantial victory.[32] This appeared to be Lavalas's moment of glory, for as one of its supporters put it,

> For months before the elections, opposition leaders in Haiti cried foul: It's their favorite thing to do, and the one thing they do well. They alleged that Aristide's supporters and Lavalas were using violence to try to put off scheduled municipal and legislative elections as long as possible, hoping to postpone the vote until the end of this year, when presidential elections are also slated to take place. The reason the opposition gave for Lavalas' alleged stalling? It claimed Aristide was afraid the opposition would win the early elections and that a legislature run by his opponents would effectively paralyze a future Aristide administration. Whereas a vote taken during the presidential election would bring in a Lavalas legislature on Aristide's presumably capacious coattails.

But the opposition's analysis was wrong, partly because it was not an analysis, it was propaganda.

With Lavalas poised on the rumble of a landslide, the opposition took up the cry of fraud and has now formally demanded the election be annulled. Reflecting the vacuum of ideas and policies in which the opposition has been festering for years, the head of the Espace de Concertation (Common Ground), a coalition of five parties, called the election "a disaster" and said the vote puts Haiti in "a new crisis."

Poor opposition. First, they claim Aristide doesn't want to play the game because he can't win. Then, when he plays and wins, they pick up their marbles and say it wasn't fair. But they can't have it both ways.[33]

They did, however, have it both ways; for soon after hailing the elections free and fair, the international monitors reversed their judgment when they realized that the vote counting was tainted by considerable fraud.[34] Fanmi Lavalas, after all, was not satisfied with a triumph; wanting more, it sought the annihilation of the opposition. What Lavalasians desired, and indeed engineered with the Préval administration's complicity, was a massive landslide whose disproportionate magnitude paradoxically deprived it of legitimacy. As James R. Morrell explained, Fanmi Lavalas "snatched defeat from the jaws of victory":

Not content with merely winning, Aristide had his supporters on the electoral commission rig the count in order to deliver first-round victories to all nineteen senatorial candidates, of whom eighteen belonged to his Lavalas Family party. They did this by stopping the counting of senatorial votes at the first four top contenders, thereby contracting the field by a quarter to a third and bumping up the percentages of the front-runners so they could claim an outright majority. By cutting off the count there they unapologetically discarded some 1.1 to 1.2 million votes cast for opposition candidates—between 25 to 35 percent of the total.[35]

This fraudulent method violated the constitution and the electoral law that stipulated clearly that victory in the first round required a majority of the votes cast—that is, 50 percent plus one. Ignoring calls from the international community and the Haitian opposition to count all the votes, the electoral commission under powerful pressures from Préval and Aristide stuck to its illegal procedure and ultimately handed over to Fanmi Lavalas quasi-absolute political control of the state. This decision was very costly; in the eyes of many erstwhile Lavalasians and the international community, it discredited Préval and Aristide's democratic credentials.[36] Moreover, it disgraced the electoral commission whose independence suffered a mortal blow. Emmanuel Charles and Debussy Damier, two of the three members appointed by the opposition, resigned from the commission in protest, and its president, Léon Manus, fled into exile rather than endorse the fraudulent results.[37]

After defending the controversial method of counting the vote, Manus reassessed the matter and became convinced that it was illegal.[38] As he put it, "The final senate tally saw only five senators elected in the first round [instead of the nineteen claimed by the electoral council]."[39] He thus refused to sanction the vote and was summoned to the National Palace where he alleged receiving menaces from both President Préval in person and then Aristide on the phone. According to Manus, "They gave [him] an ultimatum" and "threaten[ed] to engulf the capital and provincial cities in fire and blood, destroying everything in their path" unless he committed to "the immediate announcement of the results."[40] Fearing for his life, Manus escaped secretly to the Dominican Republic and then the United States with U.S. and other diplomatic assistance.[41] From New York, Manus wrote a letter to Edgard Leblanc, president of the senate, to detail the irregularities, fraud, and unconstitutionality of the May elections. The letter is worth quoting at length:

> Analysis of the legislative and local elections of May 21 and July 9 shows that they are not legally valid for the following reasons:
>
> 1. massive electoral fraud
> 2. incorrect and illegal method of counting the votes
> 3. law governing runoff elections
>
> The incorrect method of calculating the votes used in the senatorial elections should not be cited as the only reason for annulation of the elections.
>
> In effect, despite the massive participation of the population, serious fraud, denounced by the political parties of the opposition (falsification of polling results, theft of ballot boxes, destruction of tally sheets), was committed on almost all the territory of the Republic, notably in the capital, Gonâve Island, the Département de l'Artibonite, the Central Plateau, and the departments of the Nord and the Nord Ouest during the evening and throughout the night of May 21. None of these challenges has been addressed as required by the electoral law (Articles 166, 167, 168, 169, 170).
>
> No official response has been given to the different parties and contenders engaged in the process by the electoral commission.
>
> The police, charged with maintaining order and public safety, unfortunately participated in a number of fraudulent acts. Illegal interventions were reported by the opposition political parties and members of the regional electoral offices in the Central Plateau and the Department of the North as well as by many other electoral offices in the Northeast and Artibonite departments. These police never intervened or took action against any of the criminals who during the night after the vote flagrantly covered the streets of Port-au-Prince with torn-up ballots and ballot boxes. Also, the method of counting the votes used by the technical department of the CEP and rejected by the OAS observation mission, was first defended by the president of the CEP who—after reflection and study— recognized that the procedure was incorrect and did not conform with the constitution and electoral law. . . .

As a result the parliament arising from this process is illegal, illegitimate, and built on false premises, and cannot be validated without perjuring the nation.[42]

Ignoring Manus's pleas for annulling the elections, as well as intense criticisms from the UN, the OAS, the United States, and Haiti's opposition, the government went ahead with the second round on July 9 and July 30. With voter turnout declining well below 30 percent, the second round became a game without stakes boycotted by the opposition. Despite their lack of legitimacy, the government announced on August 9 the official results: Fanmi Lavalas won seventy-five of the eighty-three seats in the chamber of deputies and eighteen of nineteen contested seats in the twenty-seven-member senate.[43] Moreover, Lavalas captured 80 percent of mayoral contests and a majority of seats in urban and rural district assemblies. While Aristide's party had achieved complete control of the sites of state power, its triumph was contested and lacked legitimacy since the vote counting had been clearly manipulated. The manipulation, however, had been unnecessary given Lavalas's huge popularity and the certainty that it would have won without resorting to fraud. In fact, it may ultimately have engendered a Pyrrhic victory.

The puzzling question then is why did Fanmi Lavalas feel the need to cheat when it would have gained a significant majority in free and fair elections? Why did it risk international and domestic condemnation when most of its candidates were poised to win in the second round? In short, why the pointless, gratuitous, and counterproductive use of fraudulent means when victory was assured?

In the first place, the government and Fanmi Lavalas denied that fraud occurred at all.[44] They maintained that the method used to count the vote in 2000 was the same that was used in the previous elections of 1990, 1995, and 1997. There was no malice in the procedures and thus no reason to challenge the results. In front of the OAS, Haitian foreign minister Fritz Longchamp argued that the procedures had been publicized and that Léon Manus himself had defended the integrity and honesty of the electoral council.[45] Longchamp added that the government of Haiti did not understand "the exasperating idea of how a controversy over only ten senatorial seats would invalidate a whole election in which several hundred other seats were up for tenure throughout the country."[46] Moreover, he did not see how the government could reverse the "autonomous decision" of an "independent institution" like the electoral council. In fact, the international community was interfering in the domestic affairs of the country by seeking to impose its own wishes on a sovereign people. In Longchamp's eyes that was simply intolerable.

Foreign supporters of Fanmi Lavalas echoed this view and claimed that the United States and other international organizations were "blackballing" Aristide and Préval and "squabbling over a technicality."[47] According to the Council on Hemispheric Affairs, the United States and its allies were seeking to "humiliate" the Préval administration in order to deprive it of legitimacy.[48] The council contended that these powerful forces were resorting again to some visceral anti-Lavalas reflexes:

> [They were engaged in] an unprincipled scheme to discredit a relatively free and fair election process, given the island's impoverished circumstances. In lockstep manner, the OAS [was] effortlessly following U.S. policy objectives, which in Haiti consist of preventing at all costs the fulfillment of the will of the vast majority of the country's citizens: the return of former President Aristide to office as the result of next November's presidential ballot.[49]

Thus, for Fanmi Lavalas and its friends, the elections, in spite of a few irregularities, were basically free and fair and represented the will of the Haitian people. In their eyes, the domestic opposition was simply incapable of accepting defeat and the reality that it had little if any support among the masses. Finally, they maintained that the international community headed by the United States was bent on demonizing Aristide and demolishing his radical project.[50] While anti-Aristide forces were weak, fragmented, and opportunistic as Lavalasians argued, they nonetheless gathered a significant number of votes according to the electoral council's own tabulations. It is not only that the opposition managed respectable scores, but also that the electoral council simply discarded about 1.2 million votes—a third of all the votes cast in the senate's ballots.

Moreover, in spite of proclamations to the contrary, the council's counting methods violated its own laws; and its claims that the 2000 elections were following previous electoral procedures are simply not correct.[51] Finally, it is ironic that Lavalasians should resort to some ultranationalist rhetoric about external interference when they owe their return to power to a massive deployment of U.S. forces and other forms of foreign assistance. What they hailed in 1994 as a triumph of internationalism is now decried as an international imperialist conspiracy. The nationalist credentials of Lavalas are simply not credible. Similarly, the claim that the electoral council was autonomous and independent flies in the face of reality: President Préval and former president Aristide patently interfered in the proclamation of the official results. Not only did they request Léon Manus to endorse these results, but also they threatened him if he failed to do so. It is difficult to understand why Manus would have gone into exile if he had the liberty and independence to make his own decision. The council was clearly controlled by the executive branch and Fanmi Lavalas; to argue otherwise is disingenuous.

The government's engagement in, and defense of, electoral manipulations must have responded to certain strategic objectives and interests; otherwise they would be incomprehensible. It is clear that at least since 1997 Fanmi Lavalas has been seeking a hegemonic position that can only be satisfied by controlling at a minimum two-thirds of parliament—the threshold required to introduce major changes in the 1987 constitution. Aristide is thus establishing the terrain for an imperial presidency through the electoral omnipotence of Fanmi Lavalas. In this instance, he will be able to rely on his parliamentary supermajority to have a prime minister of his own choosing. An unmitigated form of presidential monarchism could thus be restored through the ballot box. As Claude Moïse has explained,

> When the parliamentary majority and the presidential majority come together, the formation of a homogeneous government dominated by the president can be expected. The chief of state who exercises the preponderant influence in that government then plays a decisive role in the conduct of the affairs of state.[52]

A mere majority is simply insufficient, however, for the establishment of presidential monarchism. This is why fraud became necessary to ensure both the annihilation of the anti-Lavalasian parties and the two-thirds majority for Aristide. An overwhelming victory in the first round was thus the means to that end. The logic was simple: while in the first round Fanmi Lavalas had an easy task since it faced a thoroughly divided opposition, in the second round things could have fallen apart because it would have had to contend against a single and possibly united anti-Aristide front. In these circumstances, the final outcome might have diluted the scope of Lavalas's victory, making the coveted two-thirds majority an impossibility.

The optimistic interpretation of these electoral manipulations was that Fanmi Lavalas's takeover of the fundamental institutions of the political system—the presidency, the senate, and the chamber—was an attempt to eliminate the governmental gridlock that has plagued Haiti since the fall of Jean-Claude Duvalier. In this view, Lavalas would finally be able to institute the difficult political, social, and economic reforms required to modernize the country without the permanent *blocage* of the opposition. While this process may have violated the high ideals of democracy, the argument continues, it nonetheless represented the best and most realistic solution for a country like Haiti that has always been mired in despotic rule. Moreover, any serious attempt to compel the government into reversing the fraudulent results would be counterproductive; another round of international sanctions would simply end up hurting Haiti's poor rather than its irresponsible rulers. An editorial in the *Miami Herald,* seeing no other option but acquiescing to electoral fraud, summarized well this sentiment:

Discouraging is the word that best describes the bogus second-round of voting in Haiti's parliamentary elections. . . . In rigging the outcome to benefit the ruling party, the country's leadership again is testing the forbearance of the international community that has tried time and again to provide humanitarian aid. Each attempt has been thwarted by governmental corruption or, more recently, the venal politics of former-and-future president Jean-Bertrand Aristide.

Yet it is the people of Haiti, this hemisphere's poorest nation, who suffer the consequences. For that reason, the international community—including the Clinton administration and Congress—should quell its anger and remain patient.

Sadly, there may be no alternative but to accept the reality that in Haiti a little bit of democracy is preferable to none at all.[53]

In short, the optimistic scenario is that, in spite of cheating, Fanmi Lavalas has no intention of imposing a new despotism on the island and that in fact it is bent on serving the vast majority of Haitians. Irregularities did occur, but they were of limited significance and reflected the effects of a lingering authoritarian habitus and the inevitable organizational deficiencies of a poor and debilitated country. It is clear, however, that this benign view of Lavalasian power has serious flaws. The rise of its Chimères, its absolutist rhetoric, the alarming levels of governmental corruption and incompetence, the emergence of a "narco-state," and the political *magouilles* (fraud) of its leaders bode very poorly for a successful Lavalasian democracy.

While it would be wrong to equate the current situation and Préval's or Aristide's rule with Duvalierism or the "de facto" regime of the military dictatorship, there is an increasing sense of déjà vu, of a descent into hell and a new authoritarianism. It is not merely that key figures of the democratic movement have abandoned Lavalas and criticized pointedly Aristide for his *dérive totalitaire*, but there is also the reality of collusions between Lavalas and old antidemocratic foes.[54] The sense of things falling apart is well captured by Gilles Danroc:

From 1994 to now, we have been witnessing a curious mixture of authoritarianism . . . and anarchy. The latter can be understood as the central power's inability to govern without structural intermediaries. Disorder, negligence in public services, corruption, and nepotism flourish to the point of undermining in a lasting manner a democracy in its infancy. In this respect, the erosion of the democratic sector and the recent structural divisions of Aristide's Lavalas Party—or rather the impossibility for this current to structure itself into a modern political party—explain the current uncertainties of politics and the disarray of the populace.

Nevertheless, in the country, certain sectors of civil society or certain elements of the political class are laying out ever more specific criticism against the menacing authoritarianism of ex-president Jean-Bertrand

Aristide and his close associates. Certain alliances that are difficult to understand are being established with Haitian army members such as Fourel Célestin, a Fanmi Lavalas candidate for the senate from Jacmel; Josef Médard, a candidate in the Artibonite; and Dany Toussaint from the Ouest—and with certain business interests. Rumors are flying concerning the uncontrollable corruption of the state and the institutions of the Republic.[55]

Fanmi Lavalas, however, is not the only obstacle to the full democratization of Haiti; in fact the opposition as a whole is as responsible for the current predicament confronting the country. The opposition—former allies of Aristide as well as old Duvalierist and reactionary bourgeois—has consistently behaved opportunistically. Its different sectors have all changed allies and enemies without paying attention to ideology or principle, seeking little else than the crude conquest of power. Indeed, many of those who are now crying foul and castigating Lavalas benefited in the past from similar electoral *magouilles*. So, for instance, when the OPL was still in alliance with Préval and Aristide, it won the legislative elections of 1995 under very dubious circumstances. In truth, there is no reason to believe that the irregularities that marred the 2000 ballot, egregious as they were, had a greater impact on the final results than those that marked previous elections, including those of 1995. And yet, the international community, and the United States in particular, deemed the latter "free and fair." This decision opened the door to persistent fraud and the perception that what really mattered was the regular rituals of elections rather than popular participation or the rigors of electoral honesty. Thus, both the opposition and the international community lack credibility; they legitimate electoral processes according to their ever shifting interests and changing dispositions toward alleged "winners" and "losers."

In these conditions, Haiti's ills cannot be blamed exclusively on Aristide and/or his Fanmi Lavalas; they are also the product of the collective failure of the political class and its external allies. The emphasis on the rituals of elections has exacerbated the zero-sum-game tradition of the island's politics and placed a high premium on winning at any cost. It is not surprising therefore that those who have executive power use it to maximize their opportunities, reward their clientele, and punish their adversaries. The international community, especially the United States, has tended to turn a blind eye to electoral irregularities so long as its leaders believed that the winners would promote their favored policies. Thus, the Clinton administration backed the results of both the presidential and legislative elections of 1995 in spite of serious and numerous irregularities and a turnout of less than 30 percent. The assumption then was that President Préval and his government would implement the program of structural adjustment advanced by the World Bank and the International Monetary

Fund and strongly supported by the United States. When full implementation of the program failed to materialize, generating a governmental crisis and the resignation of Prime Minister Smarth, the United States began to look more critically at the electoral process. What was acceptable in 1995 was no longer so in 1997 and 2000.

While in both instances fraud was pervasive and voter participation extremely low (barely 5 percent in 1997), the Clinton administration and the international community initially characterized the elections as "free and fair." They rapidly changed their tune, however, when it became apparent that Aristide's Fanmi Lavalas was on the verge of an overwhelming victory. Michel-Rolph Trouillot's analysis of the legislative elections of April 1997 and the U.S. reaction to them captures equally well events surrounding the elections of May 2000:

> [The] first round [of these elections] . . . was first accepted by the State Department as "an important step in the process of consolidating democracy in Haiti." In a briefing the day after the elections, spokesman Nicholas Burns noted: "Available reports to us, including from our embassy, indicate the elections were free and fair." Prompted by a journalist who suggested that the low turnout was "not a ringing endorsement of democracy," Burns replied: "That sometimes happens in the United States as well for local elections." Successive official assessments did not accord any significance to the 5 percent turnout.
>
> Reactions came later, when it became clear that the results of this dismal first round clearly favored Aristide's newly formed Lavalas Family, and that a second round would give the family veto power in the Senate. Such veto, in turn, would place Aristide in an ideal position to govern behind the scenes, to prepare a probable bid for the next presidential campaign and to interrupt implementation of the economic package backed by the Smarth government. All three prospects may provoke panic among Haiti policymakers in Washington and may explain the untypical outcry about alleged fraud. . . .
>
> Yet it is not clear that the irregularities that marked these latest elections, obvious as they were, affected the results more markedly than in recent cases on which Haiti handlers in Washington kept silent. Having insisted on democratic rituals rather than democratic debates on policy, Washington's Haiti handlers now see these rituals used to subvert their most favored policies.[56]

The hesitations and shifts of the Clinton administration were not merely an expression of its unhappiness with Aristide's ambiguous positions toward structural adjustment; they were also the manifestation of its fears that what it hailed as a "foreign policy success" might well turn into a disaster. It is also true that Clinton's Haitian policy could not remain unscathed from the extreme scrutiny and opposition of rabid right-wing conservatives after the Republicans gained control of Congress in the 1994 elections. In the eyes of these conservatives, the policy was a catastrophe: it returned to power a left-wing demagogue and squandered a unique opportunity to facilitate the emergence of a broad-based Haitian government. In addition, it constituted a massive waste of resources.[57] Facing this harsh barrage of congressional criticisms, the president's policy options became progressively more constrained. Thus, the lack of a Washington consensus generated an unsettling lack of programmatic consistency and an increasingly ad hoc posture on Haiti.[58]

Moreover, after spending $2 billion to restore Aristide to the presidency, the United States expected that a totally pliant Haitian government would usher in a smooth transition to a credible democratic order and a rationalized market economy.[59] In fact, the United States saw these two objectives as mutually supportive; economic "reforms" and democratic consolidation were to become the opposite sides of the same coin. The problem, however, was that such reforms had little popular support and that consolidation entailed nothing more than the ritual of elections. In reality, democratization, let alone its consolidation, may be hard put to withstand the destructive and polarizing pressures of the structural adjustment program (SAP) that the United States is seeking to impose on Haitian society. It is indeed difficult to understand how such an SAP can be compatible with growth, equity, and democratic governance.

Based on the triumphalism and hegemony of the neoliberal doctrines of the World Bank and the IMF, the Haitian SAP is anchored in a series of deeply flawed assumptions. It posits that development can be "private-driven," and that the Haitian bourgeoisie can suddenly have a change of heart and become the engine of the takeoff, even though the bourgeoisie has never shown any commitment to sustained productive investment. It posits that privatization leads necessarily to rational economic decisions and that private agents are inherently more virtuous and efficient than public servants, even though revenues derived from the sale of state assets can be stolen and squandered, and private agents are bent on defending their own selfish interests rather than the collective good.[60] It posits that democratic governance is compatible with the imposition of fiscal austerity in an environment that is already suffering from acute material deprivation, even though the huge social costs of SAPs are unlikely to be tolerated even by a docile and passive population. Finally, it posits that trade liberalization will promote a more efficient Haitian economy, even though the small national industrial base is incapable of withstanding and surviving foreign competition without public protection.[61]

As Adam Przeworski has explained, the neoliberal foundation on which the SAP rests "is but a conjecture, based on a mixture of evidence, argument from first principles, self-interest and wishful thinking. Moreover, this is not even the model that developed capitalist countries follow in their own practice: Western advisors are in the duplicitous situation of having to say, as Stiglitz put it, 'Do as we say, not as we do.'"[62] In reality, the current Haitian SAP can only generate the complete denationalization of the economy. It is true that both Préval and Aristide have been cognizant of these realities and have attempted to mitigate their effects. More specifically, Aristide has given to the notion of development a theological and spiritual boost and emphasized a "third way" privileging "investing in people" to satisfy their basic needs.[63] He has also argued "as long as Haitian governments continue to receive instructions from international institutions we will move from the same to the same, the same program to the same program, from bad to worse."[64] There is no doubt that these are fine and noble sentiments leading perhaps to "a greater focus on the plight of Haiti's desperately poor majority population."[65] Indeed, Aristide's programmatic ambiguity may be a deliberate means to extricate from the main international financial organizations more resources for the education, health, and safety of the poor.

On the other hand, Aristide's third way is so vague that it hardly represents an alternative program to the current SAP; it is a mere expression of a hope for a better future. In fact, it is a desperate call for survival in a harsh and cruel international environment. As Aristide himself put it,

> Either we enter a global economic system, in which we know we cannot survive, or, we refuse, and face death by slow starvation. With choices like these the urgency of finding a third way is clear. We must find some room to maneuver, some open space simply to survive. We must lift ourselves up off the morgue table and tell the experts we are not yet dead.[66]

Given these huge constraints, it is hard to conceive how any Haitian government can have the power to modify significantly the typical economic adjustment imposed by international financial institutions. The likely scenario is that powerful foreign monopolies in alliance with politically "connected" Haitian entrepreneurs will make a huge financial bonanza by acquiring control of the handful of truly profitable public firms, such as the telephone and electrical companies as well as the port and airport. The massive selling of state assets seems certain to result in a form of casino capitalism, where productive investments are minuscule and thoroughly overwhelmed by the rise of a small mafia of international and local financial speculators engaged in massive forms of private and public corruption, and in the making of easy money through oligopolistic controls of imports and the illegal exports of narcotics.[67]

The emergence of this late-twentieth-century form of piracy is likely to spawn urban and rural discontent as potential losers—bureaucrats, peasants, workers, and nationalist Haitian businesspeople—will organize to defend their interests against foreign-imposed state policies. In such conflictive conditions the authoritarian temptation will resurface again, as the imposition of the SAP will require political surrender to the dictate of international financiers, rule through decrees, and the autocratic style of technocrats educated in the dogmatism of the World Bank and IMF. As William Robinson has explained,

> [International] agencies are secretive, anti-democratic, and dictatorial in the imposition of their policies, with absolutely no accountability to the mass publics to which under polyarchic systems states are ostensibly accountable. New institutions required for the management of globalized production have come into being, conceived here as components of an internationalized state, but they are even less democratic and less accountable than nation-states. These institutions have usurped the functions of economic management from the public sphere (governments) and transferred them to their own private, and almost secretive spheres.[68]

In Haiti, foreign donors and their representatives have persistently threatened to withdraw their support if Haitian institutions and politicians fail to submit to the stringent requirements of the SAP. This is the process that transforms state administrators into "the pimps of global capitalism."[69] For example, Michel Camdessus, managing director of the IMF, traveled to Haiti to warn parliament of the dire consequences of rejecting privatization. He asserted that such a rejection "would mean that the people are rejecting the support that they need, [support] that the international community sees as necessary for Haiti. It will mean that Parliament rejects these policies and this support at a very heavy cost [for the country]."[70] Threats, however, are not the only weapons in the donors' arsenal; gentler means of persuasion have also been used. The U.S. Agency for International Development (USAID) spent close to a million dollars to "sell" privatization and the SAP to Haiti's reluctant public.[71] Foreign menaces and propaganda are, however, unlikely agents of democratization. They can only engender cynicism and resentment.

At a minimum, the survival and consolidation of democracy demand that national economic policy be credible in the eyes of those who will experience its consequences and thus that it be the result of a national consensus reached between state and representative organizations. This in turn can only imply the minimization of the social costs of the SAP and the continued and indeed increased role of the state in the provision of resources for education and health as well as for the maintenance and expansion of the physical infrastructure. Moreover, the state must coordinate an industrial policy that would generate the necessary incentives for private investment in both agriculture and industry. To advocate the withdrawal of the state and the supremacy of the market in a country like Haiti is to invite economic, political, and social disaster. Such a withdrawal seeks to expose an already devastated society to the harsh rules of unregulated markets, rather than protecting it from their further social ravages.

We are thus witnessing the return of what Karl Polanyi called the "stark utopia" of the savage period of early capitalism.[72] According to Polanyi, the stark utopia consisted of a system of production in which the state abdicated its social responsibility and came under the subordination of the laws of the self-adjusting market. When society is governed by such a regime, Polanyi warned, inequalities increase dramatically, the ecological balance is dismantled, and democracy is dilapidated. In fact, the regime of the self-adjusted market cannot "exist for any length of time without annihilating the human and natural substance of society" and without "[destroying] man and [transforming] his surroundings into a wilderness."[73]

In a politically accountable environment, the state must play a central role in organizing production and investments, in correcting market failures, in reducing obscene material inequalities, and in securing public peace through the enforcement of predictable rights and obligations. The fundamental lesson from East Asian newly industrialized countries (NICs) is that economic growth is not the result of "free markets," but rather the product of planned and sustained governmental intervention in the market.[74] Far from engaging in this task, the Haitian state is shrinking its institutional arena. It is erasing itself through privatization to the best-connected bidders and through budgetary reductions; it is becoming an irresponsible and unaccountable apparatus incapable of protecting its citizens from violence, poverty, and disease. Its growing social and economic retreat may well cause a descent into chaos. As Przeworski explains,

> When the state is reduced to the point that it cannot provide physical protection and access to basic social services, public order collapses: material survival and even physical safety can be only privately secured. Private systems of violence are then likely to emerge; violence is likely to become decentralized, anomic, and widespread. Under such conditions, it is not only democracy that is threatened, but the very bases of social cohesion.[75]

In Haiti, the accelerated development of private security systems for the wealthy and the recent wave of criminality—the Zinglendos phenomenon—affecting rich and poor alike, are the harbinger of a Hobbesian world. By denying any meaningful sense of citizenship, the social and economic emasculation of the state is generating a descent into a "war of all against all" that a constitutional design alone cannot easily stop. The privatization of essential functions that have traditionally been the preserve of any responsible and accountable state has led to a proliferation of morbid symptoms. As Beatrice Pouligny has argued,

More than ever, Haiti is, as the people in the street say, "yon machin ki pa gen chofè" [a car with no driver], the state an empty shell with its essential functions taken over by certain private networks embodying NGOs or veritable organized mafias that are tied in particular to drug trafficking and ever increasingly controlled by nouveaux riches from the diaspora. These are now the most flourishing groups in the Haitian economy. These excesses have been fed by decades of an economy based exclusively on predation and the four years of international embargo that finally ruined the economy. The absence of constitutional power, since June 1997, has aggravated the situation, considerably slowing aid programs.

This criminalizing of the economy also feeds part of a new type of insecurity that has developed in recent years. Formerly, the violence now propagated by various actors (including the police) is connected with politico-mafioso milieus, where it formerly came primarily from a repressive apparatus. Some of the former military have taken up banditry again, sometimes in association with former members of the paramilitary groups. This form of "insertion" also includes younger members, including gang leaders expelled from the United States and Canada, where they were born and have been sentenced to prison. The latter have introduced into Haiti, in particular, new forms of criminality and organization. Unemployed youth, discouraged by the lack of results obtained by their elders in the political struggle, envious of modes of rapid fortune, and seeking sites for identification and socialization, constitute an ideal pool of recruitment. They are the ones now called the *chimères,* and they resemble youth gangs in most of the poor neighborhoods in all the great cities in the world.[76]

There is thus little doubt that the extreme logic of privatization that structural adjustment entails will have gravely debilitating effects on the democratization of Haitian society. These effects will in all likelihood accentuate the impact of the lingering authoritarian legacy. The return to electoral politics and the partial neutralization of the repressive organs of the state are not sufficiently institutionalized to ensure the success of democratic consolidation. Moreover, the virtual absence of democratic debate on economic policy or on any other major issue confronting the country has aggravated an already severe democratic deficit. The only thing that seemed to matter was the electoral moment, which itself became increasingly contested, if not illegitimate, as Haitians turned their back on a failed political class.

The nation was left in Aristide's populist, unpredictable, and opportunistic hands. Indeed, he lacked a clear plan for the future, and whatever policy he advocated seemed to be ad hoc, vague, and reactive to the vagaries of an ever changing environment.[77] For instance, his position toward structural adjustment has varied according to the constituency he addressed. Constrained by the conditions of exile into supporting a structural adjustment program, Aristide prevaricated once he returned to power and then, unencumbered by the official trappings of the presidency, opposed the program. Now that he has been reelected, he seems to have moved again toward accepting the inevitability of adopting some form of structural adjustment. Aristide is advocating a "third path," but within the narrow limits of "globalization." As he put it, "Haiti cannot isolate itself from the rest of the world. The geo-economic reality must provoke a deep reflection—to maintain equilibrium, maintain calm, and find a middle way. This is what we call a partnership between the two sectors, private and public."[78] Aristide, however, remained at best vague on how he will effect such a partnership and how he will negotiate his way into the third path with international financial institutions. There is no reason to believe that his previous policy oscillations will come to a halt in his second administration; indeed, they are likely to persist and exacerbate the existing crisis of governability.

Paradoxically, however, the fear of a catastrophic outcome might well generate the conditions for a historic compromise between Aristide and his enemies. Without a pact ensuring that all parties will follow the "rules of the game" and ultimately respect electoral results, a turn to a new despotism or generalized chaos is likely. Recent Haitian history demonstrates that in the absence of such a pact, victory at the polls by any party unleashes immediate denunciations of voting fraud and calls for new elections on the part of the losers. In fact, since the fall of Duvalier, the country has been engulfed in a permanent state of electoral crisis that has generated political instability and a slow descent into hell. The organization, supervision, and ballot counting must thus gain the support of all parties before, during, and after the vote itself lest the electoral process lose legitimacy and cause further social polarization and violence. It is difficult to see, however, how the different Haitian political forces can reach a workable compromise and minimize their deep divisions. In the next chapter I analyze the major reasons for these divisions and try to elucidate the potential political alternatives for the future.

Notes

1. For the story of the complicated and ambiguous events leading to the peaceful U.S. occupation of Haiti, see Kate Doyle, "Hollow Diplomacy in Haiti," *World Policy Journal* 11, no. 1 (spring 1994): 53–55; Ian Martin, "Haiti: Mangled Multilateralism," *Foreign Policy,* no. 95 (summer 1994): 80–85; see also John Ballard, *Upholding Democracy: The United States Military Campaign in Haiti, 1994–1997* (Westport, Conn.: Praeger, 1998).

2. In a letter to Boutros Boutros-Ghali, the UN secretary-general, Aristide ultimately acquiesced to a U.S.-led military intervention by calling for "swift and determined action" to restore him to power. The letter supported UN Resolution 940, which authorized "the use of all necessary means" to topple the military junta. See AP@clarinet, July 29, 1994.

3. Aristide's relations with the United States have always been quite contradictory; while in his "first" presidency he attacked U.S. imperialism and capitalism, his exile in Washington and his U.S.-led return to Haiti transformed him into a staunch ally of the Clinton administration. In fact, upon his restoration to the presidency, Aristide started calling Clinton his twin brother. The United States, on the other hand, had always been ambivalent about the power shift that Aristide's election symbolized and had traditionally supported the elite and the army.

4. Elizabeth Gibbons, *Sanctions in Haiti: Human Rights and Democracy Under Assault* (Westport, Conn.: Praeger, with the Center for Strategic and International Studies, 1999), p. 99.

5. Ibid., p. 73.

6. David Malone, *Decision-Making in the UN Security Council: The Case of Haiti* (Oxford: Clarendon, 1998), p. 172.

7. Jorge G. Castaneda, *Utopia Unarmed* (New York: Vintage, 1994). The economists advocating structural adjustment are not only in key positions of power both in the government and international institutions, but they are also behaving with the missionary zeal of "fundamentalists." Anyone questioning or challenging their worldview is immediately branded an "ideologue" incapable of understanding the "science" of economics. As Adam Przeworski has noted in his book *Sustainable Democracy* (Cambridge: Cambridge University Press, 1995), pp. viii–ix,

> The neoliberal ideology emanating from the United States and the multinational agencies claims that the course to follow is obvious. This ideology is based on a belief about the virtues of markets and private ownership that is not justifiable in the light of contemporary economic theory, including neoclassical theory. It values efficiency over distribution to the extent of justifying social horrors. It places economic considerations over political ones, willing to sacrifice other economic and political values at the altar of efficiency. It is based on a profound conviction that there is only one way and that this way must be followed: not only any opposition but even disagreement is portrayed as self-interested, "populist" reaction. Proponents of this ideology argue as if they possessed a Last Judgment archetype of the world: a general model of economic and political dynamics that allows one to evaluate the ultimate consequences of all the partial steps.
>
> Yet this model is but a conjecture, based on a mixture of evidence, argument from first principles, self-interest and wishful thinking. Moreover, this is not even the model that developed capitalist countries follow in their own practice: Western advisors are in the duplicitous situation of having to say, as Stiglitz put it, "Do as we say, not as we do."

8. Patrice Backer, "Yes, Haiti Needs a Structural Adjustment," January 2000, online at Windows on Haiti. As Backer explains,

> [It] is hard to imagine how a reduction in government spending would affect the poor as negatively as people claim. A quick look at the current situation suggests that
>
> • The majority of the 45,000+ government employees that would be affected by layoffs do not belong to the lower strata of Haitian society, simply because the poor in Haiti are chronically unemployed. A study of the compensation structure in the government would suggest that the lower-paid employees still earn much more than those who are defined as "poor."
> • It is estimated that about 3.4 million Haitians, mostly poor or very poor, are employed in the informal sector. It is this sector of the Haitian economy that is the least served by the government today.

• In a country of roughly seven million inhabitants, the layoff of even half of the government workforce will hardly affect the overall poverty picture although the impact on those let go and their families will be very real and very painful. According to the Haiti's Plan d'Action Gouvernemental published in early 1999, more than 70% of the population lives below the absolute poverty level. It is hard to imagine this broad segment of the population gainfully employed, much less employed within the government.

• Decreased spending will not result in a reduction of government services to the poor. Haitian public administrations have rarely if ever delivered an adequate level of service to the Haitian population to begin with, let alone to the poor who have suffered from discrimination and humiliation at the hand of our civil service system.

The claims that Haiti's poor would suffer from a decrease in the size of government just do not add up. The recent implementation of an early retirement and voluntary departure program by the Haitian government confirms that they too are aware of their bloated payrolls and need an adjustment, SAP or not.

9. Alex Dupuy, "A Neo-Liberal Model for Post-Duvalier Haiti," unpublished manuscript, p. 21; see also Leslie Delatour, *Propositions pour le Progrès* (Port-au-Prince: Fondation des Industries d'Haïti, 1990). Aristide has so far been able to "sell" this most conservative economic program as if it were supportive of the poor; in an amazing performance, Aristide received a hero's welcome when he recently visited La Saline—one of the most destitute urban slums of Port-au-Prince—with James Wolfensohn, president of the World Bank; see *Haiti Progrès*, July 19–25, 1995, pp. 6–15.

10. See "Privatization: What the Haitian People Can Expect," *Haiti Info,* February 25, 1995.

11. In *Democracy and the Market* (Cambridge: Cambridge University Press, 1991), Adam Przeworski explains the paradoxes of the release from authoritarianism in conditions of dire material scarcity (p. 189):

Structural transformations of economic systems are a plunge into the unknown; they are driven by desperation and hope, not by reliable blueprints. For political reasons, the reform strategy most likely to be undertaken is not the one that minimizes social costs. . . . Inflation is likely to flare up again under inertial pressures. Unemployment, even if temporary, is difficult to tolerate. Increasing inequality stokes conflicts with suspicions that the support of some groups for reform is simply self-serving. And in the face of political reactions, governments are likely to vacillate between the technocratic style inherent in market-oriented reforms and the participatory style required to maintain consensus. . . . Ultimately, the vacillations of financially bankrupt governments become politically destabilizing. . . . Authoritarian temptations are thus inevitable.

12. "Carnaval Grands Mangeurs," *Haïti en Marche,* February 12–18, 1997, pp. 1–8; *Haïti en Marche,* February 19–25, 1997, p. 12.

13. Agence Haïtienne de Presse en Ligne, April 30, 1997, and May 15, 1997; Haiti Online, May 15, 1997.

14. The former prime minister of St. Lucia, John Compton, who served as head of the Caribbean Community (CARICOM) observer mission during the elections, estimated that the turnout was very low, "between 15 and 20 percent in the best of cases." See "CARICOM Observers Dispute Official Turnout in Haitian Elections," *EFE,* December 4, 2000. On the other hand, a U.S. group, the International Coalition of Independent Observers, confirmed official results and

pegged voter participation at about 60 percent. See "Some Americans Did Monitor Haiti's Presidential Vote," *Haitian Times,* December 2000. For additional perspectives on these estimates, see "La Presse Internationale sur les Présidentielles Haïtiennes," Haiti Online, December 1, 2000; and "Turnout Light in Aristide Bid for Haiti's Presidency," *Miami Herald,* November 27, 2000.

15. Karl Marx and Frederick Engels, *The German Ideology* (New York: International Publishers, 1947), pp. 29–30; see also Karl Marx and Frederick Engels, *Karl Marx: Selected Writings in Sociology and Social Philosophy,* translated by T. B. Bottomore, edited by T. B. Bottomore and Maximilien Rubel with a foreword by Erich Fromm (New York: McGraw-Hill, 1964), p. 240.

16. Karl Marx and Frederick Engels, *The Marx-Engels Reader,* 2d ed., edited by R. C. Tucker (New York: Norton, 1978), pp. 529–532, 537–538.

17. Michel-Rolph Trouillot, *Haiti: State Against Nation* (New York: Monthly Review Press, 1990).

18. *Bo tab la* and *en ba tab la* are Creole words meaning, respectively, to be at the table and thus capable of sharing in society's wealth, and to be under the table and thus not only to be excluded from that sharing but also to be exploited by those who are doing the eating.

19. See Jean and Maesschalck, *Transition Politique en Haïti;* and Raoul Peck, *Monsieur le Ministre . . . Jusqu'au Bout de la Patience* (Port-au-Prince: Éditions Velvet, 1999).

20. Kern Delince, *Les Forces Politiques en Haïti* (Paris: Karthala, 1993), p. 91. Translated from the original French by Carrol Coates:

> L'objectif fondamental de l'aspirant au pouvoir est évidemment l'accession à la présidence de la République. Pour parvenir à cette fin, il rassemble l'ensemble de ses partisans dans une petite structure d'action politique collective, généralement de type informel, chargée de l'organisation de la campagne électorale et de l'exécution de tâches politiques les plus diverses. En effet ce ne sont pas . . . de vrais partis politiques qui rivalisent pour la conquête et l'exercice du pouvoir, mais plutôt des chefs politiques disposant de l'appui d'une clientèle personnelle restreinte, venue à eux principalement dans un but lucratif. Le moteur principal de l'activité politique . . . consiste dans l'intérêt personnel camouflé plus ou moins adroitement derrière la recherche apparente de l'intérêt général du pays.

21. Robert White, "Haiti: Democrats vs. Democracy," *International Policy Report,* November 1997, pp. 2–3.

22. The source of these comments prefers to remain anonymous.

23. Gabriel Charles-Antoine, "Une Lecture de la Crise," *Haïti en Marche,* November 19–25, 1997, pp. 3–18.

24. "Political Feuds Ravage Haiti: So Much for Its High Hopes," *New York Times,* October 18, 1998.

25. "Haitian President Installs Premier," MSNBC, March 26, 1999.

26. OPL, "OPL Press Communiqué," Port-au-Prince, June 2, 1999.

27. "Haiti Approves New Elections," Reuters, July 20, 1999.

28. "Fights Disrupt Haiti Election Rally," Reuters, November 30, 1999.

29. Don Bohning, "Radio Commentator Shot Dead," *Miami Herald,* April 4, 2000. The mystery surrounding Dominique's killing has generated claims that some factions of Lavalas that are allegedly involved in narco-trafficking were responsible for his assassination. Journalist Ana Arana summarizes her report on Dominique's case to the Inter American Press Association in "Impunity, Haiti: The Case of Jean Léopold Dominique," Inter American Press Association, January 2001 (online at http://www.impunidad.com/cases/jeanleopoldE.html):

The first list of suspects was long—former supporters of the Duvalier dynasty as well as corrupt businessmen. But recently, the investigation indicates that Dominique, a key advisor to former President René Préval, and a friend of President Jean Bertrand Aristide, apparently was a victim of an internecine conflict among members of Aristide's Fanmi Lavalas political party.

An investigation by the Inter American Press Association (IAPA) has found that Dominique, a man who spent his life defending Haiti's poor, combining journalism with leftist political activism, was killed in a political conspiracy apparently planned and conceived over several months by leading political figures tied to Aristide. Among those named in the investigation as possible suspects are Sen. Dany Toussaint, a Machiavellian figure who commands a lot of power inside Lavalas, and several of his allies who serve in the Aristide government or are members of the Haitian Senate. These officials, evidence indicates, viewed Dominique's independence and honesty as a threat to their quest for power, and their involvement in corrupt businesses, according to sources close to the investigation. . . .

Most sources with knowledge about the Dominique investigation said they believe President Aristide was not interested in getting rid of Dominique, the most prominent Fanmi Lavalas leader killed to date. But foreign and Haitian sources believe sectors within Lavalas are completely independent of Aristide. They point out that Aristide's failure to publicly denounce the Dominique murder, other political assassinations, and attacks against the opposition and the press, have only encouraged more abuses.

See also Reporters Sans Frontières, "Who Killed Jean Dominique? 3 April 2000–3 April 2001" (online at Center for International Policy, http://www.ciponline.org/Haiti/March-May%202001/rsf.htm, March 2001). In an open letter addressed to Arana, Dany Toussaint denied any involvement in Dominique's killing and requested a public apology from her ("Réponse de Mr. Dany Toussaint à Madame Ana Arana," Haitiwebs.com, March 29, 2001).

30. Don Bohning, "Vote Turnout High in Haiti Despite Risk," *Miami Herald,* May 22, 2000. Henry F. Carey, a political scientist and a member of the three-person Center for International Policy observers' delegation to the elections, commented in "Not Perfect, but Improving," *Miami Herald,* June 12, 2000:

I have observed elections in Haiti in 1990, 1991, 1995 and 1997. Last month's were the best so far. Still they were substandard, generating ambiguity on two levels. Should progress be recognized? Or the lack of democratic credibility denounced? . . . As for the polls, it has been the same for three elections: Right up to the midnight counts, Election Day goes well, leading observers to pass positive judgments. In other countries, elections often are rigged after midnight. In Haiti, sheer incompetence takes over and opponents misinterpret the unintended chaos as bad intent.

31. Believing that their defeat was caused by electoral fraud, seventeen parties of the opposition regrouped in the Convergence Alliance and appealed for "option zero," which called for the resignation of President Préval and his government, the formation of a government of national unity, and new elections with an impartial and new electoral council. See Michael Norton, "Haiti Government Urged to Resign," Associated Press, June 21, 2000.

32. Michael Dobbs, "Aristide's Party Poised for Haitian Election Win: International Observers Satisfied Vote Credible," *Ottawa Citizen,* May 23, 2000, p. F7.

33. Amy Wilentz, "It's a New Day for Haiti, If U.S. Would Accept It," *Los Angeles Times,* June 4, 2000.

34. Mark Fineman, "As Tallying Drags On, Haiti Election Is Called Unfair,

Flawed," *Los Angeles Times,* May 27, 2000, p. 5; "'Serious Error Is Discovered in Haiti's Election," *Miami Herald,* June 3, 2000.

35. James R. Morrell, "Snatching Defeat from the Jaws of Victory," *International Policy Report,* August 2000, p. 1.

36. See, for instance, Organization of American States, "The OAS Electoral Observation Mission in Haiti: Chief of Mission Report to the OAS Permanent Council," July 13, 2000. See also Joanne Mariner, "Haiti's Tarnished Election Results," FindLaw, online at http://writ.findlaw.com/commentary/20000721_mariner.html.

37. Léon Manus, "Declaration," June 21, 2000, available on the website of the Center for International Policy, www.ciponline.org.nxlklost.com/Haiti/Archives/June-August 2000/monus.htm; see also his radio interview in which he recounts his ordeal—it can be accessed on Haiti Online, http://www.haitionline.com/2000/manus725.ram; see also SICRAD, "Élections: Résultats Définitifs dans une Atmosphère de Tension," Port-au-Prince, June 6, 2000.

38. Letter of Léon Manus to R. Orlando Marville, ambassador, chief of mission, Organization of American States, June 6, 2000. Manus wrote that Marville's publicized letter informing him that the vote count was tainted by "a serious error which if not corrected can place in doubt the validity of the whole electoral process" represented an "act of interference." Manus also let it be known that "the interference is more serious because [Ambassador Orlando Marville], speaking in the name of a respected international institution, through reckless declarations, on questions of national importance, has induced the Haitian people to error and sought to discredit the CEP in the eyes of the nation." Marville's letter is online at the Center for International Policy, http://www.ciponline.org/oas6.htm. See also Melinda Miles with Moira Feeney, *Elections 2000: Participatory Democracy in Haiti,* Haiti Reborn/Quixote Center, February 2001 (http://www.quixote.org/haiti/elections/index.html).

39. Manus, "Declaration."

40. Ibid.

41. Mark Fineman, "Haitian's Flight Shows Democracy's Slide," *Los Angeles Times,* July 25, 2000.

42. Léon Manus, letter to Edgard Leblanc, president of the senate of the Republic of Haiti, New York, August 8, 2000.

43. "Results of Partial Elections Confirm Aristide Party Sweep in Haiti," Associated Press, August 8, 2000.

44. In an article entitled "A Clarification on the Vote Calculation, US and European Interference Violates Recent UN Resolution," the pro-Aristide *Haïti Progrès* (June 28–July 4, 2000) explains Préval's and the electoral council's position as follows:

> In the first-round's final count, the CEP used a formula which calculated senatorial percentages on the basis of the top four contenders . . . as it did in previous elections.
>
> The CEP adopted this formula because it wanted an even multiple of the number of seats in contention. Otherwise, by dividing an odd number of single candidates' votes in half (or in thirds) "you will create fictitious votes, and then you are not dealing with votes cast," explained Luciano Pharaon, the CEP's director of electoral operations. "You end up giving a series of people votes they did not get."
>
> Pharaon notes that there is a "void at the level of procedure" in the Constitution and Electoral Law, which says that victors need an absolute majority of 50% plus one of the vote but doesn't tell you how to arrive at this figure."
>
> "So the Electoral Council, which is the sole judge in this matter, had to devise

a procedure which would be the most fair to both the electors and the candidates," Pharaon concluded. In short, the "debate" over what formula to adopt is a false one, since the CEP has the final word on electoral matters.

See also "An Explanation of the CEP's Partial-Vote Methodology." Attributed to director of operations Luciano Pharaon, courtesy of John Kozyn. Originally appeared on Robert Corbett e-mail list. Copied by permission. Online at the Center for International Policy, http://www.ciponline.org/pharaon.htm.

45. Speech by Fritz Longchamp, "Intervention dans le Cadre du Processus Électorale en Haïti," Washington, D.C., July 13, 2000.

46. Ibid. (author's translation).

47. The Council on Hemispheric Affairs, "Much to Do About Nothing: Two-Faced OAS Refusal to Observe Second Round Haitian Balloting Taints a Relatively Fair Election Process," Washington, D.C., July 13, 2000.

48. Ibid.

49. Ibid.; see also press release of the National Organization for the Advancement of Haitians, "NOAH Scores Any Attempt to Tarnish the Legitimacy of the Victory of Haitian People," June 19, 2000.

50. Wilentz, "It's a New Day for Haiti, If U.S. Would Accept It."

51. See Organization of American States, "The OAS Electoral Observation Mission in Haiti: Chief of Mission Report to the OAS Permanent Council"; Mariner, "Haiti's Tarnished Election Results"; Morrell, "Snatching Defeat from the Jaws of Victory," pp. 2–4. Laurent Beaulieu, in a careful review of the evidence, shows clearly that the "top-four concept" was never used in the elections of 1990 and 1995. As he put it ("Élections: Quid de l'Invention de Pharaon?" Haiti Online, August 22, 2000, author's translation),

> The method that counts only the first four candidates is an invention of the 2000 CEP [provisional electoral council]. It changes virtually a two-rounds election into a one-round election because the top candidate is elected even if he/she does not get an absolute majority. The method betrays not only the letter but also the spirit of the electoral rules established in July 1999 adopted by this very CEP.

52. Claude Moïse, *Une Constitution dans la Tourmente* (Montreal: Éditions Images, 1994), p. 33. Translated from the original French by Carrol Coates:

> Quand la majorité parlementaire et la majorité présidentielle se confondent, on doit s'attendre à la formation d'un gouvernement homogène à dominante présidentielle. Le Chef de l'État, qui y exerce une influence prépondérante, joue alors un rôle décisif dans la conduite des affaires de l'État.

53. "Haiti's Discouraging Elections: Aristide's Party Could Have Won Without Cheating," *Miami Herald,* July 11, 2000.

54. Arthur Mahon, "Haïti: Une Dictature Rampante," *Rouge,* December 7, 2000.

55. Gilles Danroc, "Imbroglio, Précarités et Démocratie," Diffusion de l'Information sur l'Amérique Latine, Dossier 2358, March 1–15, 2000, pp. 1–2. Translated from the original French by Carrol Coates:

> De 1994 à nos jours, nous assistons à un curieux mélange de pouvoir autoritaire . . . et d'anarchie. Cette dernière se comprend comme l'impossibilité du pouvoir central à gouverner sans intermédiaires structurels. La pagaille, l'incurie des services publics, la corruption et le népotisme s'en donnent à coeur joie au point de saper durablement la toute jeune démocratie balbutiante. A cet égard l'effritement depuis des années du secteur démocratique et les divisions structurelles du parti "Lavalas"

de J.B. Aristide, ou plutôt l'impossibilité de ce courant à se structurer en parti politique moderne, expliquent le flou actuel de la politique comme le désarroi de la population. . . .

Pourtant sur place . . . certains courants de la société civile où des éléments de la classe politique élaborent une critique de plus en plus précise devant la menace d'un pouvoir autoritaire concentré entre les mains de l'ex-président Jean-Bertrand Aristide et son entourage. Là se sont nouées des alliances peu compréhensibles avec des éléments de l'armée d'Haïti comme Fourel Célestin, candidat au Sénat pour "Lafanmi Lavalas" à Jacmel, Josef Médard, candidat dans l'Artibonite et Dany Toussaint à l'Ouest—où avec certain milieux d'affaires. Les rumeurs vont bon train sur fond de corruption non maîtrisée de l'État et des institutions de la République.

56. Michel-Rolph Trouillot, "The Way I See It: Traps and Trappings of Haitian Democracy," *The Gazette* (Johns Hopkins University), July 1997, pp. 3–4; see also Henry F. Carey, "Electoral Observation and Democratization in Haiti," in Kevin J. Middlebrook, ed., *Electoral Observation and Democratic Transitions in Latin America* (San Diego: Center for U.S.-Mexican Studies, 1998), pp. 141–166.

57. In the House, Dan Burton, chairman of the Western Hemisphere Subcommittee, and his Republican colleagues Porter J. Goss and Benjamin A. Gilman, and in the Senate, Jesse Helms, the powerful and archconservative chairman of the Foreign Relations Committee, led an organized and persistent opposition to Aristide and Clinton's Haitian policy.

58. See James Morrell, "Haiti: Success Under Fire," online at Center for International Policy, www.us.net/cip/haiti01.htm, January 1995; and Robert E. White, "Haiti: Policy Lost, Policy Regained," online at www.us.net/cip/cosmos3.htm.

59. The $2 billion amount is quite misleading; most of that money was not invested in Haiti, let alone targeted at the very poor majority. The bulk of the money went to pay U.S. soldiers, companies, and consultants. As Ira Kurzban has explained in "A Rational Foreign Policy Toward Haiti," Haiti Online, February 6, 2001,

For example, it is not true that we have spent 2 billion dollars on or in Haiti. Over $750,000,000 of that money went toward the interdiction of Haitians seeking to leave Haiti during the most repressive stage of the military coup in that country. These funds cannot fairly be included in any calculus regarding our assistance to Haiti. If anything, our forced repatriation of Haitian children from Guantanamo while welcoming Cuban children to the United States from that military base at the same time will remain an indelible stain on our national character. Nor can we count as "aid" to Haiti the hundreds of millions of dollars that were spent by the United States military in corporate giveaways to U.S. companies such as Brown and Root for everything from laundry for our troops to communications systems which were ripped out and probably discarded when the U.S. troops left Haiti. Included in the 2 billion dollar figure is the vast psy-ops or psychological operations program that was performed on the Haitian people by our men in green during Aristide's return.

This is not to say that the presence of U.S. troops during the first days before and immediately after Aristide's return did not perform an important function of stopping the massacres and permitting the Aristide government to destroy the hated Haitian Army once and for all. Nevertheless, the excessive costs and the lavish nature of spending by U.S. companies and the U.S. military in Haiti should hardly be attributed to Haitians as some form of U.S. "aid" to them. Nor should we ignore the fact that the remainder of the hundreds of millions of dollars in U.S. aid that went to Haiti as part of that 2 billion dollar figure mostly went to beltway companies to do studies that generally have little impact or no effect, long or short-term, on the Haitian people. It is typical of USAID officials to go to Capitol Hill and boast about how our foreign aid dollars "are returned to the U.S." because they go mostly to U.S. companies conducting studies or overseeing programs.

It is not simply that most aid is returned to the U.S. that results in little impact on Haiti, it is that the aid programs themselves are generally designed to have little impact on the vast majority of Haitians who are without basic care and who live in rural areas engaged in agrarian pursuits. Rather than directing our aid to the 70% of the population that lives in poor agrarian areas, the majority of [US]AID funds are spent to bolster the "private sector," assist in the "privatization process," further the goals of the International Monetary Fund program, or develop and bolster the opposition to the government. For example, this past year, our government overtly provided to the International Republican Institute $3,000,000 in funds not simply to help opposition parties in Haiti but to "develop" opposition parties. In light of the outrage in the United States following the revelations that the Chinese government may have attempted to provide contributions to U.S. candidates, it is nothing short of bizarre that our government would spend money in a foreign country to create an opposition to the government we are supposed to be supporting. This, of course, does not include covert funds spent in Haiti to accomplish the same ends.

60. For instance, in *Democracy Undermined, Economic Justice Denied: Structural Adjustment and the Aid Juggernaut in Haiti* (Washington, D.C.: Development Group for Alternative Policies, 1997), Lisa McGowan points out how the privatization of the sugar industry has had catastrophic social consequences (p. 25):

> The concern[s] over who gets the privatized assets and what is done with them are well grounded in Haiti's own experience with the privatization of its sugar mill in 1987 and the long-term negative impacts that this sale has had on several aspects of peasant production. The Mevs family purchased the mill, immediately shut it down, and began importing cheaper sugar from the United States and selling it at a higher price than that of local sugar; by 1995, Haiti was importing 25,000 tons of sugar from the United States alone. The plant's workers and truck drivers lost their jobs, and sugar farmers lost their market. Now, almost ten years later, sugar is so expensive in Haiti that peasants cannot afford to buy it. In Milot, in the north of Haiti, peasants report that this has destroyed much of the local market for oranges and grapefruits, which traditionally are made into a heavily sugared juice. Without the sugar, people aren't drinking juice and the fruit is left to rot.

The potential for corruption in the privatization process of TELECO (the Haitian state-owned phone company) is examined in Mary Anastasia O'Grady, "Clinton's Haiti Policy Deserves Prompt Scrutiny," *Wall Street Journal,* January 26, 2001. While the article is a diatribe against Aristide, it does show the vicissitudes of privatization. In fact, the corruptions of privatization clearly go beyond Haiti or Aristide. Whether it takes place in Russia or Argentina or any other country, it leaves a trail of bribery and sleaze.

61. For an excellent review and critique of the Haitian structural adjustment program, see McGowan, *Democracy Undermined, Economic Justice Denied.*

62. Przeworski, *Sustainable Democracy,* pp. viii–ix.

63. Jean-Bertrand Aristide, *Eyes of the Heart* (Monroe, Maine: Common Courage Press, 2000).

64. Ibid., pp. 48–49.

65. James R. Morrell, Rachel Nield, and Hugh Byrne, "Haiti and the Limits to Nation-Building," *Current History,* March 1999, pp. 127–146. Online at the Center for International Policy.

66. Aristide, *Eyes of the Heart,* pp. 16–17.

67. McGowan, *Democracy Undermined, Economic Justice Denied,* pp. 7–26; see also Michel Chossudovsky, "Comment les Mafias Gangrènent l'Économie Mondiale," *Le Monde Diplomatique,* December 1996, pp. 24–25.

68. William I. Robinson, *Promoting Polyarchy* (Cambridge: Cambridge University Press, 1996), p. 375.

69. Ibid., p. 374.

70. As quoted in McGowan, *Democracy Undermined, Economic Justice Denied,* p. 26.

71. Ibid.

72. Karl Polanyi, *The Great Transformation* (Boston: Beacon Press, 1957); see also Robert W. Cox with Timothy J. Sinclair, *Approaches to World Order* (Cambridge: Cambridge University Press, 1996).

73. Polanyi, *The Great Transformation,* p. 3.

74. Alice H. Amsden, *Asia's Next Giant: South Korea and Late Industrialization* (New York: Oxford University Press, 1989); Peter Evans, *Embedded Autonomy* (Princeton: Princeton University Press, 1995); Robert Wade, *Governing the Market: Economic Theory and the Role of Government in East Asian Industrialization* (Princeton: Princeton University Press, 1990); Wade, "Japan, the World Bank, and the Art of Paradigm Maintenance: The East Asian Miracle in Political Perspective," *New Left Review* 217 (May–June, 1996): 3–36.

75. Przeworski, *Sustainable Democracy,* pp. 111–112.

76. Beatrice Pouligny, "Haïti: Deux ou Trois Raisons d'Espérer," *Libération,* February 13, 2001. Translated from the original French by Carrol Coates:

> Plus que jamais, Haïti est, comme le dit l'homme de la rue, yon machin ki pa gen chofè (une "voiture sans pilote"), l'État une coquille vide, ses fonctions essentielles étant accaparées par des logiques privées qui prennent notamment le visage d'ONG où de véritables mafias organisées, liées en particulier au trafic de la drogue et de plus en plus contrôlées par de "nouveaux riches" issus de la diaspora. Elles représentent aujourd'hui les secteurs les plus florissants de l'économie haïtienne. Ces dérives ont été alimentées par des décennies d'une économie exclusivement basée sur la prédation et quatre ans d'embargo international qui ont fini de la ruiner. La vacance constitutionnelle du pouvoir, depuis juin 1997, n'a fait qu'aggraver ce processus, en ralentissant considérablement les programmes d'aide.
>
> Cette criminalisation de l'économie alimente également une partie de l'insécurité d'un type nouveau qui s'est développée ces dernières années. Autrefois principalement le fait d'un appareil répressif, la violence émane aujourd'hui d'acteurs divers (parmi lesquels des policiers) participant aux réseaux politico-mafieux. Une partie des anciens soldats s'est également reconvertie dans le banditisme, parfois en association avec d'anciens membres des groupes paramilitaires. Cette forme d'"insertion" inclut aussi de jeunes éléments, dont des chefs de gang expulsés des États-Unis et du Canada où ils sont nés et ont été condamnés à des peines de prison. Ceux-ci ont notamment introduit en Haïti de nouvelles formes de criminalité et d'organisation. Des jeunes sans emploi, découragés par le peu de résultats de la lutte politique menée par leurs aînés, envieux de modes d'enrichissement rapides et en quête de lieux d'identification et de socialisation, constituent un vivier de recrutement idéal. Ils sont ceux qu'aujourd'hui l'on appelle les "chimères" et ressemblent aux gangs de jeunes de la plupart des quartiers pauvres de toutes les grandes villes du monde.

77. Jennifer Bauduy, "Haiti's Aristide Presents Party Platform," *Sun-Sentinel* (Fort Lauderdale, Fla.), December 15, 1999. Fanmi Lavalas published in December 1999 a 182-page platform advocating a vague notion of a partnership between the

private and public sectors. Entitled "Investir dans l'Humain" [Investing in Human Beings], the document calls for the development of a just, equitable, and humane society. It privileges a form of "participatory" politics enhancing dignity and freedom. The goal is to generate a "third path" between a stultifying statism and an irresponsible and antisocial hyperliberalism. The precise nature of this humane and participatory third path is never fully explained.

A year later Fanmi Lavalas issued a new platform, Programme Économique et Social 2001–2006, that sought to elucidate more precisely its objectives. Five sectors will be given priority: infrastructure, health, education, security, and justice. The platform promises the creation of 500,000 jobs, the "takeoff" of the economy, a revitalization of schooling, and the provision of basic health care for the rural population. And yet there are few indications on how these objectives will be achieved. The document is more a wish list of laudable projects than a serious programmatic framework for development. Aristide's own views are presented in his book *Eyes of the Heart.*

Christophe Wargny, "The Country That Doesn't Quite Exist: Haiti's Last Chance," *Le Monde Diplomatique,* July 2000, describes well the predicament of Lavalas's program:

> The Lavalas Family's programme is full of good intentions but vague, making no clear choices between a wide range of priorities. "Investing in the human side" is a title full of promise: but the content underestimates the fragility of an anaemic country in a globalised economy, and its extreme dependence on those putting up the money. It has no known mineral wealth, an agriculture that is inadequate for an excessive population (the farmed area has shrunk by half over the last 25 years while the population has doubled), and a spendthrift oligarchy—the money sent by two million expatriates to their eight million relatives back home ends up in the pockets of a dozen well-entrenched private monopolies.

78. Ibid.

6

The Antagonistic Present and Future Alternatives

Lavalas and the Challenge of Convergence Démocratique

The overwhelming victory of Aristide in the presidential elections of November 26, 2000, has exacerbated the antagonisms afflicting Haitian politics.[1] Facing no serious challengers and limiting his campaign to a single short public appearance, Aristide gained little legitimacy or credibility by winning an election that can only be called farcical. The election took place in the violent aftermath of a complete breakdown in negotiations over the contested May legislative ballots and further aggravated conflicts between Fanmi Lavalas and the Convergence Démocratique (CD).[2]

CD crystallized in the days following the legislative elections as an umbrella organization regrouping fifteen opposition parties. It put forward initially the so-called option zero, which demanded the resignation of President Préval and his government, the annulment of the legislative elections, the postponement of the presidential ballot, the installation of a new and impartial electoral council, and the formation of an interim ruling body charged with organizing new general elections. Moreover, CD refused any cooperation with what it considered the illegitimate Fanmi Lavalas regime. Option zero was thus a maximalist position that had little likelihood of materializing.

Facing a complete and dangerous impasse, however, the contending parties agreed to engage in a "dialogue" sponsored by the Organization of American States. Engineered by the OAS assistant secretary-general, Luigi Einaudi, the dialogue occurred in late September and October but failed to generate the desired political compromise. The two sides had unbridgeable positions; while CD modified its option zero, it persisted in demanding the creation of a provisional government of "national unity," the installation of a new and impartial electoral council, the holding of entirely new legislative elections, and a postponement of the presidential elections set for

141

November 26. These demands were simply unacceptable to Fanmi Lavalas. They would have meant the probable early departure of René Préval, the dismissal of all parliamentarians, and the delay of Aristide's virtually certain victory in the presidential polls.[3]

Not surprisingly, with the collapse of the dialogue and the ensuing presidential election of Aristide, the huge divide separating the opposition and Fanmi Lavalas deepened further. While Aristide's campaign slogan was "Lapè nan tet, lapè nan vant" [peace in the head, peace in the belly], CD would have none of it. Moreover, the vast majority of CD's constituents rejected out of hand Aristide's postelectoral olive branch. Attempting to be conciliatory and to dispel fears that he would become a tyrant, Aristide declared, "There will be a place for everyone in my government. . . . To have a peaceful Haiti, the opposition is indispensable. . . . It is part of our democratic fate."[4] In a letter dated December 27 to President Clinton, Aristide went on to confirm in writing his commitment to creating a government of national consensus that would include technocrats and members of the opposition. Aristide wrote the letter under strong pressure from the United States and after a series of meetings with Special Envoy Tony Lake and the State Department's special Haiti coordinator, Donald Steinberg. In the letter, he promised a long list of reforms that he had hitherto rejected; he pledged to "rectify the problems associated with the May 21 elections, create a credible electoral council, enhance counterdrug cooperation, professionalize the police force and judiciary, strengthen democratic institutions and protect human rights, install a broad-based government, initiate a new dialogue with the international financial institutions, and negotiate a new agreement for the repatriation of illegal migrants."[5]

Aristide had thus acquiesced to major concessions. He seemed to have accepted the idea of holding new elections for the disputed parliamentary seats Fanmi Lavalas won in the contested legislative ballot of May 2000, and to have agreed to form a new provisional electoral council with the help of the opposition. Moreover, he was undermining his own hegemonic status by vowing to appoint opposition figures to senior cabinet positions. Also, by contemplating the dismissal of many of the senators elected in the contested May ballot, and making his peace with the IMF and the World Bank, Aristide was bound to generate major divisions and struggles within his own Fanmi Lavalas. Finally, his apparent agreement to fight drug traffickers and repatriate boat peoples by allowing the U.S. Coast Guard to patrol Haitian waters could only alienate his own nationalist followers and inevitably exacerbate such internecine divisions. The obvious question then is why did Aristide change his mind? Why was he submitting to conditions he had earlier rejected, and why was he now prepared to pay the high political price of surrendering to U.S. pressure?

In reality, Aristide had little choice lest he be isolated completely from the international community, lose all foreign assistance, and transform Haiti into a pariah nation.[6] By accepting the agreement, he hoped to regain the $500 million promised in international aid that had been suspended as a result of the persistent political crisis. Aristide was also trying to smooth relations with Washington and the incoming George W. Bush administration. The goal was to minimize the Republican Party's strong antagonism to his rule and persona. Aristide had always been perceived as a dangerous, mad, crypto-communist demagogue by right-wing Republicans—especially Senator Jesse Helms, the Senate Foreign Relations Committee chair, and Representative Benjamin Gilman, the House International Relations Committee chair.

In fact, on December 8, Helms and Gilman, joined by Congressman Porter Goss, the House Intelligence Committee chair, issued a joint statement saying that Aristide's election "marked a tragic day in Haiti's long and troubled quest for pluralism and representative democracy. Haitian President René Préval and his one-party electoral commission organized a sham election with the sole purpose of delivering absolute control over Haiti's government to Mr. Jean-Bertrand Aristide."[7] Moreover, added Helms, Gilman, and Goss,

> Under Mr. Aristide's leadership and influence, Haiti has become even more impoverished. . . . Colombian narcotics traffickers have established a firm beachhead and, with their Haitian confederates, have largely succeeded in consolidating a narco-state in Haiti.
>
> The United States must now deal with Haiti for what it has become. All direct support for the Haitian Government must end, as provided under current U.S. law. . . . Narco-traffickers, criminals and other antidemocratic elements who surround Jean Bertrand Aristide should feel the full weight of U.S. law enforcement.[8]

Not surprisingly, Gilman reacted very cautiously to Aristide's letter. As he put it, "The promises being made by Jean-Bertrand Aristide are important. The proof, however, will be in the implementation of these promises. Unfortunately, Mr. Aristide's record in this regard has not been very encouraging."[9] Gilman's skepticism was fully shared by the Haitian opposition. In fact, the opposition rejected Aristide's concessions as devious trickery, a last-minute machination to lull it into passivity and into accepting the basic outcome of the "fraudulent" May and November 2000 elections. As Gérard Pierre-Charles put it: "We don't give a lot of value to [Aristide's] words."[10]

The issue, however, was not merely a matter of trust; the opposition refused to recognize the May and November elections, which it labeled a "coup d'État."[11] It saw both Aristide and the new parliament as illegitimate and would simply not accept their "concessions." Convergence

Démocratique urged its followers to fight against the "small group of profi-teers" who usurped power. One of its leaders, Paul Denis, explained that CD's objective was "to mobilize the silent majority, which, by staying home instead of voting signified its repudiation of Aristide."[12]

In fact, CD called for the establishment of a "parallel" government that would be charged with organizing new general elections under the supervision of an impartial electoral council. To that effect, it convened, on January 3, 2001, a large forum to prepare for a national convention that would nominate the members of this alternative government. CD's goal was not only to challenge the legitimacy of Aristide's incoming administration, but also eventually to replace it. Hubert Deronceray, a leading figure of CD, went so far as to suggest that on February 7, the opposition rather than Aristide would be installed in Haiti's National Palace.[13] Not surprisingly, the Lavalas regime was both alarmed and amused by CD's call for an alternative government.

President Préval described CD's plan as "political folly," but he added that it had to be "taken seriously" because the "hunger for power can generate any act of madness."[14] He likened CD's political initiative to the January 1991 failed coup of Roger Lafontant. Similarly, while calling members of the opposition a "bunch of lunatics," Prime Minister Jacques-Édouard Alexis warned them that the government would not tolerate any illegal attempt at challenging Aristide's return to the presidency. Moreover, Fanmi Lavalas gave notice that it would mobilize its supporters and popular organizations to thwart the opposition's efforts to overthrow it. These organizations, specifically Petite Communauté de l'Église de Saint Jean Bosco (TKL) and Jeunesse Pouvoir Populaire (JPP), threatened physical violence against the opposition.[15] Their spokesman, Paul Raymond, para-phrasing Boisrond-Tonerre, a hero of Haiti's struggle for independence, declared that in writing the country's second declaration of independence, the masses will "use the skin of all of those joining the [alternative government] as parchment, their skull as inkwell, and their blood as the ink."[16] Such menaces raise the obvious question: Why would Lavalasian leaders and groups fear CD if, as they claim, it has no real popular following and represents only a reactionary elite?

It is probably true, though difficult to determine with any certainty, that Convergence Démocratique has a very limited mass following that is far smaller than Lavalas's. Moreover, CD's diverse composition, ranging from Duvalierists to socialists, invites internecine struggles hidden only by the common fight against Aristide. In fact, there are clear programmatic divisions within the opposition. MIDH leader and former prime minister in the "de facto" military regime Marc Bazin, who lost the 1990 presidential elections in spite of strong U.S. support, has emerged as the principal voice calling for toleration and compromise. He has described the plan for a parallel government advocated by his colleagues in CD as "an insurrectional movement" that would generate a dangerous "vacuum of power."[17] Moreover, he criticized their strategy of "systematic opposition" as short-sighted and counterproductive and having nothing to offer to counteract Lavalas's destructive and corrupting structural adjustment program. In Bazin's view, CD simply lacked the ideological and programmatic means to carry out its plans. Sooner or later, he added, it would be forced to negotiate with Aristide. In fact, he had himself done so and found Aristide ready to open a dialogue on all the problems paralyzing Haitian society and politics.[18]

Time will tell whether Bazin's prediction was correct, but it seemed clear that CD was convinced that the constellation of domestic and (particularly) international forces greatly favored its determined challenge to Aristide's election and legitimacy. The opposition was assuming and hoping that the incoming Republican administration of George W. Bush would be bent on neutralizing and perhaps overthrowing the Lavalas regime. As the *Washington Post* reported,

> [CD's] most determined . . . men . . . freely express their desire to see the U.S. military intervene once again, this time to get rid of Aristide and rebuild the disbanded Haitian army. "That would be the cleanest solution," said one opposition party leader. Failing that, they say, the CIA should train and equip Haitian officers exiled in the neighboring Dominican Republic so they could stage a comeback themselves.[19]

In this case, CD's "parallel government" would fill the vacuum of power. This scenario was not absolutely far-fetched; it was based on the Panamanian precedent when dictator Manuel Noriega was "surgically removed" by a U.S. military intervention. After years of close collaboration with the United States, Noriega became the target of a systematic campaign of denigration for his alleged connections to Colombian drug dealers; he soon fell out of U.S. favor and ultimately surrendered to U.S. forces. Some of the elements precipitating Noriega's fate are in place in Haiti.

Right-wing U.S. policymakers have already condemned Aristide for being a dangerous radical and an intransigent man who surrounds himself with "narco-traffickers" and encourages "thuggish violence." These accusations, which have never been substantiated, could easily become the basis for a major campaign of systematic denigration portraying Lavalas as nothing but a brutal "narco-movement" that Washington ought to overthrow. The grounds for a "surgical removal" could thus be set up rapidly.

Thus, the fear of a potential U.S. intervention has contributed to Aristide's new "flexibility"; he knows that right-wing Republicans are waiting for an opportunity to challenge and indeed overthrow him. Seeking to extricate himself from this predicament, on January 12, 2001, he wrote a letter to members of the opposition inviting them to his private residence in Tabarre for a "dialogue" that would, he suggested, "open peaceful horizons."[20] While welcoming this initiative, CD refused to recognize Aristide as the president-elect and faulted him for being silent "about the climate of terror that his partisans [were] inflicting on the country." CD was prepared to meet Aristide but only as a private citizen and leader of Fanmi Lavalas. Moreover, if there was to be a dialogue it had to take place at a neutral site rather than at Tabarre and in the presence of members of civil society as well as international observers.[21] Finally, CD invited Aristide and his party to participate in the National Conference and to contribute to creating a government of consensus that would run the country provisionally once Préval departed on February 7, 2001.[22]

Clearly, this was an invitation that Aristide could not and did not accept; it was nothing but a demand for his public abdication of power. The National Conference did, however, take place on January 27. It offered no surprise and reiterated the opposition's negotiating platform in a ten-point resolution.[23] The resolution emphasized the "illegal" nature of Aristide's election and declared that it would not recognize any attempt to inaugurate him as president. Moreover, the opposition reasserted that it would establish a provisional parallel government.

In a final effort to end the deadlock before Aristide's inauguration, "civil society" offered an initiative to mediate and facilitate the dialogue between Fanmi Lavalas and the opposition.[24] Both parties accepted the initiative, though Fanmi Lavalas was apprehensive that it would favor Convergence Démocratique. Indeed, civil society was nothing but a series of self-appointed leaders and groups composed largely of privileged members of the professional, business, and religious sectors.[25] It was a movement thoroughly separated from popular organizations that tended to be associated with Lavalas. Not surprisingly, in its "Appeal for a Solution to the Crisis," civil society clearly sided with the opposition, absolving it of any fault while blaming Fanmi Lavalas for the "serious harm and damage" it caused the country. Moreover, civil society warned Lavalas that "maintaining the elections of May 21 and November 26 as a fait accompli would carry very serious consequences," even if it did take seriously the concessions and promises of Aristide's letter to Clinton.[26]

In the end, the Facilitation Commission that civil society proposed was biased toward the opposition. It was composed of seven members, five of whom represented civil society;[27] the other two represented Lavalas and the opposition. It is difficult to see how that commission could have reflected a genuine national consensus, since it represented at best the vision of a self-appointed moral elite claiming "unquestionable integrity, impartiality, objectivity, [and] a sense of common well-being." To that extent, civil society was a fiction and an instrument of the dominant class, albeit of its "progressive" and liberal wing. It enjoyed, however, significant media access and foreign support and thus had a disproportionate impact on the making of national policies.[28] Thus, civil society's power derived not from its very limited popular base, but from the nature of its constituency, which comprised the dominant circles in business, religion, and the professions. Moreover, it was extremely well connected to influential foreign policy makers, organizations, and sources of finance. Fanmi Lavalas and Aristide could ignore it only at their peril.[29]

Not surprisingly, in the days preceding Aristide's assumption of power, "civil society's initiative" became the basis of frantic negotiations between the opposition and Fanmi Lavalas. Under intense pressure from the international community, Aristide met with his adversaries; but the talks broke down on the eve of his inauguration as president. He offered to rectify the results of the May parliamentary elections, include opposition figures in his government, and appoint a new provisional electoral council. These concessions failed to gain the opposition's support. In turn, Convergence Démocratique initially proposed installing a provisional government; then a "three-member presidential council" that would run the country until 2003 when general elections would be held; and finally a government of national consensus with Aristide serving a presidential term of two years. Furthermore, CD demanded that a prime minister picked from its own ranks be given the authority to exercise power by decree.[30] CD's proposals varied little from its so-called option zero. They were more than a test of Aristide's flexibility; they pushed him into a difficult position with virtually no room to negotiate. Not surprisingly Fanmi Lavalas rejected them.

CD's position certainly did not achieve its goal: on February 7, 2001, amid peaceful popular celebrations, Aristide became president of the Republic for a second time. While the international community shunned his inauguration,[31] the Haitian masses still perceived Aristide as "the savior," albeit a savior with a diminished aura. Equipped with brooms, they swept away garbage from the streets of Port-au-Prince and painted public plazas in the blue and red of the Haitian flag in anticipation of Aristide's inauguration.[32] It is true, however, that February 7, 2001, lacked the popular euphoria and spontaneity that had marked the same occasion ten years earlier. There was no sense that "everything was possible" and that a new beginning was at hand. While Aristide was still the only politician with a real mass following, he could no longer enjoy the absolute and unconditional adulation of the masses. His continued supremacy was a testament to the opposition's utter incapacity to articulate a program that could gain the people's adhesion.

Not surprisingly, CD's gamble to nominate a provisional president and government failed to gain any popular support and was totally eclipsed by the thousands acclaiming Aristide's return to the National Palace.[33]

Moreover, by calling for the return of the despised military chiefs in exile and the reconstitution of the dreaded Haitian army, Gérard Gourgue, in his own presidential "inauguration," exposed CD's desperate lack of popular support. Gourgue's speech was nothing but a veiled appeal for the mobilization of former military officers against the new Aristide administration.[34]

Rather than facilitating reconciliation, the opposition's call for the return of the hated military and its persistence in denying Aristide any legitimacy represented a provocation that could well end up strengthening Lavalas's hard-liners and contribute to further political polarization. This in turn could easily generate a cycle of dangerous political violence enhancing the possibility of a foreign military intervention. Clearly, Aristide has a vested interest in avoiding such an outcome and thus in finding an accommodation with the opposition. In his inaugural speech as president, he reiterated his determination to continue negotiations with CD in order to end the economic and political crisis plaguing the country. He also sought to appease the dominant class that seemed as bent as ever on blocking his ascendancy. He promised to be "the president of all Haitians. And [he added] I will be the president of everyone without exception. There is only one way to take us, and that is the road of peace. Between the opposition and Lavalas, we are the same. We are from the same mother. Haiti is our mother."[35] In addition, he vowed to rout the wave of criminal activities.[36]

Thus, Aristide appeared eager to reach an accommodation with CD, not only to reduce the threat of foreign interference and reestablish law and order, but also because he needs new allies to cut his ties with his troublesome and violent Chimères. Paradoxically, while the Chimères may have played a useful role in consolidating Fanmi Lavalas's power, they have become progressively more autonomous and are no longer a pliable instrument in Aristide's arsenal. In fact, the Chimères' "militarization" has transformed them into armed gangs with increasingly independent interests and leaders; they are escaping from Aristide's control and he knows it. The danger thus is that, having begun as a mere political instrument in the struggle for power, the Chimères have now become a power unto themselves.

Aristide confronts, then, the necessity of reining in his armed allies if he is to preserve his authority. The means to that end is a pact with the opposition that would give him the freedom to do so. Not surprisingly, the Chimères have done everything to exacerbate the divisions between Aristide and the opposition, knowing that they thrive best in conditions of permanent crisis and chaos. Aristide's problem is how to draw CD into negotiations that would not challenge the legitimacy of his controversial election to the presidency.

CD's decision to go ahead with its threat to create an "alternative government" and name Gérard Gourgue as "provisional president" will inevitably complicate efforts to reach a compromise.[37] Moreover, it demonstrated that CD remained convinced that it could effectively, in Evans Paul's words, call on Haitians to "rise up" and challenge peacefully Aristide's legitimacy.[38] It is unlikely, however, that CD's alternative government will gain any popular support, and eventually negotiations will have to start again lest the country be faced with a descent into utter ungovernability. CD's parallel-government strategy was more a tactical maneuver to draw international attention than a response to the demand of a large domestic constituency. But this was a very hazardous gamble since the diplomatic community, led by U.S. ambassador Brian Dean Curran, warned that "the formation of a provisional government [did] not advance prospects for dialogue or a solution of the political crisis."[39]

CD thus risked a fall into irrelevance; it banked on very uncertain foreign support and it had a rather voiceless domestic constituency. In spite of its claim of representing the "silent majority," it was simply unable to mobilize the masses. Only Chavannes Jean-Baptiste's Mouvement des Paysans de Papaye (MPP) showed a capacity to draw significant anti-Lavalas crowds.[40] Based in the Central Plateau department, the MPP is, however, a regional movement that lacks a national audience. In other words, while the opposition may get a fair number of voters, it failed miserably to turn them into active protesters. It simply lacked the means to generate any form of "people's power" with which to challenge seriously the Lavalas regime. The opposition's credibility was sustained more by its ability to influence foreign opinion and policy than to activate widespread internal defiance.[41] It lacked a clear program that would appeal to the majority and on which it could run the country.

Moreover, Haitians know well that before it broke with Lavalas, OPL, one of the opposition's major parties, enjoyed legislative power in both the senate and the house but did precious little with it. Its record in office was lamentable; Christophe Wargny describes it well: "The two parliamentary chambers present a pitiful picture: legal stratagems and maneuvering, calculation, short-termism and constant wheeling-and-dealing push parliamentary madness to the limit, out of contact with the ordinary citizen."[42]

The opposition has thus to contend with a legacy of incompetence and poor strategic choices. It has been unable to capitalize on Lavalas's own failures and declining popularity because of its utter incapacity to accomplish what it promises in defiant rhetoric. Simply put, the opposition lacks credibility; the masses have become progressively more indifferent to the political spectacle of "big eaters" fighting over the spoils of power, and they are fatigued by the permanent crisis and the never-ending descent into poverty and squalor.[43] Moreover, it is increasingly clear that Lavalas's internecine wars, from whose wombs emerged the opposition, had little to do with fundamental differences in policies or programs.

What is indeed striking about the opposition and Fanmi Lavalas is not their divergences but their similarities. It is true that ideological differences over the existing neoliberal economic agenda and over the substance and meaning of democratization exist, but these divisions are more fundamentally rooted in personal rivalries and in the fight for the spoils of power. On the one hand, the opposition sees Fanmi Lavalas not as a vehicle of popular change, but rather as the personal instrument of a demagogic and destructive Aristide. In fact, it is convinced that the "little priest" is bent on disrupting political life to demonstrate that he, and he alone, can restore order and peace.[44] As OPL's leading figure, Pierre-Charles, has put it,

> The heart of the matter is the use Aristide has made of his influence and his domination from the sidelines, with [Préval's] complicity, of many institutions in this country. [The worse the situation becomes] the more Aristide likes it, because he has this messianic idea that he and only he will be the one to save Haiti from chaos.[45]

Fanmi Lavalas, on the other hand, views the OPL as nothing but a coterie of corrupt, opportunistic politicians so blinded by their desire to destroy Aristide that they are capable of any political treachery and manipulation. Moreover, Fanmi Lavalas accuses the OPL and other erstwhile allies of collaborating with both old Duvalierist forces and reactionary members of the dominant class in an effort to undermine popular movements and sabotage Aristide's return to the presidency. In reality, however, few differences exist between the opposition and Fanmi Lavalas; both have accepted, albeit reluctantly, the inevitability of neoliberalism, privatization, and utter dependence on outside powers, particularly the United States.

Scarcity and Zero–Sum Politics

The internecine struggles that devoured Lavalas and resulted in its complete fragmentation reflected the desire of its petit bourgeois and intellectual notables to capture the state as a means of enhancing their class status. Kern Delince's remarks on the Haitian political class describe well the behavior of these Lavalasian notables:

> The members of the political class are very concerned about the prestige that public opinion attaches to class status or privileged social categories. Since most of them come from the upper levels of the middle class, they are seeking to gain their place in the urban bourgeoisie that they have kept as a reference model. Poltiical life offers them a means of social promotion, a trampoline for gaining access to a higher social status, a shortcut allowing them to cross the ditch separating them from various strata of Haitian society.[46]

The utter lack of resources characterizing Haitian society has meant that the top membership of the original Lavalas coalition was too large to enjoy fully the fruits of power. To maximize the benefits of its individual constituents, the coalition had to shrink in size. The ruling cadres of Lavalas were thus bent on creating minimum winning alliances, and this in turn implied exclusionary practices leading to increasingly bitter fighting between competing groups for a fixed amount of prebendary gains. Material scarcity engendered *une politique du ventre;* in order to monopolize valued public goods for their own private windfall, Lavalasian leaders became rational political entrepreneurs bent on organizing loyal followings. The Lavalas movement had increasingly evolved into an unsteady and divided "accumulation alliance," as its claims on state revenues could no longer satisfy all its constituent parts.[47]

The vicissitudes of scarcity are likely to engender not only corruption, but also the perverse environment supportive of dictatorship. As Duvalierism demonstrated, scarcity enhances the capacity of the tyrant to draw the lumpen into his own orbit with minuscule payoffs and with promises of larger future gains for a chosen few. As Michel-Rolph Trouillot has argued,

> [The] shrewdness of Duvalierist redistribution . . . was that everyone could hope to profit some day. For the majority of claimants, however, success was no more than a possibility. . . . [The] state apparatus could support an extraordinary number of cheap allegiances at the bottom of the pyramid and *at the same time* provide ever increasing incomes for the shrinking minority that reached the upper echelons. . . .
>
> Contrary to what one might think, it was not the most prominent *tonton-makout* who maintained the regime of François Duvalier, but the high number of actual or potential *makout* of second rank whom the government bought at very low price. The ferocious competition at the bottom of the ladder, which evokes the image of a basket of crabs, neutralized the potential for mass revolt. . . .
>
> Average individual gains were low, but the number of claimants for crumbs who remained convinced of their chance was always sufficient to hinder the group solidarity necessary for effective action.[48]

Hence, while material want and the ugly struggle for necessity are not absolute obstacles to democratic rule and effective collective action, they tend to favor the emergence of tyrants and populist demagogues. For instance, constitutionalism may be hard put to withstand the polarizing pressures of the persisting economic crisis that has exacerbated social tensions and fueled anomic gang violence. The proliferation of private security systems for the wealthy and the increasing levels of Zinglendo criminality, victimizing rich and poor alike, are an ominous sign of a collapsing public order and of a Hobbesian world in the making. These morbid symptoms sap any meaningful sense of citizenship and generate a seemingly unstoppable descent into a "war of all against all." While the descent may ultimately be halted, its effects are bound to have a devastating impact on the already precarious process of democratization.

The ritual of regular elections cannot mask their increasingly farcical character or the reemergence of authoritarian tendencies. The return to electoral politics and the partial neutralization of the repressive organs of the state are not sufficiently institutionalized to ensure the success of democratic consolidation.[49] While Aristide effectively emasculated the military into a "fifty-man presidential band,"[50] former soldiers and Tontons Macoutes have remained a danger. They have been able to keep their weapons and undermine public peace.[51] Old Duvalierists are not the only menace to democratic governance, however. The Chimères, which are closely linked to Fanmi Lavalas, have also contributed to a climate of insecurity by threatening and indeed using violence against political opponents.[52] Finally, the proliferation of armed gangs involved in the trafficking of drugs and other criminal activities has aggravated a morbid situation that an utterly incompetent police cannot control.

The Haitian police, which had been one of the brighter lights of the country's floundering institutions, has gradually degenerated into a politicized, demoralized, and increasingly corrupt body.[53] It also suffered from deep internal divisions that exploded in what the government described as an "attempted coup" of disgruntled officers.[54] Seven of these officers crossed into the Dominican Republic fearing reprisals from Préval and Aristide, whom they accused of ordering "some twenty captains" to do "whatever was necessary" to ensure Fanmi Lavalas's victory in the elections of May 21.[55] Lavalas denied these accusations and claimed that they were pure fabrications bent on undermining Aristide and his party.[56] The government maintained, however, that as many as 600 police officers were involved in a plot to kill Aristide and Préval and install an anti-Lavalas provisional regime.[57] The plot, according to Télévision Nationale d'Haïti (TNH) and *Haïti Progrès*, was a conspiracy involving foreign-trained officers financed by Haitian industrialist Olivier Nadal.[58] Lavalas condemned it as the machination of the old Duvalierists and reactionary bourgeois forces seeking to recover the power they had lost. As President Préval put it, the attempted coup was symbolic of the ongoing battle between "99% of the population living on the margins of society and the 1% of Haitians who control half the country's wealth."[59] It is difficult to ascertain, however, whether this turmoil in the police was indicative of class warfare, as Préval would have it, or an invention of the government itself to cover its own failings and harass the opposition, as CD claimed.[60]

What became clear was that the police force was increasingly politicized and in disarray. Moreover, it was simply incapable of protecting citizens; those who have the means have opted for more effective private security services.[61] In turn, members of the police play a dual role as they are also on the payroll of these private services. The national police from top to bottom failed to establish a distinction between public office and private property; in fact, it was in the interests of its members that public safety be privatized. In a society in which it is unnatural not to make a profit from the public office one holds, the top echelons of the police are more involved in the business of providing private security services than in guaranteeing public safety.[62]

Not surprisingly, the police force has lost whatever idealism and esprit de corps it may have had. Officers fearing for their lives and lacking basic equipment are leaving the force or joining private security agencies.[63] From a high of more than 6,500 officers in 1997 to under 6,000 in 2000, and with numbers continuing to drop, it is highly unlikely that the police department will achieve its objective of attracting 10,000 officers by 2003. Moreover, there is a high degree of corruption among those who decide to stay—since 1995 authorities have had to dismiss more than 530 officers for "abuse of power and other disciplinary infractions."[64] The secretary-general of the United Nations, Kofi Annan, summarized the situation:

> There have been worrying allegations of police involvement in robbery, extortion and abduction, as well as drug trafficking, together with reports of anarchic tax collection by newly elected local officials, and the involvement of popular organizations in protection rackets.
>
> Political pressures on the Haitian National Police (HNP), together with such incidents as the attempted lynching of a police commissioner during a pro-Aristide demonstration on 2 October, have contributed to the demoralization of HNP and eroded its operational capacity and credibility. Reports that its effective strength has fallen to alarmingly low levels have fuelled fears of a breakdown in public order.[65]

These fears were exacerbated by the Chimères' vocal threats and indeed brutal hostility to anyone perceived as anti-Lavalas. While their slogan "Aristide or death" and veiled appeals for more "Père Lebruns" have worsened social polarization, they should not mask the reality that well-known supporters of the murderous military regime have gone unpunished pursuing their political activities. In fact, the moral dilemma of seeking national reconciliation while at the same time establishing the rule of justice has remained a Gordian knot. Paradoxically, Aristide's return in 1995 had an elevated price: it required tolerating the persisting power of key sectors of the old dictatorial coalition, accepting a de facto amnesty for past crimes, and collaborating with former supporters of the authoritarian de facto regime.

It is true that such tolerance may represent the "least unsatisfactory" solution to the "torturer problem" as it corresponds to Samuel Huntington's prudent motto, "Do not prosecute, do not punish, do not forgive, and, above all, do not forget."[66] The popular development of an acute memory of the ugliness of brutal repression and of a profound sense of moral outrage at past barbarities may thus contribute to deter a future descent into hell, but it is neither a guarantee against such a descent nor a satisfying rendering of justice. In fact, memory of such events may check further democratization, for the terror it inspires paralyzes people into believing that punishing the torturers will cause their murderous return to power. As Michael Taussig has argued, "The [authoritarian] State's interest is in keeping memory of public political protest, and memory of the sadistic and cruel violence unleashed against it, alive!"[67] By simultaneously preserving the memory of the dictatorship's violent practices and the freedom of torturers, democratization engenders an ambiguous sense of normalcy. Such a sense of normalcy encroaches on the development of a more democratic alternative because it is built on the constraining legacy and continued presence of criminals. In these conditions, democratization collides with popular justice and seeks to disarm it. It becomes a mere *technique* of prudent, conservative governance that accepts coexistence with the lingering authoritarian legacy. Thus, democratization's benign rather than frontal assault on the core institutions, leaders, and beliefs of the old regime can ultimately contribute to legitimize the silent violence of daily material deprivation plaguing oppressed majorities. A lingering despotism is thus inscribed or tacitly accepted in the norms of the postdictatorial society.

The prompt return to social normalcy may buy a temporary peace, but it has meant accepting the presence of unpunished torturers and murderers and thereby may ultimately portend future victims. It is clear that the National Commission for Truth and Justice created in March 1995 by the Aristide government failed to resolve that dilemma.[68] The hopes raised by the commission for a national soul cleansing and for the development of a deep and meaningful sense of justice never materialized. In fact, the commission's report, *Si M Pa Rélé,* has been so poorly disseminated that it has utterly failed to reach its intended audience. Only a handful of Haitians have had access to the 1,200-page report. As Human Rights Watch/ Americas pointed out in September 1996,

> The Commission's mandate prohibited it from initiating prosecutions of any of the 8,652 human rights cases it documented, but expectations were high that its report would at least provide a public accounting of gross human rights violations under the military government. However, over seven months after the report's completion it has yet to be published and has had no visible impact. Only the recommendations were released, which one human rights advocate likened to a doctor providing a prescription without a diagnosis. The recommendations standing alone did little to

address the root causes of human rights abuse in Haiti, nor did they provide an opportunity for victims' stories to be told in an official forum. Meanwhile, human rights victims and the courts have no access to potentially useful documentation of human rights crimes.[69]

The National Commission for Truth and Justice has thus failed to live up to the very slogan it has used to name its report. The Creole words *Si m pa Rélé* and the proverb *Si m pa Rélé, m'ap toufé*, translate, respectively, "If I don't cry out" and "If I don't cry out, I will suffocate"—suggesting that it is necessary to express one's outrage against injustice in order to combat it. But instead of generating outrage, the report produced silence. The Haitian truth commission was thus a complete disappointment; it provided, in David Malone's words, "a case-book study of how not to launch, administer, and support similar bodies elsewhere."[70] Limited funding, incompetent staffing and management, and U.S. unwillingness to cooperate in documenting the killings committed under the military government plagued the commission.[71] The United States refused to hand over to the Aristide and Préval administrations the 160,000 pages of military and paramilitary materials its troops seized upon occupying Haiti. The details of the junta's methods and targets of repression therefore remain hidden from public scrutiny.[72]

The Préval administration managed, however, to bring some justice and closure to the victims of the Raboteau massacre. Raboteau, a seaside neighborhood of Gonaïves, was the site, on April 22, 1994, of a savage military attack against supporters of President Aristide. At least six people were murdered and many others tortured.[73] On September 29, 2000, the perpetrators of the massacre were brought to trial; among them were the exiled coup leaders Raoul Cédras, Michel François, and Philippe Biamby; the military high command; and Emmanuel Constant, the leader of FRAPH. The trial was the single successful attempt to partially cleanse the country of the terror of the 1991 coup d'état. It exposed the brutalities of the de facto regime and punished the defendants for their crimes. Twelve former soldiers and paramilitaries were given life sentences. Tried in absentia, Cédras, Biamby, François, and Constant were also condemned to life in prison with hard labor for their role in the massacre.[74]

The Raboteau trial was the sole important case where the rule of law— that intrinsic part of constitutionalism—was respected rather than denied. Despite celebrating it in written documents and rhetorical commitments, the Lavalas regime has rarely ensured or implemented it. The mere existence of a liberal constitution has not led to constitutionalism. Moreover, the material costs required for establishing constitutionalism may be so high that they severely undermine democracy itself. The enormous resources needed to create viable, functioning, and relatively honest judiciary and electoral systems have to be drawn from other critical and starving sectors of society, such as education, infrastructure, and health. In this zero-sum environment, allocative choices are extremely constrained; the costs of implanting democratic electoralism in Haiti may well collide with the improvement of social welfare.[75] Finally, the material incapacity of both the Aristide and Préval regimes to respect the law, norms, and rules that they themselves promulgate can only generate more popular cynicism and apathy. Thus, Haiti's political system has degenerated beyond Philippe Schmitter's "unconsolidated democracy";[76] it is truly a predatory democracy.

The Illusions of Constitutionalism

A liberal constitution does not make for an effective form of constitutionalism. Institutions simply do not soar above the material and political structures of society. They reflect the balance of forces governing class relations and interests, and their workings are severely constrained by the material environment within which they operate. The effectiveness of a constitution is inextricably dependent on the relationships of class power and their cultural and institutional manifestations.

It is true that the construction of institutions matters in democratizing society; in fact, the "new constitutionalism" has placed such a construction at the very center of political science.[77] The assumption is not only that institutions matter, but that they are "the most promising avenue for changing the world."[78] According to this view, in periods of regime transition, institutions become determinant in the crafting of "good societies." The establishment of appropriate constitutions is perceived as the critical factor in creating the democracies of the "third wave."[79] In turn, the design of such constitutions simultaneously causes the further development of, and is caused by, civic virtue. For new constitutionalists, it is this virtue that produces the citizens' skilled and motivated imagination enabling them to trespass their narrow self-interest and embrace the common good.

Thus, constitutions simultaneously reflect and create "political culture." Elinor Ostrom describes political culture as a form of "social capital," that is, "the shared knowledge, understandings, and patterns of interaction" that are usable for the crafting of institutions.[80] Constraining and molding each other, social capital and institutional design interact in a dialectical way to create the terrain on which citizens can expand, limit, or freeze the "boundaries of the possible." In their preface to *The Failure of Presidential Democracy*, Juan Linz and Arturo Valenzuela argue that from the perspective of the institutionalist paradigm,

> politics and institutions are viewed as independent variables in their own right, not simply as epiphenomena reflecting underlying economic and

social forces. Complex organizations are more than aggregates of individual behavior; they are social structures with their autonomy and logic, affecting and constraining individual behavior and human choice. Political options and decisions are mediated by the rules and structures of the game, rules with closely related formal and informal dimensions.[81]

In the eyes of the new constitutionalists, institutions make history, even if they are not independent variables. Institutions are in fact shaped and influenced by the dominant habits, norms, and ways of life of the polity. Political culture thus acquires great significance; it supports civic behavior, making possible democratic institutions that in turn strengthen such behavior. In a mutually reinforcing relation, political culture creates the foundations on which constitutions rest, and constitutions in turn define and open up the new social parameters molding political culture itself.

To this extent, situations in which civic competence is high are favorable to the crafting of institutions reflecting the common good and the establishment of a democratic constitutional order. In this instance, the fundamental premise is that individuals, groups, and classes can detach themselves from their material, political, and social interests to devise a genuine commonwealth. Standing in midair, as it were, they can look at the general terrain and build those institutions that will serve as the foundations of the "good" society.

Many political scientists make a stronger version of that claim; they perceive the implantation and consolidation of democracy as a matter of political "crafting"[82] and of constitutional engineering through charismatic, creative, and talented political leadership. In this perspective, structural constraints and the obdurate opposition of classes are not seen as determinant of the outcome; instead, Michael Burton, Richard Gunther, and John Higley summarize the findings of their book, *Elites and Democratic Consolidation in Latin America and Southern Europe,* with these words:

> In the final analysis . . . a central conclusion of these studies is the great responsibility of national elites for achieving, or failing to achieve, the degree of consensus and unity necessary for the establishment and consolidation of democracy.[83]

Democratization is thus increasingly viewed as a matter of political design and "constitutional knowledge."[84] From this perspective, it is not that interests are ignored, but rather that they can be rationally curbed, if not altogether eliminated, by the acquisition of knowledge of constitutional theories. By explaining the operation, norms, and consequences of constitutions and their making, such knowledge facilitates choices that transcend narrow self-interest and promote "packages" of behavior enhancing democratic governance. Advocates of "deliberative democracy," who place their

faith in people's capacity to reach moral principles through collective dialogue, advance a similar argument. Such a dialogue, in the eyes of deliberative democrats, has the potential to lead to the cultural internalization of the
"significance and legitimacy of a constitutional system based on the rule of
law."[85] Once this is achieved, the transition to and the consolidation of
democratic government are ensured.

It is true that new constitutionalists and deliberative democrats
acknowledge that class antagonisms, ethnic animosities, and dire poverty
may constrain the rise of polyarchy; but in their view, these structural factors do not constitute insurmountable obstacles to the flourishing of democracy. Constitutional crafting, moral appeals, and rational deliberations can
dissolve self-interest and generate an enlightened consensus for democratic
rule. Democratization is thus a matter of elite leadership and capacity to
effect compromise and goodwill. Guillermo O'Donnell and Philippe
Schmitter argue for the decisive role of innovative individual action:

> Elite dispositions, calculations, and pacts . . . largely determine whether or
> not an opening will occur at all, [and] the catalyst [for collective action]
> comes first from gestures by exemplary individuals, who begin testing the
> boundaries of behavior initially imposed by the incumbent regime.[86]

I argue, however, that while it may be true that constitution making
requires a political class possessing knowledge, engineering skills, and
political imagination, such faculties do not obliterate the reality that there is
a fundamental difference between writing a founding charter and adhering
to its norms and rules. There is a profound chasm between a constitution
and constitutionalism. On the one hand, constitution making takes place in
what might be termed a "moment of exception," reflecting either an
ephemeral balance of power between contending classes and groups that
are prepared to settle temporarily their conflicts, or the total victory of a
particular social segment of society. On the other hand, constitutionalism
entails an enduring equilibrium of forces that compels and eventually habit-
uates political actors into conforming to an institutionalized set of practices
and behaviors, minimizing the potential for arbitrary and personalized
authority as well as the tyranny of the majority.[87] This is the basis on which
polyarchy is established.

Neither political culture nor institutions can sustain constitutionalism.
It is the balance of class forces supporting the foundations of culture and
institutions that makes possible any type of constitutional governance.
Constitutional knowledge, civic competence, and the desire for a good
society are not unimportant in democratic transitions and consolidations,
but they cannot obliterate class interests and the privileged groups' quest
for maintaining their dominant position in the existing system of political
and economic power.

In the Haitian context, the fundamental question then is whether the establishment of the democratic constitution of 1987 in the wake of the collapse of the Duvalier dictatorship can in fact engender constitutionalism. It seems to me that by itself the constitution cannot achieve this objective; or to put the matter more clearly, the constitution is a necessary but not sufficient condition for the establishment of constitutionalism. Constitutionalism requires the regulated political unpredictability of polyarchy—a form of uncertainty contained within and structured by a predictable system of rules. Most critically, political actors have—at a minimum—to be convinced that the uncertainties of defeat do not outweigh the gains of a possible future victory. The precondition for establishing such convictions is the institutionalization of uncertainty within a predictable framework, within which outcomes would be neither permanent nor arbitrary. That in turn requires political actors to accept the rules of constitutionalism. Such acceptance, however, thoroughly depends on a relative equilibrium of power between the major competing political blocs of civil society.

Thus, constitutionalism is not merely a set of institutional constraints on majority rule, a binding limit to "passions" and arbitrary power; it is above all a pattern of predictable and civil behavior generated by a balance of class forces. The making of the constitution and the incentive to obey it both depend on power relations. Moreover, power relations can undermine constitutionalism when a privileged minority persistently uses the constitution to preserve its interests in the face of overwhelming popular opposition. In this situation, constitutionalism is nothing but the defense of the status quo and a legal obstacle to any meaningful democratization. It leads to a dangerous political immobilism that is likely to be settled by the exercise of brute force even if the contending parties make vain appeals to constitutionalism.

Constitutionalism is safe only when the parties are convinced that their respective weaknesses and strengths are such that if either of them violates the basic "rules of the game," the other would have enough power to—at least—launch a mutually detrimental war of all against all. Thus, an equilibrium of power and terror is decisive in the consolidation of constitutionalism. Unless constitution making takes place in a conjuncture where the coercive apparatus of the state is thoroughly emasculated, it is unlikely to prevent ruling classes from launching multiple coups de force to suppress the eruption of popular classes onto the political stage and the potential transformation of the existing balance of class power.

A constitution cannot on its own transform political actors into polyarchical, let alone democratic, agents; in conditions of extreme social polarization, it can offer only the fragility of written codes and regulations that are unlikely to withstand the ferocious retaliation of a threatened dominant class. The provisions of constitutional polyarchy are likely to function effectively only when subordinate and dominant classes perceive themselves as equally armed or disarmed; only such conditions create the incentives for the surrender of weapons to the moral force of written pacts and documents. A Haitian proverb expresses well this reality: "Konstitisyon se papye, bayonèt se fè" [a constitution is made up of paper, but bayonets are made up of steel]. It is sheer fantasy to believe that moral appeals can equalize the balance of power and open up a rational dialogue between dominant and subordinate classes. Without such equalization, the incentive to compromise and reach mutually acceptable governing formulas is virtually nil.

Haiti is unlikely to enjoy any meaningful democratization without a modicum of redistribution of resources and wealth.[88] This, however, is extremely difficult, given the determination of the dominant class to cling to its privileges and status. Moreover, redistribution would solve little; it would merely generalize poverty. Growth with redistribution is thus the means to achieve a more productive and humane environment, but it depends on the resolution of the persisting crisis of governability afflicting the country. If the past is any guide, then the future is at best uncertain if not altogether bleak. The hope, however, is that Aristide has now understood that the logic of democracy—in its minimal form—entails the presence and toleration of the opposition. It remains to be seen whether such novel political awakening will be enough to ensure a compromise and the resolution of Haiti's persistent crisis of governability. The next chapter explores the complicated and difficult negotiations surrounding the search for such a compromise.

Notes

1. Aristide won close to 92 percent of the vote against candidates who were virtually unknown to all Haitians. The official results are shown in the table below (source, CNN.Com/IFES):

Candidate	Affiliation	Votes Received	% of Valid Votes
Aristide	FL	2,632,534	91.81
Dumas	Independent	56,678	2.04
Nicolas	UNR	45,411	1.55
Sylvain	Independent	37,371	1.30
Dorisca	Independent	36,233	1.26
Dorce	Independent	32,245	1.12
Fleurival	Independent	31,100	1.08

2. The major parties of the CD are the following: Organisation du Peuple en Lutte (OPL), led by Gérard Pierre-Charles; Espace de Concertation (EC)—regrouping five parties; Confédération Unité Démocratique (KID), led by Evans Paul; Génération 2004, Parti National Progressiste Haïtien (PANPRHA), led by Serge Gilles; Congrès National des Mouvements Démocratiques (CONACOM), led by Victor Benoît and Micha Gaillard; Ayiti Kapab; and Mouvement Patriotique pour le Sauvegarde National (MPSN)—a coalition of Duvalierist formations of which the main ones are Mouvement pour le Développement National (MDN), led by Hubert Deronceray; Parti Démocrate Chrétien Haïtien (PDCH); L'Alliance pour la Libération d'Haïti (ALAH), led by Reynolds Georges; Mouvement Chrétien pour une Nouvelle Haïti (MOCRENHA); Rassemblement des Démocrates Nationalistes et Progressistes (RDNP); and Parti Démocrate Haïtien (PADEMH), led by Jean-Jacques Clark Parent.

As the Haiti Support Group, based in London, explained (in "What Is the Democratic Convergence?"),

> Apart from the OPL, MOCHRENA and the Espace de Concertation coalition, who recorded modest tallies in the May elections, these parties, or more accurately "particles," enjoy very little support. They are mainly vehicles for the personal ambitions of wealthy or well-connected individuals. They do not have a mass membership or a party structure.
>
> As for the others, it is worth noting that the OPL enjoyed a dominant role in the government and Parliament from 1995/6 largely thanks to its membership of the pro-Aristide PPL Lavalas coalition—this coalition broke up in 1996 when Aristide and others formed a new party, the Lavalas Family. The main members of the Espace coalition are CONACOM and PANPRHA, both members of the social democratic Socialist International, supported by European social democratic parties. MOCHRENA is a new party formed by right wing Protestant evangelical churches that are mainly funded by US evangelical groups.

3. On the failure of the OAS-sponsored "dialogue," see United Nations, "United Nations International Civilian Support Mission in Haiti, Report of the Secretary-General," Fifty-fifth session, A/55/618, November 9, 2000, pp. 2–3; see also "Crise Electorale: Aucun Accord en Vue," Métropole Haïti, October 27, 2000; "Haiti's Elections and the Truth Behind the Negotiation Process," Haiti123, November 22, 2000.

4. As quoted in Michael Norton, "Aristide Pledges Diverse Rule," Associated Press, November 28, 2000.

5. The White House, "Statement by the Press Secretary," December 28, 2000. Aristide's letter confirmed an agreement he had reached with Tony Lake and Donald Steinberg during a series of meetings in Port-au-Prince. The White House released a copy of the letter and the agreement on December 28, 2000. The agreement has the eight following points, which Aristide pledged to observe:

> 1. Rapid rectification of the problems associated with the May 21 elections through run-offs for disputed Senate seats or by other credible means. This rectification is being facilitated by the work of the Lissade Commission.
> 2. Creation of a credible new provisional electoral council (CEP) in consultation with opposition figures to rectify the problems associated with the disputed Senate seats.
> 3. Enhance substantially cooperation to combat drug trafficking, including implementation of money laundering legislation and expansion of maritime cooperation, building on the October 1997 agreement, in order to allow access to U.S.

Coast Guard anti-drug operation in Haitian waters. Strengthen efforts, in collaboration with the U.S. and Dominican Republic governments, to interdict trafficking across Haitian/DR border.

4. Nominate capable and respected officials for senior security positions, including within the HNP. Ensure that there is no interference in the professional work and conduct of the HNP by members of Parliament and others. Take steps to enhance the professionalism and independence of juridical system.

5. Strengthen democratic institutions and protection of human rights through the establishment of a semi-permanent OAS commission to facilitate dialogue among Haitian political, civic, and business leaders and through international monitoring of the protection of human rights.

6. Seek to install a broad-based government including "technocrats" and members of the opposition.

7. Initiate new dialogue with international financial institutions concerning sound budgetary proposals and economic reforms to enhance free markets and promote private investment. Such measures will be aimed at reducing poverty and stimulating growth.

8. Negotiate agreement for repatriation of illegal migrants.

See also "Another Chance for Haiti," *Washington Post,* December 29, 2000; "US Waits for Aristide's Haiti to Deliver on New Promises of Reform," *Washington Post,* December 29, 2000; "Aristide Pledges Opening to Opposition," *Miami Herald,* December 29, 2000.

6. As Aristide put it to Catherin Orenstein, "If the international community is not for us, one thing is sure: We will fail." As quoted in Orenstein, "Aristide, Again," *The Progressive,* January 2001.

7. House International Relations Committee, "Gilman, Helms and Goss Issue Statement on Haitian Election," December 8, 2000.

8. Ibid.

9. As quoted in "US Waits for Aristide's Haiti to Deliver on New Promises of Reform," *Washington Post,* December 29, 2000.

10. As quoted in "Alliance to Challenge Haiti's Rulers," *Miami Herald,* January 5, 2001.

11. Democratic Convergence, "Declaration of Marlik," December 13, 2000.

12. As quoted in "Opposition Alliance Forms in Haiti," Associated Press, January 3, 20001.

13. "Another Coup in the Making?" *Haïti Progrès,* January 3–9, 2001.

14. "L'Exécutif Haïtien Lance une Mise en Garde Contre Tout Mouvement de Désordre dans le Pays," Flash InterVision2000, January 4, 2001 (author's translation).

15. "Menaces Contre Plusieurs Personnalités d'Opposition," AFP International, January 10, 2001. The Petite Communauté de l'Église de Saint Jean Bosco and Jeunesse Pouvoir Populaire claimed that the opposition was in the process of creating a Conseil National de Salut Public that would replace the Lavalas regime. The Conseil had generated a long list of Haitian personalities who were supposed to compose its membership. Curiously, Jean-Bertrand Aristide's name and that of other Lavalasians were included in the list. TKL and JPP concentrated their attack, however, on prominent figures of the opposition such as Leslie Manigat, Gérard Pierre-Charles, Gérard Gourgue, Evans Paul, Serge Gilles, Hubert Deronceray, and Claude Roumain. The document informing the country that the Conseil had been created was published on the Web and can be accessed through Haiti Online, January 10, 2001. See also "Les OP Lavalas s'Attaquent à l'Opposition et à la Presse," Métropole Haïti, January 10, 2001. The Préval admin-

istration through Camille Leblanc, the minister of justice, condemned the declarations of TKL and JPP. Fanmi Lavalas joined in the condemnation and claimed that its peaceful principles were at odds with the violence preached by these popular organizations. See "Les OP Lavalas Doivent Répondre Devant la Justice," Métropole Haïti, January 11, 2001; "Le Parti Fanmi Lavalas Condamne les Agissements de TKL de Saint Jean Bosco," Flash InterVision2000, January 11, 2001.

16. "Les OP Lavalas s'Attaquent à l'Opposition et à la Presse," Métropole Haïti, January 10, 2001.

17. "Marc Bazin Qualifie de Mouvement Insurrectionnel la Décision de l'Opposition," Flash InterVision2000, January 10, 2001.

18. "Transcript d'Interview: Marc Bazin avec Robert Philomé," Haiti Online, December 8, 2000; "Marc Bazin Reçu en Audience par le Président Elu," Métropole Haïti, December 5, 2000.

19. Edward Cody, "Haiti Torn by Hope and Hatred as Aristide Returns to Power," *Washington Post,* February 2, 2001, p. A1.

20. Jean-Bertrand Aristide, "Letter to Convergence Démocratique," January 12, 2001. Hatuey De Camps, president of the Dominican Revolutionary Party (PRD), greatly facilitated this attempted mediation. He met first in Santo Domingo with the leaders of the opposition, Leslie Manigat, Gérard Pierre-Charles, Evans Paul, Serge Gilles, and Victor Benoît, and then in Port-au-Prince with Aristide. The Center for International Diplomacy in Washington summarized the findings of the PRD's intervention ("Effects of Dominican Republic Mediation," January 18, 2001):

> According to [De Camps], Aristide hopes that resurrection of dialogue with the opposition can lead to nominating a consensus prime minister, integration of members of the opposition into the government, and organization of new legislative elections. Aristide repeatedly told the PRD president that everything was on the table in his discussion with the opposition except his own election as president, since he recognized that the success of his government would greatly depend on the support and respect of the opposition.
>
> The leader of the PRD gave Aristide some specific political advice and told him one could not speak of democracy in a country with elections where only one party takes part and wins all the legislative seats, the judiciary and the election commission. He also told Aristide the days of Latin American dictators such as Chile's Pinochet and Peru's Fujimori were over. Informed of Aristide's letter to President Clinton he told Aristide that was not enough, it did not provide any real assurances to the opposition of his flexibility.
>
> He said he gave equally specific advice to the opposition. He noted that the opposition itself was divided on creation of its shadow government. He told the opposition that Aristide would have won anyway no matter who monitored the election.

21. See "Jean-Bertrand Aristide Invite l'Opposition au Dialogue," Haiti Online, January 16, 2001; "La Convergence Démocratique Répond Positivement à l'Appel au Dialogue du Leader de Fanmi Lavalas," Flash Intervision2000, January 18, 2001.

22. See CD's letter responding to Aristide; the text of the letter signed by Gérard Pierre-Charles (OPL), Victor Benoît (Espace de Concertation), Hubert Deronceray (MPSN), Leslie Manigat (RDNP), Clark Parent (PADEMH), and Luc Mesadieu (MOCHRENAH), can be found at Flash Intervision2000, January 18, 2001.

23. The text of the resolution (translated by Carrol Coates) follows (original text at Haiti Online, "Résolution de la Journée d'Ouverture des États Généraux," January 29, 20001):

1. Recalling the Universal Declaration of Human Rights, the United Nations' charter, the Organization of American States' charter, the various international conventions, agreements concerning economic, social, cultural, political rights of the human being to which Haiti is a party;
2. Recalling the ten years (1991–2001) during which the Lavalas government has choked Haiti's national economy, undermined democracy, imposed the rule of a single political party, frustrated the Haitian population, unjustly imprisoned and exiled honest citizens, increased unemployment, insecurity, poverty, social unrest, and despair;
3. Recognizing that from 1997 to 2000, legislative, municipal, local, and presidential elections were characterized by the arbitrary decisions of the provisional electoral councils totally subdued to the Lavalas regime, marked by the absence of electoral campaigns, by physical violence, by the systematic violation of the electoral law, and by all sorts of fraud and scandalous irregularities, including the invention of a method of tabulation favoring the Lavalas party;
4. Considering that the Haitian population by refusing to endorse the electoral crime of May 21, 2000, by abstaining to take part in the electoral coup of November 26, 2000, has manifested its full adhesion to the efforts undertaken by Convergence Démocratique;
5. Considering that repeated calls of the opposition, civil society, and the international community for a dialogue have run against the dilatory maneuvers of the Lavalas clan, and to a politics of fait accompli that is likely to result in the further isolation of Haiti and entail irreparable socioeconomic and political consequences for our country;
6. Considering that Haitians from all social backgrounds are pressing for the designation of the head of the provisional government;
7. [The members of the National Conference] remain open to negotiate;
8. Declare unacceptable and of null effect any attempt to inaugurate the illegal and illegitimate presidency of J. B. Aristide at the Palais National on February 7, 2001;
9. Have decided to fill the institutional void by forming a provisional government of national consensus and unity, the composition of which will be announced shortly;
10. Hereby invite the international community to acknowledge this national decision.

24. "La Société Civile Encourage une Solution à la Crise," Métropole Haïti, January 19, 2001; see also "Bombs Explode in Port-au-Prince," Associated Press, January 19, 2001.

25. "La Société Civile Veut Ramener les Hommes Politiques à la Raison," Haitian Television Network, January 19, 2001.

26. Civil Society Initiative, "Civil Society Appeal for a Solution to the Crisis," January 18, 2001, online at the Center for International Policy, http://www.ciponline.org/Haiti/Dec%202000-%20Feb%2001/civil.htm.

27. The five members of "civil society's" facilitation commission were Mgr. Joseph Serge Miot, president of the Commission Épiscopale Justice et Paix; Reverend Seth Pierre-Louis, president of the Fédération Protestante d'Haïti; professor Rosny Desroches, president of the Fondation Haïtienne de l'Enseignement Privé; Ambassador Guy Alexandre, coordinator of Initiatives Démocratiques; and Maurice Lafortune, vice president of the Chambre de Commerce et d'Industrie d'Haïti.

28. U.S. representative Benjamin A. Gilman gave his immediate support to civil society's initiative while warning Aristide to fulfill his promises (U.S. House of Representatives, "Gilman Supports Haiti Civil Society Dialogue, Calls on Aristide to Match Words with Actions, January 18, 2001):

> The dialogue announced by leaders of Haiti's civil society is a courageous and welcome initiative. An old Creole saying reminds us that a river cannot run upstream. Accordingly, a real dialogue among Haitians is fundamental to taking the necessary steps to secure space for political pluralism, the rule of law, and legitimate governance in Haiti. A broad dialogue is the only path that can lead to the serious reforms and investments in education and healthcare that are so desperately needed for all Haitians to benefit from the global economy.
>
> The government of Haiti and its ruling Lavalas Family party will bear the principal burden for the success or failure of this dialogue initiative. Regrettably, Mr. Jean Bertrand Aristide's promises to President Clinton and public call for dialogue have only been words. Mr. Aristide must go beyond words now and take concrete, constructive steps.
>
> Mr. Aristide remains silent while his partisans continue to threaten violence against journalists, civil society and democratic political leaders. In Limbe, Haiti, individuals directly related to Mr. Aristide's political party are threatening to seize and destroy the "Hôpital Bon Samaritain," a charitable, American-run institution that serves Haiti's poor people. It is time for Mr. Aristide to exercise leadership and stop the violence.

Colin Powell, the new U.S. secretary of state, was more conciliatory; he declared in his testimony to the Committee on Foreign Relations that Aristide's promises to Clinton constituted "an appropriate road map to get started." He added that the Bush administration will "have to engage with President Aristide. It seems that our goals remain what they were 10 or 12 years ago, how to get that democracy and that economy started and how to keep the Haitian people at home and not on the seas heading toward Florida" (Committee on Foreign Relations, United States Senate, Secretary of State Nomination Part II, January 17, 2001, Washington, D.C.).

The new U.S. ambassador to Haiti, Brian Dean Curran, pointed out, however, that the United States would not have normal relations with the Aristide administration unless the "problems with the May elections are resolved." See "U.S. Deals Blow to Aristide," Associated Press, February 6, 2001.

29. Béatrice Pouligny ("Haïti: Deux ou Trois Raisons d'Espérer," *Libération,* February 13, 2001) emphasized correctly the significance of foreign support in making Convergence Démocratique at all viable:

> La "communauté internationale" a contribué à remettre en selle une opposition hétéroclite, complètement discréditée et qui ne peut se prévaloir d'aucune base électorale. Elle est essentiellement constituée d'individualités, en l'absence de réels partis politiques organisés comme tels. Ceux qui se présentent aux ambassades et délégations de passage à Port-au-Prince comme les représentants de la "société civile" répondent souvent aux mêmes caractéristiques. Du reste, nombre d'entre eux cumulent les fonctions, changeant de casquette au gré des opportunités. Les plus progressistes, intellectuels souvent formés à l'étranger, pro-Aristide en 1990, qui ont parfois occupé des fonctions politiques et sont restés intègres, sont aujourd'hui divisés, ont quitté le pays ou ont fait le choix de se replier sur des engagements concrets auprès des organisations communautaires. Mais même ceux-là continuent, à de rares exceptions près, à éprouver d'énormes difficultés à se situer à la fois vis-à-vis du pouvoir politique et de la majorité de la population.
>
> L'essentiel des débats de ces élites n'a rien à voir avec les préoccupations des 90% de la population dont, le plus souvent, ils ne parlent même pas la langue.

Leurs discours séducteurs à l'égard des étrangers tendent trop souvent à masquer l'existence des réseaux d'organisations communautaires qui, depuis le début des années 80, ont servi de cadre à l'émergence de la majorité de la population sur la scène politique.

[The "international community" has contributed to putting back into place a heteroclite opposition that is completely discredited and that cannot take advantage of any electoral base. It is essentially composed of individualities in the absence of real political parties organized as such. The people who present themselves to embassies and passing delegations in Port-au-Prince as representatives of "civil society" often fit the same description. Besides, many of them collect roles, changing hats as circumstances allow. The more progressive among them, intellectuals who have often been educated abroad, who were pro-Aristide in 1990 and have often had political positions and have retained their integrity, are now divided, have left the country, or have made a choice of falling back on their concrete commitments to community organizations. But even these people continue, with rare exceptions, to experience enormous difficulties in assuming a position with respect to political power and the majority of the populace.

The essential aspect of debates among these elites has nothing to do with the preoccupations of 90 percent of the population and, most often, they do not even speak the same language. Their discourse, which entices foreigners, too often tends to hide the existence of the networks of community organization that, since the beginning of the 1980s, have served as a framework for the emergence of the majority of the population onto the political scene.] (Translated by Carrol Coates)

30. "La Convergence Démocratique Annonce la Nomination d'un Président Parallèle," Agence Haïtienne de Presse, February 6, 2001; "Échec des Négociations Initiées par des Secteurs de la Société Civile en vue de Résoudre la Crise Post-Électorale," Agence Haïtienne de Presse, February 6, 2001; David Gonzalez, "Haiti's Opposition Proposes 3-Member Presidency," *New York Times,* February 6, 2001; "Talks Break Down Between Haiti's Opposition and Aristide's Party," Associated Press, February 6, 2001; David Gonzalez, "Haitian Opposition Says It Will Form Alternative Government," *New York Times,* February 7, 2001; "Négociations Politiques Infructueuses à la Veille du 7 Février," Service d'Information du Centre de Recherche et d'Action pour le Développement (SICRAD), February 6, 2001. According to SICRAD,

Les négociations entre Fanmi Lavalas et la Convergence Démocratique se sont soldées par un échec, au cours de la nuit du 5 au 6 février. Les parties qui avaient débuté des pourparlers dans la soirée du 3 février s'étaient données deux jours pour trouver une solution à la crise politique qui s'est accentuée depuis les élections de l'année 2000.

Des propositions et contre-propositions se sont succédées. Fanmi Lavalas et la Convergence Démocratique se rejettent mutuellement la responsabilité de cet échec et l'opposition a désigné M. Gérard Gourgue comme "président provisoire de la République" pour 24 mois, afin d'organiser "des élections générales".

Un face-a-face Aristide et Convergence avait finalement eu lieu a la Nonciature à Port-au-Prince pour inaugurer les échanges. La rencontre s'était déroulée dans une atmosphère cordiale, en présence des membres de la commission de facilitation dite de la société civile et des membres du corps diplomatique. Les deux parties s'étaient entendues sur un agenda de négociation pour résoudre la crise électorale, garantir la stabilité de l'état et favoriser la réconciliation nationale.

Les pourparlers se sont poursuivis a l'Hôtel El Rancho, en banlieue de la capitale. Des rencontres séparées se sont déroulées entre les membres de la Commission de facilitation, les représentants de la Communauté internationale et chacune des parties, avec le ferme espoir d'aboutir à un accord politique.

Le 5 février vers midi, la Convergence remet a Fanmi Lavalas une proposition en 17 points, axée sur la formation d'un gouvernement de consensus et d'union nationale avec un mandat de deux ans. Ce gouvernement devrait inclure des membres des deux parties ainsi que ceux de la société civile avec à sa tête un conseil de 3 membres, dont Jean Bertrand Aristide. Cette présidence tricéphale devrait prendre fonction ce 7 février et choisir son premier ministre dans les rangs de la Convergence.

La proposition de l'opposition mentionne aussi un Conseil Consultatif, formé des membres de la société civile et des parties qui ont pris part aux élections de l'année dernière, qui ferait office de contre-pouvoir.

La proposition de la Convergence a été examinée durant environ 6 heures de temps par l'équipe de négociation de Fanmi Lavalas qui a fait une contre-proposition en reprenant les principaux points d'un accord conclu récemment entre Aristide et des envoyés spéciaux de l'ancien président américain William Clinton. Ce document en 8 points, prévoit, entre autres, la correction des problèmes liés aux élections du 21 mai, la formation d'un nouveau Conseil Électoral, la mise en place d'un gouvernement d'ouverture.

Suite à cette contre-proposition, la Convergence a fait un pas en acceptant Aristide comme président, mais ce dernier devrait avoir un mandat de deux ans et prêter serment devant la Cour de Cassation. Inacceptable pour Fanmi Lavalas qui a rejeté sans ambages la dernière proposition de la Convergence, demandé l'ajournement des négociations et la reprise des pourparlers dans la matinée du 6 février. Position contraire de la partie adverse qui était plutôt favorable a une poursuite sans relâche des consultations.

Il était 3 heures du matin lorsque la Commission de facilitation, dans un communiqué distribué à la presse, a constaté l'échec des négociations, à environ 24 heures de la date prévue pour la prestation de serment du nouveau président.

[The negotiations between Fanmi Lavalas and Convergence Démocratique (Democratic Convergence) ended up in a stalemate on the night of February 5–6. The parties that had begun talks on the evening of February 3 had given themselves two days to find a solution to the political crisis that had become worse since the elections of 2000.

Propositions and counterpropositions followed one another. Fanmi Lavalas and Convergence Démocratique mutually blamed each other for the stalemate, and the opposition designated Mr. Gérard Gourgue as the "provisional president of the Republic" for twenty-four months for the purpose of organizing "general elections."

There was finally a meeting between Aristide and Convergence at the Nonciature in Port-au-Prince in order to open the negotiations. The meeting was carried on in a cordial atmosphere, in the presence of members of the facilitating commission presumably representing civil society and members of the diplomatic corps. The two parties had agreed on a business agenda for resolving the electoral crisis, guaranteeing the stability of the state, and favoring national reconciliation.

The talks took place at the Hotel El Rancho, in the suburb of the capital. Separate meetings took place between members of the facilitating commission, the representatives of the international community, and each of the parties in the firm hope of reaching a political agreement.

On February 5, toward noon, Convergence handed to Fanmi Lavalas a proposal with seventeen points, aimed at the formation of a government of consensus and national unity with a mandate of two years. This government would include members of both parties as well as of civil society, with a council of three members, including Jean-Bertrand Aristide, at its head. This tripartite presidency would take office on February 7 and would choose its prime minister from the ranks of Convergence.

The proposal from the opposition also mentions a consultative council formed of members of civil society and the parties that took part in the elections of the previous year, serving the purpose of a counterpower.

The proposal by Convergence was examined for some six hours by Fanmi Lavalas's negotiating team, which made a counterproposal by repeating the principal points of an agreement recently concluded between Aristide and the special envoys of the former American president, William Clinton. This eight-point document provides, among other things, corrective measures for the problems linked with the elections of May 21—the formation of a new electoral council and the establishment of an inaugural government.

Following this counterproposal, Convergence took a step toward accepting Aristide as president, but the latter would have to accept a mandate of two years and take his oath before the Cour de Cassation (appeals court). This was unacceptable to Fanmi Lavalas, which unambiguously rejected Convergence's last proposal and moved for adjournment of negotiations and the resumption of talks the morning of February 6. This position was contrary to that of the opposing party, which preferred pursuing the talks without interruption.

It was 3 a.m. when the facilitating commission, in a communiqué distributed to the press, recognized the collapse of the negotiations, about twenty-four hours before the new president was to take his oath of office.] (Translated by Carrol Coates)

31. The United States, France, and the European Union remained extremely critical of Aristide and warned him that normal relations with the international community and foreign assistance were dependent on the resolution of the political crisis generated by the elections of May and November 2000. France blamed Aristide for the collapse of civil society's initiative and declared in a communiqué, "It is a pity that Mr. Aristide and his party have not demonstrated the will for making the compromises necessary to get an accord" (Ministère Français des Affaires Etrangères, Point de Presse, February 7, 2001, published on the website of the Center for International Policy).

See also Shelley Emling, "Aristide's Inauguration Tainted by Pessimism," eCountries website at www.ecountriescorporate.com, February 7, 2001; Mark Fineman, "Aristide Takes Office Again as President. Haiti: Opposition and World Leaders Boycott Inauguration in Wake of Controversial Election," *Los Angeles Times,* February 8, 2001; "La Communauté Internationale Bloque son Aide à Haïti," *Le Monde,* February 7, 2001.

32. "Aristide Starts Second Term in Haiti," Associated Press, February 7, 2001. According to many Haitian observers, however, the cleaning of Port-au-Prince was not a spontaneous affair; poor people engaged in the process because the government simply paid them. In addition, the Préval administration requisitioned the vans and buses of *service plus* to mobilize pro-Aristide crowds for his inauguration.

33. As *The Economist* put it ("Another Half-Chance for Aristide and Haiti," economist.com, February 10, 2001),

> The Convergence said that it would form an alternative government, led by a former presidential candidate, Gérard Gourgue, and invited Mr. Aristide to join it.
>
> That is high farce. No foreign governments will recognise the Convergence alternative. But the donors' demands are pretty farcical too. Even if the election last May had been held properly, Lavalas would have won most or all of the disputed seats. The opposition is fragmented, ranging from former Marxists to ex-Duvalier supporters, and lacks the power to scrutinise aid spending.
>
> The opposition mostly represents the upper-middle class and intellectual elite. By contrast, Lavalas Family is a tightly-run and powerful movement. It has deep roots in Haiti's poorest communities through such groups as COMICS [a neighborhood organization of poor people in Cité Soleil], as well as rara bands that sing about political and social issues, and the chimères—violent young agitators who seem to be Mr. Aristide's budding version of the Tontons Macoutes, the Duvaliers' notoriously thuggish enforcers. "We've heard of the opposition," says Mr. Louinel in Cité Soleil, "but they've never come down here."

See also Richard Chacón, "Taking Office, Aristide Urges Unity," *Boston Globe,* February 8, 2001

34. "Le "Président" Nommé par la Convergence Démocratique Promet la Constitution de l'Armée," Agence Haïtienne de Presse, February 7, 2001; "Jean Bertrand Aristide Prête Serment Comme Nouveau Président d'Haïti," Haiti Online, February 7, 2001; "Intronisation Egalement ce Mercredi du Président Proclamé de l'Opposition," Flash InterVision2000, February 7, 2001; Yves Colon, "Haiti's Aristide Sworn in as Foes Pick Own Leader," *Miami Herald,* February 8, 2001.

35. As quoted in David Gonzalez, "Vowing Peace, Aristide Is Sworn in Again as Haitian President," *New York Times,* February 8, 2001.

36. "Le Président Aristide Réitère son Appel à l'Entente aux Partis de l'Opposition," Agence Haïtienne de Presse, February 7, 2001; "Prestation de Serment du Président Jean-Bertrand Aristide," Agence Haïtienne de Presse, February 7, 2001; "Discours d'Investiture d'Aristide: des Objectifs Très Ambitieux," SICRAD, February 7, 2001.

37. "La Convergence Démocratique Proclame Gérard Gourgue, Président Provisoire de la République d'Haïti," Flash Intervision 2000, February 6, 2001.

38. "Talks Break Down Between Haiti's Opposition and Aristide's Party," Associated Press, February 6, 2001; "Échec de Négociations pour une Issue à la Crise Politique en Haïti," Flash InterVision 2000, February 6, 2001.

39. Ibid.

40. "8000 Personnes Marchent Contre le Régime Lavalas," Haiti Online, September 19, 2000. The MPP organized the sole major anti-Lavalas manifestation in Hinche, where 8,000 people heard Chavannes Jean-Baptiste condemn Aristide and Préval for their totalitarian leadership and utter incompetence in promoting Haiti's development. Apart from this protest, the opposition has been utterly unsuccessful in its attempts to mobilize a large and committed following. The national forum it organized to prepare for the establishment of the "parallel government" took place behind the privileged walls of the Hotel Montana near Pétionville and included only the "political class." It was an elite affair.

41. Ira Kurzban, general counsel in the United States for Haiti's Aristide and Préval administrations, pointed out correctly that the opposition's influence was to a large extent due to international and particularly U.S. funding ("A Rational Foreign Policy Toward Haiti," Haiti Online, February 6, 2001):

> [In 2000, the U.S.] government overtly provided to the International Republican Institute $3,000,000 in funds not simply to help opposition parties in Haiti but to "develop" opposition parties. In light of the outrage in the United States following the revelations that the Chinese government may have attempted to provide contributions to U.S. candidates, it is nothing short of bizarre that our government would spend money in a foreign country to create an opposition to the government we are supposed to be supporting. This, of course, does not include covert funds spent in Haiti to accomplish the same ends.

42. Christophe Wargny, "The Country That Doesn't Quite Exist: Haiti's Last Chance," *Le Monde Diplomatique,* July 2000.

43. Manno Michel, "Les Elections du 21 Mai 2000," online at Windows on Haiti website. As Michel puts it,

> En résumé, l'opposition semble être à bout de souffle, toujours en quête de quelque chose qui lui permettra de se maintenir à flot. Il lui est très difficile d'ajuster sa stratégie à la nouvelle conjoncture et elle se complaît à opposer des obstacles à

chaque coin de rue, se cantonnant dans des positions si négatives que même lorsqu'elle a raison, elle est si peu crédible et si inconsistante qu'elle est constamment passée en dérision par la majorité.

[In summary, the opposition seems to be out of breath, ever seeking some means by which to remain afloat. It has great difficulty in adjusting its strategy to the new circumstances and it is satisfied with setting up obstacles at every street corner, taking refuge behind such negative positions that, even when it is in the right, the reasoning is so minimally credible and so inconsistent that the majority is constantly derisive of it.] (Translated by Carrol Coates)

44. Although Aristide is no longer a priest and is now married with two children, he is still referred to in rather pejorative terms as the "little priest" by many in the opposition and the dominant classes.

Expelled from the Salesian order in 1988 for allegedly inciting "hatred and violence" and "glorifying" class struggles, Aristide formally resigned from the priesthood in 1994. In 1996, he married Haitian-American attorney Mildred Trouillot. Aristide's wedding was not welcomed by all; many Haitians, particularly his mass constituency, saw it as a betrayal and indeed a divorce from the "people" with whom he was supposed to have an exclusive relationship. The fact that Mildred Trouillot was a member of the Haitian diaspora and a lighter-skinned woman contributed to the problem. On Aristide's expulsion from the Salesian order, see Aristide, *Autobiography,* pp. 105–106; on his wedding, see "For Love, Aristide Puts Political Career on the Line," Associated Press, January 20, 1996.

45. As quoted in "Political Feuds Ravage Haïti: So Much for Its High Hopes," *New York Times,* October 18, 1998.

46. Kern Delince, *Les Forces Politiques en Haïti* (Paris: Karthala, 1993), p. 97. Translated from the original French by Carrol Coates:

Les membres de la classe politique sont très soucieux du prestige attaché par l'opinion publique à la condition des classes ou des catégories sociales priviligiées. En provenance la plupart des couches supérieures de la classe moyenne, ils se préoccupent de leur insertion dans la bourgeoisie urbaine retenue comme modèle de référence. La vie politique leur offre une voie de promotion sociale, un tremplin pour l'accession à un statut social supérieur, un raccourci permettant de franchir le fossé qui sépare les différentes strates de la sociéte haïtienne.

47. Jacky Dahomay ("Où en Est la Démocratie en Haïti?" Haiti Online, January 14, 2001, p. 11) faults Lavalas's intellectuals for joining the *grands mangeurs* and failing to warn Aristide and his followers of the dangers of state power:

Les cadres lavalassiens se sont mués en militants à cravate et se sont contentés de manger à la table de l'État. Celui-ci a été réduit à un butin dont il faut s'accaparer, à une table et il est significatif d'ailleurs que Jean-Bertrand Aristide ait baptisé son mouvement "bo tab-la." "Venez avec moi, chers amis qui me supportez, manger à la table de l'État!" Avec de telles pratiques et une telle vision de l'État et du bien public, on ne pouvait pas s'en sortir. Les intellectuels lavalassiens auraient dû éclairer Aristide et Préval sur les graves dérives dans lesquelles ils entraînaient le pouvoir politique en Haïti.

[The Lavalas leaders have changed into militants wearing ties and have been satisfied with dining at the table of the state. The state has been reduced to booty that must be seized, into a table, and it is significant moreover that Jean-Bertrand Aristide has baptized his movement "bò tab la." "Come with me, dear friends who are supporting me, come to eat at the table of the state!" With such practices and such a vision of the state and public property, there is no escape. The Lavalas intellectuals should have enlightened Aristide and Préval about the grave excesses into which they were taking political power in Haiti.] (Translated by Carrol Coates)

48. Trouillot, *Haiti: State Against Nation* (New York: Monthly Review Press, 1990), pp. 155–156.

49. Irwin P. Stotzky, *Silencing the Guns in Haiti* (Chicago: University of Chicago Press, 1997), pp. 42–43, 159–181.

50. Ibid., p. 180.

51. Ibid., p. 44. See also Robert Maguire, "Demilitarizing Public Order in a Predatory State: The Case of Haiti," *The North South Agenda Papers*, No. 17, December 1995.

52. According to Human Rights Watch (Human Rights Watch Backgrounder, "Aristide's Return to Power in Haiti," February 2001),

> Members of popular organizations supporting Fanmi Lavalas were responsible for violent street demonstrations and other mob actions that went largely unchallenged by the Haitian National Police. . . . The most dramatic pre-election incident of mob violence occurred on April 8, when some one hundred protesters burned down the headquarters of the opposition coalition, *Espace de Concertation.* Earlier in the day, at funeral services for Jean Dominique, members of the mob had publicly announced their plans to burn the building and kill opposition leader Evans Paul (whom they were unable to find). Police, who were on the scene, did not interfere, nor did they make any arrests.

53. In 1996, there was great optimism for the Haitian police force. Susan Joanis, a member of the Ontario Human Rights Commission in Toronto, expressed the prevailing view ("Haiti: Hopes for Democracy Rest on Police," *Compass, a Jesuit Journal* 13, no. 6 (January-February 1996):

> Now the entire population is putting its faith in a new independent, civilian, professional police force, the cornerstone of Haiti's hopes for democracy. In the past, Haiti's "police" were members of the army and the dreaded paramilitary forces— Papa Doc's Tontons Macoutes and more recently the attachés. Far from respecting the law, these thugs created it according to their own whims. They were the law, and they ruled through fear and intimidation, using extortion, theft and torture as their tools.
>
> The new Haitian National Police agents are young and have no previous military experience. About 5 per cent of them are women, presenting yet another brand new phenomenon in Haiti. They are well-intentioned and highly motivated. While many if not most are fresh from school, a good number of them have experience in teaching, journalism, medicine, engineering and various trades. A few have returned recently to Haiti from Canada. Many of them suffered personally or through the experiences of close friends and family members under the previous regime, and they are eager to help bring about positive changes for their country.

Soon afterward, however, things started to fall apart. The police force was politicized and came under the increasing control of the executive and Fanmi Lavalas, especially after the "resignations" of some high-ranking officers. Luc Eucher Joseph (the general inspector), Wilfrid Léger, Pierre Fortin, Jean Denis, and Aramick Louis quit the force following the forced departure in October 1999 of Robert Manuel, secretary of state for public security, who had attempted to preserve the independence of the institution. See "Police: Le Cycle des Démissions se Poursuit," SICRAD, May 1, 2000; see also Amnesty International, "Haiti: A

Worrying Increase in Violence Against the Police Force," news release, AMR 36/06/99, 1999.

See also Rachel Nield, ed., and Juan L. Guiller, trans., *Demilitarizing Public Order: The International Community, Police Reform and Human Rights in Central America and Haiti* (Washington, D.C.: Washington Office on Latin America, 1995); and Rachel Nield, *Policing Haiti: Preliminary Assessment of the Civilian Police Force* (Washington, D.C.: Washington Office on Latin America, 1995).

54. According to *Haïti Progrès'* confidential sources ("The Autopsy of a Failed Coup, Would-Be Coup Leader Hiding in U.S. Embassy," October 25–31, 2000),

> All began at two meetings which were held at the private residence of a U.S. Military Attaché in Haiti, a certain Major Douyon, on Oct. 8 and Oct. 11. In the course of the first meeting, there was discussion of delivering visas to certain police chiefs. At the second meeting political matters were introduced, such as the necessity for the police chiefs to take action in the face of the Lavalas demonstrators ("Chimères") who were attacking them. . . . Certain policemen said they had expected the discussion to be about the delivery of visas. Participating in the meeting were former soldiers, civilians, and former police chiefs who had been fired. Also present or at least expected, according to an unconfirmed report by Radio Kiskeya on Oct. 24, was the U.S. Chargé d'Affaires Leslie Alexander. Kiskeya also reported that a leading member of the group was Didier Seïde, a former soldier and police chief at the Palace. He was fired from the PNH for alleged involvement in drug trafficking.
>
> Unfortunately for the would-be putschists, a sector in the U.S. Embassy alerted Haitian authorities about the subversive meetings at Douyon's home. . . . Meanwhile, the Palace received complementary information confirming that a coup d'état was being prepared. Peasants in Fermathe had noted the movement of armed men, as many as 200 by one count, at the residence of Patrick Dormeville, the former police chief at the Airport.

In a slightly different version, the *Washington Post* confirmed that the United States warned the Haitian government of the potential coup. According to Edward Cody ("Haiti Torn by Hope and Hatred as Aristide Returns to Power," *Washington Post,* February 2, 2001, p. A1),

> The problems with Haiti's National Police came to a head last October when Aristide showed up at Provisional Electoral Council headquarters to register officially as a candidate for election, joined by a crowd of cheering supporters.
>
> The local police commissioner, Jean-Jacques "Jackie" Nau, had his men go through the crowd looking for weapons. A street leader known to be an Aristide supporter, nicknamed Ronald Cadaver in tribute to his reputation for violence, refused to relinquish his gun. In the confrontation that ensued, Cadaver and his gang disarmed Nau and other officers and put tires around their necks in apparent preparation for one of the gruesome burnings known as "necklacing."
>
> The standoff was resolved without anyone being killed. But Cadaver was never called to account, and the infuriated Nau began meeting with another police commissioner, Guy Philippe, and other officers to discuss what should be done.
>
> By the middle of November, in an account confirmed by a senior U.S. official, Prime Minister Alexis said he was visited by Don Steinberg, a Lake aide then on temporary duty in Port-au-Prince. Steinberg relayed intelligence that Nau, Philippe and the others were discussing what could be the beginnings of a coup. Several days later, Alexis said, Steinberg went to see Aristide at his home with the information, warning that Aristide and Préval could be assassination targets.
>
> Called in to explain themselves, Alexis went on, Nau and Philippe denied

they were contemplating a coup. But within days, they and a half-dozen other officers fled to the Dominican Republic.

Two other officers implicated in the reports sought refuge in the Dominican Embassy in Port-au-Prince. Haitian authorities wanted to wait them out. But Alexis said they were allowed instead to travel unmolested to the Dominican Republic—at the request of the U.S. Embassy.

55. Two of the implicated officers, Dormevil Jacques Patrick and Guy Philippe, told the press in Santo Domingo that the twenty police captains met at Aristide's residence in Tabarre days before the elections and were instructed "to fire at polling places in the northern city of Cap-Haïtien and blame the opposition for it." Philippe added, "I am a professional and I could not follow those orders. Besides they were criminal orders against the people and the police department itself," adding that he felt that he had been followed ever since. This account is contained in "Haitian Police Flee Reprisals by Aristide," *EFE,* October 25, 2000.

56. "Un Sénateur Rejette les Accusations Contre M. Aristide," Métropole Haïti, October 26, 2000.

57. See "The Autopsy of a Failed Coup; Would-Be Coup Leader Hiding in U.S. Embassy," *Haïti Progrès,* October 25–31, 2000.

58. "Is a Coup d'État Looming?" *Haïti Progrès,* October 18–24, 2000.

59. "The Autopsy of a Failed Coup."

60. See "Coup Monté, Coup d'État ou Auto-Coup?" Haiti Online, October 19, 2000; "Frustran Golpe de Estado en Haiti," *Listin* (Santo Domingo), October 19, 2000.

61. There are multiple reports on the police refusing to come to the rescue of victims of crimes. In several instances, the police informed callers that it would not be able to help because its vehicles were broken down or had run out of gas.

62. Pierre Denizé, the police chief, who seemed to have tried to bring some level of honesty and competence to the force, has, however, his own problems and conflict of interests. Denizé owns a private security agency and is enmeshed in a web of powerful personal "connections" who are bound to gain if the police are incapable of guaranteeing law and order. As Charles Lane has pointed out ("Cop Land," *New Republic,* September 29, 1997, p. 23),

> [Denizé] owns Cobra, a company that provides armed protection to those with enough money to pay. Of course, Cobra's financial success depends upon a public perception that the National Police can't do their job fully—which is precisely the perception Denizé is supposed to be eradicating. . . . [Far] from discouraging Denizé, the government of Haiti hired Cobra to protect Teleco, the state-owned telephone monopoly. . . . Teleco says Cobra got its contract through competitive bidding. Or relatively competitive: Denizé's partner, Serge Calvin, is President Préval's brother-in-law.

63. Many officers have complained that they themselves have to pay for their equipment, most of which was donated to the Haitian government. See Lane, "Cop Land," p. 23.

64. "Haiti's Police Accused of Lawlessness, Murders, Drug Offenses Laid to U.S.-Trained Force," *Washington Post,* September 28, 1999; p. A1.

65. United Nations, "United Nations International Civilian Support Mission in Haiti, Report of the Secretary-General," Fifty-fifth session, A/55/618, November 9, 2000, p. 3.

66. Samuel Huntington, *The Third Wave* (Norman: University of Oklahoma Press, 1991), p. 231.

67. Michael Taussig, *The Nervous System* (New York: Routledge, 1992), p. 48.

68. The report—without the annex—can be accessed through the website of the Haitian Embassy in the United States at www.haiti.org/index.html. Paradoxically it is virtually impossible to obtain a copy of it in Haiti itself; see also Human Rights Watch/Americas, *Thirst for Justice: A Decade of Immunity in Haiti* (New York: Human Rights Watch, 1996), pp. 18–19; Commission Nationale de Vérité et de Justice, 1998; Jean-Germain Gros, "Compensation as a Justice Tool in the Post-Conflict Era," in Peter Cross and Guenola Rasamoelina, eds., *Conflict Prevention Policy of the European Union, Yearbook 1998/99* (Baden-Baden: Nomos Verlagsgesellschaft, 1999), pp. 197–199.

69. Human Rights Watch/Americas 1996, p. 18.

70. Malone, *Decision-Making in the UN Security Council: The Case of Haiti* (Oxford: Oxford University Press, 1998), p. 125.

71. Audrey R. Chapman and Patrick Ball, "The Truth Commissions: Comparative Lessons from Haiti, South Africa, and Guatemala," *Human Rights Quaterly* 23 (2001): 1–43. As Chapman and Ball point out (pp. 16–35),

> [The] Haitian Commission probably operated on a little more than $1 million, and the report complains that the lack of sufficient funds greatly reduced their ability to complete their work.
>
> Acknowledgement, the translation of a private into a public truth, requires widespread dissemination of the findings of a truth commission. . . . [The] experience of the Haitian National Commission for Truth and Justice testifies to its breakdown. The final report transmitted to President Aristide during his last hours in office in February 1996 was not published until September 1996, and then only seventy-five copies were made. Conflicts between the supporters of Aristide and the administration of President René Préval made the report something of an embarrassment for President Préval. A second edition of 1500 copies was published in March 1997, but these were circulated only in Haiti.

72. Human Rights Watch/Americas 1996, pp. 24–25. On September 29, 2001, in a speech marking the tenth anniversary of the 1991 coup, Aristide announced that the United States had finally released the documents that it had seized. The Haitian government received the documents in March 2001 and thus waited six months to acknowledge this fact. The secrecy with which Aristide handled the matter bodes poorly for any serious judicial investigation or public disclosure of the content of the documents. Moreover, the Haitian government continued to encourage an international campaign calling for the release of the documents while it was already in their possession. See "Haiti Marks 10th Coup Anniversary," Associated Press, September 29, 2001.

73. Michelle Karshan, foreign press liaison of Haiti's government, describes the horror of Raboteau ("Haiti's Raboteau Massacre Trial Will Try 22 Defendants in Detention and 36 in Absentia Including *FRAPH*'s Toto Constant and the Military High Command," e-mail release, September 24, 2000):

> The attackers forcibly entered dozens of homes, beating and arresting those found within, including the elderly and small children. Many people were arrested and tortured, others were tortured or humiliated on site. Some were forced to lie in open sewers, or out in the hot sun for hours, some were forced to tear down a house with their bare hands. Those who fled to the sea, Raboteau's traditional refuge, were shot at, some were killed.
>
> Although six murders are sufficiently documented to be part of the prosecu-

tion, it is likely that many more were killed. The military authorities prevented the victims' families from retrieving bodies from the sea or burying them, so some bodies may have floated away, while others were reportedly eaten by animals on the beach.

The Raboteau massacre took place during a particularly harsh period of Haiti's brutal 1991–94 military dictatorship. As the international community tightened sanctions against Haiti in the first half of 1994, the army responded with attacks on areas of non-violent resistance throughout the country. Gonaïves, especially Raboteau, had always prided itself on refusing to accept the dictatorship, and in calling for the return of democratically elected President Jean-Bertrand Aristide. The massacre was intended to terrorize the area's residents into abandoning their democratic hopes.

74. "Soldiers' Murder Convictions Seen as Boost to Justice in Haiti," *Miami Herald,* November 11, 2000; "Ex-officers Sentenced in Haiti," *Miami Herald,* November 17, 2000.

75. Guy Pierre, former Haitian ambassador to the OAS, has argued that the government's expenses for the May and November 2000 elections contributed to a huge deficit; see "El Pueblo Haitiano en Busca de un Mejor Devenir Histórico Inmediato," December 18, 2000. Available online at www.ciponline.org. nxlkhost.com/Haiti/Dec2000-Feb01/pierre.htm.

76. Philippe C. Schmitter, "Transitology: The Science or the Art of Democratization?" in Joseph S. Tulcin with Bernice Romero, eds., *The Consolidation of Democracy in Latin America* (Boulder: Lynn Rienner, 1995), p. 16.

77. Stephen L. Elkin and Karol Edward Soltan, eds., *A New Constitutionalism* (Chicago: University of Chicago Press, 1993).

78. Karol Edward Soltan, "Introduction: Imagination, Political Competence, and Institutions," in Karol Edward Soltan and Stephen L. Elkin, eds., *The Constitution of Good Societies* (University Park: Pennsylvania State University Press, 1996), p. 2.

79. In *The Third Wave* (pp. 15–16), Huntington argues,

A wave of democratization is a group of transitions from nondemocratic to democratic regimes that occur within a specified period of time and that significantly outnumber transitions in the opposite direction during that period of time. A wave usually involves liberalizing or partial democratization in political systems that do not become fully democratic. Three waves of democratization have occurred in the modern world. Each wave affected a relatively small number of countries, and during each wave some regime transitions occurred in a nondemocratic direction. In addition, not all transitions to democracy occurred during democratic waves. History is messy and political changes do not sort themselves into neat historical boxes. History is also not unidirectional. Each of the first two waves of democratization was followed by a reverse wave in which some but not all of the countries that had previously made the transitions to democracy reverted to nondemocratic rule.

80. Elinor Ostrom, "Covenants, Collective Action, and Common-Pool Resources," in Soltan and Elkin, *The Constitution of Good Societies,* p. 31.

81. Juan J. Linz and Arturo Valenzuela, "Preface," in Juan Linz and Arturo Valenzuela, eds., *The Failure of Presidential Democracy* (Baltimore: Johns Hopkins University Press, 1994), p. xii.

82. Guiseppe Di Palma, *To Craft Democracies* (Berkeley: University of California Press, 1990).

83. Michael Burton, Richard Gunther, and John Higley, "Elites and Democratic Consolidation in Latin America and Southern Europe: An Overview,"

in Richard Gunther and John Higley, eds., *Elites and Democratic Consolidation in Latin America and Southern Europe* (Cambridge: Cambridge University Press, 1992), p. 342; see also Youssef Cohen, *Radicals, Reformers, and Reactionaries* (Chicago: University of Chicago Press, 1994), pp. 119–120.

84. Viktor J. Vanberg and James M. Buchanan, "Constitutional Choice, Rational Ignorance and the Limits of Reason," in Soltan and Elkin, *The Constitution of Good Societies,* pp. 39–56.

85. Irwin P. Stotzky, *Silencing the Guns in Haiti* (Chicago: University of Chicago Press, 1997), p. 85.

86. Guillermo O'Donnell and Philippe C. Schmitter, *Transitions from Authoritarian Rule: Tentative Conclusions About Uncertain Democracies* (Baltimore: Johns Hopkins Press, 1986), pp. 48–49; see also Doh Chull Shin, "On the Third Wave of Democratization: A Synthesis and Evaluation of Recent Theory and Research," *World Politics* 47, no. 1 (October 1994): 138–139.

87. Jon Elster, "Introduction," in Jon Elster and Rune Slagstad, eds., *Constitutionalism and Democracy* (Cambridge: Cambridge University Press, 1993), pp. 1–17. Elster contends that "[constitutionalism] refers to limits on majority decisions; more specifically, to limits that are in some sense self-imposed" (p. 2).

88. In his book *Counterpoints* (Notre Dame: University of Notre Dame Press, 1999), Guillermo O'Donnell argues forcefully that the huge disparities of wealth, income, and power dividing Latin American societies make the implantation of mutually acceptable democratic rules improbable. He suggests that a "new species" of democracy has emerged in Latin America: delegative democracy. This type of democracy exhibits extreme forms of presidentialism, majoritarianism, and individualism. Accordingly, delegative democracy, for O'Donnell, "could hardly be less congenial to the building and strengthening of democratic political institutions" (p. 166).

7

Toward a Compromise?

Since his presidential inauguration on February 7, 2001, Aristide has attempted to lure the opposition into his own orbit. He appointed Jean-Marie Chérestal as his prime minister and formed a so-called *gouvernement d'ouverture* reflecting his commitment to include opposition members into his administration. Incapable of drawing members of Convergence Démocratique into the cabinet, the leader of Lavalas had to settle on the incorporation of former supporters of Jean-Claude Duvalier into his new regime. This incorporation of erstwhile Duvalierists was not welcomed by all; Michèle Montas, the widow of Jean Dominique, condemned it as embodying

> unholy alliances not only between victims and former torturers but also between those aspiring to positions of power and the fierce and proven enemies of democratic principles, including the moneyed interests who inspired the [Cédras] coup d'état. These alliances . . . are budding and blossoming . . . in the midst of the *Convergence* as well as within *Fanmi Lavalas*.[1]

Aristide, however, confronted the dilemma of meeting contradictory demands. On the one hand, he wanted some opponents in his government, but on the other hand, he was not prepared to make the type of concessions that CD had called for. He thus settled on an alliance with Duvalierist enemies in an effort to satisfy the international community's call for political pluralism and in response to CD's refusal to join the Chérestal government.

The return to power of old Duvalierists indicates an opportunistic attempt to isolate CD from other opposition groups and force it into the periphery of the political system. Ultimately, Aristide hopes that the tactical partnership with *Jean-Claudisme* will neutralize CD and lead to its breakdown and complete emasculation. The partnership is to be a prelude to the eventual co-optation of the major elements of the opposition into the

Lavalasian project. For the moment, however, Aristide's *ouverture* is confined to a small but significant circle of former adversaries. Four important ministries went to men identified with either the opposition, the private sector, or *Jean-Claudisme:* Stanley Théard was named commerce minister, the same position he held under Duvalier in the early 1980s; Garry Lissade, an "independent lawyer," was appointed justice minister;[2] Marc Bazin, leader of the MIDH, who had a short tenure as Duvalier's finance minister in 1982 and was Aristide's principal adversary in the presidential elections of 1990 and a prime minister in the "de facto" Cédras military dictatorship, became minister of planning and external cooperation; and, finally, Gustave Faubert, a former director of a development bank funded by USAID, became minister of the economy and finances.[3]

Aristide's quest to bring the opposition "back in" extended to the formation of a new CEP that mirrored the cabinet's political profile. On March 2, he appointed four *Jean-Claudistes* to the nine-member council.[4] Clearly he intended to demonstrate that the Haitian opposition was not limited to CD. He also sought to prove that he could govern without it and that CD was neither indispensable to the formation of a national government of consensus nor representative of a large popular constituency. In fact, it is likely that had it not been for intense external pressures, Aristide would have governed alone—*Lavalassement*—excluding all and any opposition. As a "rational" politician seeking to maximize his hegemonic position, he is simply reluctant to make major concessions to his adversaries, let alone share power with them.[5]

Not surprisingly, Aristide chose to include in his government a few *Jean-Claudistes* who were politically feeble, had an extremely small popular base, and were of little danger to his presidential monarchism. A leading Haitian official told me that some of Lavalas's *Jean-Claudistes* were financially trapped and that enlisting them into the government was truly symptomatic of *la politique du ventre*. The question then was why did CD or some of its key members not succumb to the powerful attraction of government office? Why did *la politique du ventre* fail to whet their appetite?[6]

Several reasons explain CD's determined opposition to Aristide and Lavalas. In the first place, it receives significant financial support from abroad, particularly from the International Republican Institute (IRI), which assisted in its creation.[7] So far, this flow of resources has allowed CD to curb its craving for high administrative and political functions. In other words, CD can afford to ignore Lavalas's olive branch as long as its foreign connections continue to feed it adequately. External financial assistance is a temporary substitute for the domestic play of *la politique du ventre*.

The international constellation of power is thus having a decisive impact on the persisting crisis and its potential resolution. The vagaries of external decisions may speed up the resolution of the current impasse or exacerbate it. Continued foreign assistance to CD would inevitably give it the means to insist on the implementation of option zero, whose demand for the annulment of both presidential and legislative elections of 2000 is clearly unacceptable to Lavalas. While Aristide has offered to make concessions, he is not prepared to give up everything. He sees himself as the duly elected, legitimate, and constitutional president of Haiti who intends to fulfill his regular term in office. CD's call for an early presidential ballot is, as he put it, an option with zero chances of materializing.[8]

Aristide, however, has offered to organize anticipated legislative elections as a means of rectifying the fraudulent results of May 2000.[9] Moreover, it is likely that he may agree to dissolve parliament and call for general legislative elections within the next year. Such a concession would go a long way in satisfying not only Haitian "civil society" but also the major foreign powers. Indeed, both the United States and the OAS have rejected publicly option zero.[10] They seem to advocate the March 7 Centre pour la Libre Entreprise et la Démocratie (CLED) proposition that recognizes the legitimacy of Aristide's presidency but appeals for the organization of general legislative elections within the next twelve months.[11] To the great consternation of CD,[12] the international community has thus blessed Aristide's authority. It is a blessing, however, that comes with very significant conditions.

In late April, Aristide was invited to and participated in the Quebec Summit of the Americas as one of the "democratically elected Heads of State" of the region. He was asked, however, by the summit host, Canadian prime minister Jean Chrétien, "to take rapid action on all of the commitments made in December" to former president Clinton.[13] The prime minister acknowledged that Aristide had made some effort to resolve the crisis; he added, nonetheless, that he was "also aware of the efforts of other political parties and other sectors of political life, notably members of civil society."[14] Thus, while the international community was pressuring Aristide for more concessions in an attempt to curb his authoritarian tendencies, it was also asking CD to abandon its intransigent stand on new presidential elections. As a result, there were signs that a forthcoming agreement between the parties might crystallize.

On April 23, upon returning from the Summit of the Americas, Aristide declared, "Without the opposition, Haiti does not have a future," and he predicted optimistically that by May 2 the crisis would be resolved.[15] In fact, on April 27, in an attempt to reach a political compromise, CD and Lavalas met at the Hôtel Villa Créole in Pétionville for a four-hour discussion. The meeting ended, however, in failure, with the two parties blaming each other for the continuing impasse.[16] Still calling President Aristide "citizen Aristide," CD condemned him for failing to come in person to the negotiating table. Moreover, it demanded that any future meeting with Aristide take place in a neutral location and certainly not in the National Palace.[17]

On the other hand, Lavalas's spokesman, Jonas Petit, accused the major figures of CD of nourishing themselves from the crisis. He indicted them for nurturing their self-serving intransigence with foreign funding; and Petit added that they were bent on exacerbating the crisis because it benefited their selfish personal material interests.[18] The relations between CD and Lavalas are poisoned by personal animosities and recriminations; their antagonistic character reflects more this simple reality than a profound ideological divide. As Edzer Pierre, a former Lavalas militant, put it, "The conflict between Fanmi Lavalas and the opposition isn't a real conflict. . . . It's comparable to two intellectuals sitting down and not being able to get along because one is coming on to the other's girlfriend. The conflicts between Aristide and Gérard Pierre-Charles amount to ego and bullshit."[19]

The antagonism is, however, very real. Some of the key leaders of CD see Aristide as an evil force capable of committing any crime to stay in power. Ironically, they have come to believe the most virulent anti-Aristide propaganda that they had themselves rejected until recently. Now they share Lynn Garrison's extravagant and bizarre portrayal of Aristide as a demented psychopath responsible for virtually all the murders that have taken place in the country since 1990.[20] Garrison, who had been a personal adviser to Cédras's military dictatorship, played a major role in the elaboration of a controversial and discredited 1993 CIA psychological profile that claimed that Aristide was a "psychotic manic depressive with proven homicidal tendencies."[21]

Former allies are using the profile to wage bitter attacks against the president. Rosny Mondestin, a former senator and a leader of the Mouvement de la Reconstruction National (MRN), has accused Aristide of seeking to implant a new totalitarianism through the full *chimérisation* of Haiti. In his view, Aristide seeks to give control of the national police to his Chimères and embark on a reign of terror to silence the opposition. He is the new Duvalier who is in the process of establishing "the peace of corpses."[22] Similarly, Chavannes Jean-Baptiste, a former friend and ally of Aristide, describes the president as

> nothing but a political cadaver who will pass like garbage through the history of Haiti. He has only one chance, and that is to come out and say that there was no election in 2000, and agree to start the process over again. He should say, "I will win, but I'll win a fair election." I know that he's too sick with power to say that. I would tell him to enter the palace provisionally and organize clean and fair elections. But if not, he will bury himself face down in the history of the country and humanity.[23]

Mondestin and Jean-Baptiste's views highlight the opposition's genuine fears about Aristide's project and authoritarian tendencies. In turn, the Lavalas government has described the main figures of CD as "enemies of the Republic" who are "usurping the title of President" and violating the law by forming an alternative government.[24] This mutual demonization points to the extreme difficulties facing any breakthrough to a lasting solution to the Haitian quagmire. It has also generated dangerous moments of violence between Aristide and CD supporters.[25] Lavalas's Chimères and followers are threatening the opposition because they believe that it is purposefully exacerbating the crisis to generate a chaos that would nurture the return of the military.[26] They fear that CD's ultimate objective is to overthrow Aristide, and they are committed to using violence to prevent such an outcome. They are calling for the arrest of Gérard Gourgue and his key associates, whom they see as dangerous provocateurs.[27]

The role of the Chimères in the current conjuncture is, however, ambiguous. Are they merely Aristide's pliable instrument of intimidation, or are they becoming an increasingly autonomous and volatile force with its own independent strategy and leaders? While it would be naïve to assume that Aristide has no authority over them, it would be equally simplistic to think that he fully controls them. The relationship between Chimères and Aristide seems to be based on an opportunistic convergence of interests. On the one hand, Aristide appears to have broad power over their activities, but the exercise of that power is curbed and shaped by his concern for the Chimères' adverse impact on his own capacity to rule effectively. On the other hand, once unleashed, the Chimères acquire a dynamic of their own and can begin to actively voice and negotiate their own corporate demands on the president himself. They can become a power unto themselves.

The interaction between Aristide and the Chimères is typical of the phenomenon of clientelism. Clientelism as René Lemarchand has argued is an "alternative means for integration where coercive power is not sufficiently coercive to command widespread compliance and where conceptions of legitimacy are as yet too weak or circumscribed to produce consensus."[28] It is clear, however, that in spite of his temptation to depend on the Chimères for enforcing his political agenda, Aristide would prefer to establish a consensus through compromise rather than violence. This is not to say that he does not find them a useful vehicle for intimidating the opposition; on the contrary, he has an interest in keeping them going as a reminder of Lavalas's ever present menace to friends and foes alike. Always lurking in Haiti's shadowy politics and always on the verge of activation, the Chimères constitute Aristide's weapon of deterrence.

The opposition's fears that Lavalas has the capacity to unleash

Aristide's Chimères and engulf society into brutal chaos are paradoxically a potent incentive for a political compromise. While Aristide can manipulate the Chimères to compel CD into his own negotiating orbit, he knows that given the domestic and (especially) international constellation of forces, he has no other option but negotiations. The Chimères, however, give him a preponderance of power. This is why Aristide can continue to look favorably to negotiations and consultations. He has little to lose; not only does he have the coercive means on his side, but he also enjoys undisputed and overwhelming popularity.[29]

It is this context that explains Aristide's May 3 convocation at the National Palace of all sectors of Haitian society and politics. Although CD refused to participate,[30] the meeting produced an important and promising consensus among key interlocutors. Based on the key principles of CLED's propositions, the consensus appears to set the stage for legitimizing Aristide's presidency and organizing new parliamentary, and perhaps municipal and local, elections.[31] On the one hand, Lavalas would accept the invalidation of its controversial legislative victory, and on the other hand, the opposition and CD in particular would recognize Aristide as the president entitled to complete his constitutional five-year term. A new electoral council selected by Fanmi Lavalas, CD, and credible civil society institutions would supervise these elections.[32] The significance of these propositions is that the most powerful forces of Haiti's business elite and international community now back them.[33] It is unlikely that CD will be able to oppose them and impose its own option zero.

Not surprisingly, "President" Gérard Gourgue began to acknowledge this political reality. For the first time, in a May 2 address to CD's directorship, he did not directly challenge the legitimacy of Aristide; instead, he proposed that the 2000 presidential election be "evaluated" by a new and independent electoral council composed of nine members equally drawn from Lavalas, CD, and civil society.[34] A compromise is thus in the making; it remains to be seen whether it will indeed crystallize and then survive the vicissitudes of *la politique du ventre*. At the moment, however, the country is paralyzed, plagued by an economy in free fall, and besieged by a wave of criminal violence. Morbid symptoms abound, but both CD and Lavalas seem prepared to wage a war of attrition and hope that exhaustion and external pressures will force one to eventually concede defeat at the negotiating table.

It is clear, however, that key domestic actors as well as the international community are losing patience. In mid-May, after another failed mission to end the stalemate, members of the OAS and the Caribbean Community (CARICOM) expressed their exasperation about the political situation. Upon departing Haiti, Luigi Einaudi, the OAS assistant secretary-general, declared, "We leave with the conviction that it's time to begin. This thing has gone on too long, with everybody posturing and paralyzed. . . . It's time to cut the Gordian knot. Of course, we haven't figured out how to do it."[35]

The difficulties were magnified when the protagonists began fighting over seemingly inconsequential matters, such as the interpretation of what constituted a "neutral" site for negotiations. After rejecting the National Palace and Tabarre as appropriate locations for meeting Aristide, CD refused his invitation to meet at the Museum of the National Pantheon because it was not "neutral enough." According to Evans Paul, a CD leader, "Neutral ground can't be chosen by just one of the parties. . . . Mr. Aristide together with the facilitators, meaning the civil society and the OAS, along with the Convergence must all agree on what is neutral ground."[36] In spite of these rather frivolous equivocations, there is a sense that a compromise is inevitable lest a descent into utter chaos and civil war become acceptable to the protagonists. Yet, while compromise is necessary because it holds the promise of a better future for a country that has hitherto flirted with catastrophe, it will not materialize unless Convergence Démocratique comprehends that it cannot aspire to rule the country and replace Lavalas on the sole basis of its foreign connections. The hegemonic status of Aristide and Lavalas responds not only to electoral *magouilles*, but to the real constellation of domestic support as well.

The two principal international actors, the United States and the OAS, seem to have finally acknowledged these realities; in early June, they accepted five concrete steps put forward by Aristide as the negotiating basis for resolving the persisting impasse.[37] The five steps unveiled by Aristide entailed (1) the resignation of the seven contested senators; (2) the creation of a new and independent provisional electoral council composed of nine members nominated by the main political forces of the country—including CD and Fanmi Lavalas; (3) elections for the contested seats in the senate before the end of the year 2001; (4) the organization of early elections for all members of parliament elected May 21, 2000; and (5) the establishment of a special OAS/CARICOM mission to facilitate negotiations between Haitian protagonists and guarantee the fairness of the electoral process.[38]

With these five points in mind, and under the mediation of César Gavira, secretary-general of the OAS, Fanmi Lavalas and Convergence Démocratique resumed negotiations and achieved a potential breakthrough. After three days of discussions that began on July 14 at the Hotel Montana, they agreed to hold new legislative and local elections and approved a formula for the creation of a new electoral commission. The elections would serve to replace all local government officials, the chamber of deputies in its entirety, and eighteen of the twenty-seven seats in the senate. Moreover, they approved a series of measures to ensure the development of a safe political environment for the free and fair exercise of the ballot. Fanmi Lavalas and Convergence Démocratique did not sign an agreement, however, because they were still at odds over the nature of the "political climate" and the date to hold the elections. While Lavalas proposed that legislative and local elections take place in November 2002 and May 2003, respectively, CD demanded that both elections be set for November 2002.[39]

The existing disagreements were therefore minimal, and the two parties adjourned with the clear understanding that a final compromise was at hand. In fact, rather than insulting each other as had been customary, government and opposition leaders joined together and praised each other for the patriotic and cooperative spirit prevailing during the talks. As Gérard Pierre-Charles put it, "We have advanced in the direction of a total agreement. We've made a lot of progress. We're negotiating in good faith. Both sides have understood the importance of getting out of the crisis." In the same vein, Prime Minister Jean-Marie Chérestal declared, "We took a commitment to keep talking. This is a major step and it's clear we are not far from resolving the crisis."[40] Soon afterward, however, old demons began to resurface, undermining prospects for concluding the agreement.

The talks, which were supposed to have continued in the wake of the Hotel Montana meetings, came to a virtual halt as the protagonists waited for the return of foreign mediators. In the interregnum, the situation deteriorated suddenly; on July 28, members of the disbanded military launched a series of violent attacks against several police stations, killing five officers.[41] While the attackers failed miserably to challenge Aristide's power and fled into exile in the Dominican Republic,[42] they contributed to a further exacerbation of the already tense political climate.

Not surprisingly, Lavalas's leaders accused CD, which had called earlier for the restoration of the Haitian armed forces, of conspiring with the despised military to overthrow the government. According to Lavalas's spokesman, Senator Yvon Neptune, "a coup [was] underway, in its political and military guises." The interior minister, Henri-Claude Menard, asserted confidently, however, that "the days when coup d'états were staged to crush democracy are behind us."[43] CD denied any involvement in the alleged plot; in fact it claimed that the government itself had staged the whole episode. According to Micha Gaillard, Lavalas engineered the attacks to "block the negotiations and to raise the population against [the opposition]."[44] Moreover, CD leaders claimed that Aristide would use the attacks as a pretext to incarcerate and intimidate them.[45] When the government arrested thirty-five suspects—the majority of whom supported the opposition—in connection with the violent assaults,[46] they quickly condemned it for creating "an environment of persecution and terror."[47] CD warned that it would not resume negotiations under these circumstances. As one of its key figures, Evans Paul, put it,

How can Lavalas ask us to sit and talk in order to guarantee the future of democracy in an atmosphere that is undemocratic? How can this happen in an atmosphere where police officers died in strange circumstances, where other police officers are kept in prison, oddly enough, where our militants are murdered without any explanation, where others are kept in jail and where others had to go into hiding?[48]

CD was thus setting new conditions for a resolution of the crisis: it would not return to the discussion table unless the government released its supporters who it claimed had been arbitrarily detained. While Lavalas denied that it was engaging in illegal and repressive measures and called for the resumption of negotiations, it could ignore CD's demands only at its own peril. Indeed, the United States through its ambassador, Brian Dean Curran, expressed support for CD's position and emphasized that the current political climate was not conducive to negotiations. Curran added, however, that he was encouraged by Lavalas's commitment to finding a solution to the crisis.[49] In fact, despite all his detours, Aristide seems to have embarked on a path leading to the implementation of a modified option zero. It is likely that he will have to settle for new legislative and local elections under the supervision of an autonomous electoral council and under the surveillance of international observers. In return, the opposition will reluctantly concede that he is the president of all Haitians, and the foreign community will fund the country's economic "rationalization." Aristide's profound desire to legitimize his presidency both at home and abroad and to acquire badly needed foreign assistance leaves him with very little choice. He is virtually condemned to make major concessions.

It remains to be seen, however, whether these concessions will suffice for arriving at a historic compromise. On the one hand, the opposition knows that new elections will bring it, at best, only limited success and few legislative seats. The persistence of the crisis might therefore serve its interests best, since it gives it a disproportionate amount of power over national decisions. On the other hand, the Lavalas "base" might fear that future political arrangements with certain sectors of the opposition might exclude it from the prebends of public office. It might therefore choose to preserve the status quo in spite of its vicissitudes and difficulties.

The future is therefore uncertain, and the necessity of a compromise by no means guarantees it. The omnipresent and universal poverty of society may invite the naked and intransigent protection of selfish material interests and provoke dangerous miscalculations that otherwise could have been avoided. The staggering disillusionment of vast sections of the population eking a miserable living in a ruined economy and amid the alarming violence of Zinglendos, Chimères, and other armed gangs, bodes poorly for any genuine democratic outcome. Tired and disenchanted, Haiti is in disarray and its people are increasingly cynical. These are neither triumphal nor happy times; but as Hegel warned us long ago, "History is not the realm of happiness"; on the contrary, "periods of happiness are [history's] empty pages."[50] For good or ill, since their independence in 1804, Haitians have always filled these pages and there are no reasons to believe that they will cease do so in the immediate future.

Notes

1. Michèle Montas, "An Open Letter to My Husband, Jean Léopold Dominique," Center for International Policy, May 3, 2001; see also the editorials of *Haïti Progrès* following the creation of the *gouvernement d'ouverture*. Ben Dupuy, editor of *Haïti Progrès* and leader of the left-wing National Popular Party, who supported Aristide's reelection, has now come full circle and condemned both Lavalas and CD; he has also questioned the legitimacy of civil society's representatives and argued that the current crisis is artificial, a distraction from the real structural problems facing the country. As he explained (cited as quoted in "The Soap Opera Continues," *Haïti Progrès,* May 9–15, 2001),

> [The] so-called crisis, which many people including ourselves call a false crisis, a synthetic crisis, seems more like a soap opera or what we might call a television series. [Moreover, representatives of "civil society" are not impartial mediators.] We don't know who gave these so-called representatives of the "civil society" their mandate. Was it in an election? Were they democratically chosen to represent what they call the "civil society"? Or is it people who have parachuted themselves in as representatives of the so-called "civil society"?
>
> [In reality the "crisis" is partly a power struggle between the Convergence and Lavalas Family, both of which] have the same boss. Both are agreed to apply the death plan, the neoliberal plan. [Dupuy added, this power struggle] is not just for political power. As we know in Haiti's case, political power means enrichment. We see a lot of people come into politics without a penny and then—presto—they are building big houses, they have big institutions.
>
> We see that more and more those who struggled for the ideals of [Aristide's first election on] Dec. 16, 1990—Justice, Transparency, and Participation—are increasingly sidelined and replaced by Duvalierists and Tonton Macoutes.
>
> We think that the real crisis in Haiti is a social crisis, a structural crisis which has been with us for about 200 years where there is a small elite which exploits the vast majority of the people and is leading the country into a veritable catastrophe today. [The] fundamental problems facing the country are not on the table. They are all just focused on dividing up the cake.

2. Garry Lissade was identified by several Haitian newspapers as an "organic intellectual" of the "liberal" wing of Duvalierism, but he has publicly denied any linkage with the regime of Jean-Claude Duvalier. He defines himself as an independent figure having no affiliation to political parties or organizations.

3. "Le Nouveau Cabinet Ministériel est Composé de Technocrates, pour la Majorité, des Proches de Fanmi Lavalas," Flash InterVision2000, March 2, 2001; "Is Aristide Hostage of the International Community?" *Haïti Progrès,* March 6–13, 2001; "Weekly News," *Haiti Reborn Home,* March 21, 2001; "Haiti's Prime Minister and Cabinet Sworn In," Reuters, March 2, 2001.

4. The four *Jean-Claudistes* are Volvick Rémy Joseph, a leader of the neo-Duvalierist party Mouvman Kombit Nasyonal (MKN), who was health minister in

Jean-Claude Duvalier's administration; Yves Masillon, Duvalier's former chief of protocol; Domingo Théronier, a police commissioner under Duvalier's reign; and Pierre André Anélas, a well-known supporter of *Jean-Claudisme*.

5. The classical statement on the "rationality" of maximizing power can be found in Anthony Downs, *An Economic Theory of Democracy* (New York: Harper and Row, 1957). According to Downs (p. 28),

> [Party members] act solely in order to attain the income, prestige, and power which come from being in office. Thus politicians in our model never seek office as a means of carrying out particular policies; their only goal is to reap the rewards of holding office *per se*. They treat policies purely as a means to the attainment of their private ends, which they can reach only by being elected.

6. Micha Gaillard, a key figure in CD, celebrated his group's capacity to resist the temptations of power. As he put it in "A First Response to the Center for Free Enterprise and Democracy and Democratic Initiatives—For a Truly New Departure," Center for International Policy, March 20, 2001,

> All the political parties and civil-society organizations, all of them patriotic, do not cease to call for an agreement among the political actors. The question remains, what kind of political agreement? An agreement confined to the electoral question alone . . . will not be enough to effectively end the hostilities among the different protagonists. The opposition grouped around the Democratic Convergence has declined—something new in our history—the jobs offered as consolation prizes in the Aristide-Chérestal government and the Lavalas/Macoute electoral council. It holds out for a true agreement or none at all. Given that the parties in conflict cannot agree to a comprehensive political deal setting the rules of the game of a state of law which the armed elements would have to respect, Haiti continues its descent into the shadows.

The question, however, is whether CD's refusal to integrate Chérestal's government is indeed principled. Can it withstand a cut of foreign assistance, mainly from the IRI, and the contradictory pulls of ideological divisions? As I have argued in this book, the opportunistic character of the opposition and *la politique du ventre* are likely to lead to the explosion of CD and the incorporation of some of its factions in Aristide's regime.

7. "Haiti Looms as Early Foreign Policy Headache for Bush," *Washington Post,* February 3, 2001; Ira Kurzban, "A Rational Foreign Policy Toward Haiti," Haiti Online, February 6, 2001. The post-Duvalier and controversial history of U.S. attempts to "export" democratic norms to Haiti is analyzed in a short document published by the Washington Office on Haiti, "Democracy Intervention in Haiti," March 1994. The document is available online at http://www.igc.org/reports/democenh.html. According to the Washington Office on Haiti, these attempts at exporting democracy have served to "undermine genuine democracy in poor countries. The kind of 'democracy' sought is not that which reflects self-determination, popular participation, or the interests of the poor majorities in Third World countries."

8. "Le Président Aristide Appelle de Nouveau l'Opposition à Favoriser avec Lui le Déblocage des Fonds Destinés à l'Amélioration du Sort de la Population Haïtienne," Agence Haïtienne de Presse en Ligne, April 23, 2001.

9. Michelle Karshan, "The Elements of President Jean-Bertrand Aristide's Most Recent Position to Reduce the Terms of All Members of Parliament Elected May 21st, 2000," Center for International Policy, April 17, 2001, http://www.

ciponline.org/. Karshan, foreign press liaison of the Haitian government, summarizes Fanmi Lavalas's concessions:

> President Aristide, in keeping with the eight-point agreement with the United States, has been willing to work out a compromise regarding the dispute arising from the May 21st elections and has taken many steps to demonstrate his commitment to this end. For example, the creation of the Lissade Commission, personal participation in a meeting with the Democratic Convergence, engagement of Fanmi Lavalas in intense negotiations to reach accord on the appointment of a new provisional electoral council able to schedule new runoff elections, the enlisting of the support of five Fanmi Lavalas senators and one independent senator to abstain from Senate activities, securing the resignation of the old electoral council and the formation of a new provisional electoral council, all illustrating the good faith efforts made by President Aristide and the government of Haiti to resolve the electoral crisis.
>
> Going further, President Aristide's most recent offer, made as part of his pursuit of a negotiated settlement with the opposition to end the crisis, would accelerate the electoral calendar by two years and reduce the terms of all senators and deputies elected on May 21st. The government proposed the following calendar to the OAS last month.

> - Early elections in November 2002 to renew the 1/3 of the Senate elected May 21st whose terms would have otherwise expired in January 2004;
> - Elections in November 2002 for all deputies elected May 21st whose terms would have otherwise expired in January 2004;
> - Elections in November 2004 for the other 1/3 of the Senate elected on May 21st whose terms would have otherwise expired in January 2006;
> - Organize complementary elections to arrive at a definitive solution to the controversy raised in the May 21st election.

> This proposal goes well beyond the recommendations made by the OAS and exceeds the commitments already made by President Aristide in the eight-point agreement signed last December. The OAS never questioned the legitimacy of the May 21st elections and in fact affirmed them as free and fair with a 60% turnout. The OAS has never recommended that overall elections be held again. This is like throwing out the baby with the bath water! The Democratic Convergence has stubbornly stuck to their "option zero" strategy that calls for the elimination of the May 21st elections and the holding of entirely new elections. They also do not recognize any subsequent elections to the May 21st elections despite the international community's position.

Haiti's minister of foreign affairs, Joseph Philippe Antonio, first proposed Aristide's concessions in a speech to the Permanent Council of the OAS on March 14, 2001.

10. See the resolution of the Permanent Council of the OAS, "Support for Democracy in Haiti," CP/RES. 786 (1267/01), March 14, 2001; see also "Le Conseil de l'OEA Rejette Tout Appel à l'Option Zéro et Prône une Solution Passant par la Correction des Législatives du 21 Mai," Agence Haïtienne de Presse en Ligne, March 15, 2001; "L'OEA ne Supporte pas la Théorie de la Page Blanche et Appelle les Secteurs en Conflit à Consentir des Sacrifices pour le Déblocage de la Crise," Flash InterVision2000, April 16, 2001; "Le Président Américain Rend Hommage au Numéro II de l'OEA pour les Efforts Déployé en Vue de Favoriser le Dialogue Entre les Partis en Conflit en Haïti," Agence Haïtienne de Presse en Ligne, April 18, 2001.

11. CLED has put forward these major propositions ("Statement in Support of

the Civil Society Initiative," Port-au-Prince, March 7, 2001, posted on the website of the Center for International Policy, http://www.ciponline.org/):

> To revive the confidence of the Haitian people in this system and to consolidate the foundations of democracy in Haiti, it is essential that President Aristide proceed to the designation of a new CEP on the basis of a consensual agreement with the opposition political parties and with civil society organizations. It would be desirable for the members of this new CEP [to] be chosen or delegated according to the spirit and the method of selection adopted in the creation of the 1987 CEP.
>
> As numerous irregularities have flawed the electoral process since May 21, 2000, we believe that only general legislative elections are capable of endowing the parliament as a whole with irrefutable legitimacy. These elections should be organized within the next twelve months. We recommend that, during this period, the contested parliament abstain from:
>
> (a)   making the least modification, however minor, to the Constitution of 1987;
> (b)   voting on any bill which has not been introduced by a consensus government resulting from successful negotiations between President Aristide and the opposition political parties;
> (c)   taking the initiative in drafting laws countering this spirit of consensus that must prevail during the transition period.
>
> We suggest that members of the Territorial Collectivities elected on May 21, 2000 remain in their positions until the end of their term. However, they should refrain from designating those members who should take part in the Departmental Assemblies. Thus, there will be no permanent CEP before new elections are held to renew the Territorial Collectivities.
>
> The International Community should play an active role in the process of organizing the next elections and in that of consolidating democracy in Haiti.

12. "Des Organisations Politiques et de la Société Civile s'en Prennent Vivement aux Organisateurs du Sommet Qui ont Invité Jean Bertrand Aristide," Flash InterVision2000, April 17, 2001.

13. "America's Leaders Urge Haiti to Press On with Reform," Reuters, April 22, 2001. It is worth noting again Aristide's eight promises to President Clinton (White House, "Statement by the Press Secretary," December 28, 2000):

> 1. Rapid rectification of the problems associated with the May 21 elections through run-offs for disputed Senate seats or by other credible means. This rectification is being facilitated by the work of the Lissade Commission.
>
> 2. Creation of a credible new provisional electoral council (CEP) in consultation with opposition figures to rectify the problems associated with the disputed Senate seats.
>
> 3. Enhance substantially cooperation to combat drug trafficking, including implementation of money laundering legislation and expansion of maritime cooperation, building on the October 1997 agreement, in order to allow access to U.S. Coast Guard anti-drug operation in Haitian waters. Strengthen efforts, in collaboration with the U.S. and Dominican Republic governments, to interdict trafficking across Haitian/DR border.
>
> 4. Nominate capable and respected officials for senior security positions, including within the HNP. Ensure that there is no interference in the professional work and conduct of the HNP by members of Parliament and others. Take steps to enhance the professionalism and independence of juridical system.
>
> 5. Strengthen democratic institutions and protection of human rights through the establishment of a semi-permanent OAS commission to facilitate dialogue

among Haitian political, civic, and business leaders and through international monitoring of the protection of human rights.

6. Seek to install a broad-based government including "technocrats" and members of the opposition.

7. Initiate new dialogue with international financial institutions concerning sound budgetary proposals and economic reforms to enhance free markets and promote private investment. Such measures will be aimed at reducing poverty and stimulating growth.

8. Negotiate agreement for repatriation of illegal migrants.

14. Ibid.; see also "Summit Leaders Urge Haiti Reform," BBC, April 22, 2001; and "OAS Looks to Ease Haiti's Turmoil," *Miami Herald,* April 24, 2001.

15. "OAS Looks to Ease Haiti's Turmoil"; see also "Haiti's President Optimistic His Country Can Resolve Political Crisis," Haiti-Info, April 23, 2001.

16. "Haiti: Talks Between the Ruling Party and Opposition Fail," Associated Press, April 27, 2001; "Crise Politique: La Rencontre Préparatoire aux Nouvelles Discussions Convergence/Fanmi Lavalas Bloquées à Villa Créole," Agence Haïtienne de Presse en Ligne, April 28, 2001; "Echec de la Réunion de la Convergence Démocratique, ce Jeudi, à l'Hôtel Villa Créole" Flash InterVision2000, April 29, 2001.

17. "Echec de la Réunion de la Convergence Démocratique"; "Déclaration de la Convergence Démocratique Suite à la Réunion, ce Vendredi, à l'Hôtel Villa Créole," Flash InterVision2000, April 29, 2001.

18. "De Nouveaux Écueils sur la Voie de la Reprise du Dialogue en Haïti," Agence Haïtienne de Presse en Ligne, April 26, 2001.

19. As quoted in Michael Deibert, "Notes from the Last Testament," windowsonhaiti.com, May 1, 2001.

20. Lynn Garrison, *Voodoo Politics* (Los Angeles: Leprechaun, 2000).

21. Ibid., p. 173; for an excellent analysis of the sources, motivations, and fabrications of the right-wing smearing of Aristide, see Paul Farmer, *The Uses of Haiti* (Monroe, Maine: Common Courage Press, 1994); see also Nicolas Jallot and Laurent Lesage, *Haïti: Dix Ans d'Histoire Secrète* (Paris, Éditions du Félin, 1995), pp. 149–150.

22. Rony Mondestin, "Plan de Chimérisation de la PNH et de l'Appareil Judiciaire par le Pouvoir Lavalas: Les Prémisses d'une Dictature de Basse Intensité: Document de Travail," Center for International Policy, April 2001, http://www.ciponline.org/.

23. As quoted in Deibert, "Notes from the Last Testament."

24. In a speech following two days of violent confrontations between supporters of Lavalas and CD, Aristide declared, "The state cannot have people thumbing their nose at the law. . . . The law is the law." In a rather menacing allusion, he added, "In 63 B.C. Cicero, by foiling Cataline's plot, scored a political success" ("Speech by Jean-Bertrand Aristide on Events of the Past Two Days," March 21, 2001, Center for International Policy, http://www.ciponline.org/). Leaders of the opposition interpreted the allusion as a threat to their own lives, since Cicero used assassinations as the means to silence his detractors. See also "Haiti President's Supporters Set Flaming Barricades," CNN News, March 17, 2001; "Anti-Opposition Demonstrations Rock Haiti," *Haïti Progrès,* March 21–27, 2001; "Branle-bas Populaire Contre la Convergence," *Haïti Progrès,* March 21–27, 2001; "Protests Intensify in Haiti," *Financial Times,* March 21, 2001; "La Région Métropolitaine Devient la Proie des Chimères," Haiti Online, March 22, 2001.

25. Ibid.; see also "Affrontement Entre des Partisans du Pouvoir et Ceux de

l'Opposition: Plusieurs Blessés," SICRAD, Haiti Correspondance, Série 2, No. 95, March 19, 2001; "Des Responsables de la Convergence Nient Leurs Responsabilités dans les Violences Ayant Fait au Moins Deux Blessés Graves à Port-au-Prince," Agence Haïtienne de Presse, March 20, 2001; "Mobs of Aristide Backers Bully a Frail Foe in Haiti," *Sun-Sentinel* (Fort Lauderdale, Fla.), March 24, 2001.

26. Gérard Dalvius, a former major in the Haitian military, led a protest demonstration of retired soldiers and officers who claimed their allegiance to Gourgue and demanded the exit of Aristide. Shouting "long live Gérard Gourgue! long live the army," and "down with the criminals! down with Lavalas!" the protesters echoed CD's demand for the restoration of the Haitian army (see "Former Soldiers Demand Army's Return," *Haitian Times* (online edition), March 19, 2001).

27. While the interior minister, Henry-Claude Menard, declared that Gourgue should be arrested for usurping the title of president, he never issued a warrant. Aristide knew that arresting Gourgue would have created sympathy for the "provisional president" and generated massive international condemnations (see the editorial "Acceptons la Vérité," Agence Haïtienne de Presse, March 26, 2001). In a *Miami Herald* interview, Gourgue acknowledged this much ("Rival Leader Challenges Aristide to Arrest Him," *Miami Herald,* March 25, 2001). See also "Haiti President's Supporters Set Flaming Barricades," CNN News, March 17, 2001.

28. René Lemarchand, "Political Clientelism and Ethnicity in Tropical Africa: Competing Solidarities in Nation-Building," in Steffen W. Schmidt, James Scott, Carl Landé, and Laura Guasti, eds., *Friends, Followers, and Factions* (Berkeley: Universty of California Press, 1977), p. 101.

29. According to a Gallup poll taken on the eve of the November 26 presidential elections, more than half of Haitians thought that Aristide was the politician they trusted most; about 70 percent of the population gave their preference to Aristide over any other political leader (see "Un Sondage de CID/Gallup Réalisé en Octobre 2000 Relève que Jean Bertrand Aristide Est la Personnalité à Bénéficier des Opinions les Plus Favorables de la Population Haïtienne," Agence Haïtienne de Presse en Ligne, May 2, 2001).

30. Evans Paul, "Evans Paul Responds," Center for International Policy, March–May 2001 (http://www.ciponline.org/), gave this explanation for CD's absence:

> We say that we are ready to participate in any meetings held on a neutral field. I already said that we do not invite people to the Convergence premises in Pont Morin, and we would never invite people to discuss solutions at the residence of president Gérard Gourgue. Similarly, we cannot be asked to come to any appointment or to participate in any meeting that takes place either in Tabarre or at the National Palace.

31. Marc Bazin, Aristide's minister of planning, argued that the legislative elections should be reheld and that the contending parties should make the necessary concessions to resolve the crisis ("Aristide Sets May 18 as Next Date for Resolution of Electoral Crisis," Center for International Policy, May 4, 2001); see also "Vers la Relance du Processus de Dialogue: Le Président Aristide Invite Différents Secteurs à une Rencontre au Palais National," Agence Haïtienne de Presse en Ligne, April 30, 2001; "Aristide Tente de Prendre le Leadership des Négociations," SICRAD, Série 2, No. 101, April 30, 2001; "Consensus sur l'Urgence d'une Sortie de Crise," Agence France Presse, May 3, 2001.

32. On May 10, CLED, with the collaboration of other organizations of the

business community, revised its earlier initiative and put forward a new set of propositions. The key propositions are the following ("The Business Community's Position on the Political Situation," May 10, 2001, summary/translation by Center for International Policy):

> [We] live in a nation that is exhausted, bled dry, and without hope. The degree of immiseration of the country is greater than ever. The degradation of the environment continues apace. The democratic institutions inscribed in the constitution of 1987 have not been created, and the state is disintegrating.
>
> The elections of May 21, 2000 and the elections of 2000 did not bring a solution but on the contrary exacerbated the situation. The consequence is the blockage of the forces of production that is visible to all and the degradation of the living standards of all citizens. . . .
>
> We note the proposal formulated by CLED on March 7. Despite the nuances in our position we all ardently desire a compromise to end this crisis. We take the CLED proposal as our basic position and modify it so:
>
> 1. Elections
>
> In addition to completely new legislative elections we think there should be new municipal and local elections.
>
> 2. Electoral commission (CEP)
>
> To achieve an impartial commission we propose that the protatgonists' negotiators reach a consensus on nine representative and credible civil-society institutions which will nominate the nine members of the CEP along the lines and criteria established by the negotiators to guarantee the credibility, honesty and competence of those chosen.
>
> 3. Mediation
>
> The negotiations should be conducted under the aegis of the OAS and the Civil Society Initiative.
>
> 4. Principal interlocutors
>
> The Lavalas Family and the Democratic Convergence.
>
> The accord should:
>
> 1. Establish strict rules of the game for the democratic process and the credibility of elections.
>
> 2. Assure political stability and governability.
>
> 3. End all challenge to the legitimacy of the state.
>
> 4. Create conditions for normalizing politics, resuming economic activity, and creating social peace.

33. Ibid.; see also "Après la Rencontre du Palais National," *Haïti en Marche,* May 7, 2001.

34. "Adresse du Gouvernement Provisoire de Consensus et d'Unité Nationale, Me. Gérard Gourgue, Président, aux Membres du Directoire de la Convergence Démocratique," Haitiwebs.Com, May 3, 2001; "Gérard Gourgue Soumet aux Leaders de la Convergence une Proposition en 7 Points sur Laquelle Devront Être Orientées Toutes Éventuelles Négociations," www.haitiwebs.com, May 3, 2001.

35. "OAS Mission to Haiti Ends with Little Progress," *Miami Herald,* May 14, 2001.

36. As quoted in "The Soap Opera Continues . . .," *Haïti Progrès,* May 9–15, 2001; see also "Après la Rencontre du Palais National"; "Joint Mission to Haiti Seeks to Help Solve Crisis: Advance Group from CARICOM, OAS Headed to Assess Situation," *Miami Herald,* May 10, 2001.

37. The OAS adopted at its fourth plenary session held in San José, Costa Rica, the resolution *Support for Democracy in Haiti,* OEA/Ser.PAG/doc.4044/01, June 5, 2001. The OAS resolved:

1. To reiterate its deep concern at the continuing political crisis in Haiti, arising from the elections of 21 May 2000.

2. To take note of the initiative, consisting of five elements, contained in the letter of the President of Haiti . . . with regard to the process toward a definitive resolution to the current political crisis.

3. To acknowledge the concerns expressed in said letter regarding the urgency of normalizing relations between Haiti and the international financial institutions.

4. To urge the Government of Haiti to follow the resignations of seven Senators with the expeditious constitution of a credible, independent and neutral Provisional Electoral Council (CEP), composed of nine members nominated by the Executive, Judiciary, political parties—including the Convergence, Fanmi Lavalas, and other political parties—and churches, both Catholic and Protestant, by 25 June 2001. This is a necessary step to create a climate of confidence conducive to a broad based agreement among the Government of Haiti, political parties and civil society, and other relevant institutions of Haitian society, with a view to resolving the political crisis and strengthening democracy and respect for human rights in Haiti.

5. To call upon the Government of Haiti, political parties, and civil society and other relevant institutions of Haitian society to commit themselves fully to this end.

6. To instruct the Secretary General to monitor and report to the Permanent Council on implementation of the commitments contained in [Aristide's letter].

7. To instruct the Secretary General to increase his efforts, in consultation with CARICOM and with other interested countries, to contribute further to the resolution of the existing political crisis in Haiti, to its social and economic development, the strengthening of democracy and the respect for human rights in that country.

8. To invite the Secretary General to establish a Group of Friends on Haiti from interested OAS member states and permanent observers to assist him in these efforts.

9. To request the Permanent Council to examine, as a matter of urgency, the mandate, modalities, budget, financing and other arrangements concerning the establishment of a possible Mission to Haiti.

10. To instruct the Secretary General to work jointly with member states towards normalizing relations between Haiti and the international community, including the international financial institutions, as progress is achieved in reaching a sustainable solution to the crisis arising from the 21 May 2000 elections.

11. To instruct the Secretary General to report to the Permanent Council or the General Assembly as appropriate on the implementation of this resolution.

38. Jean-Bertrand Aristide, president, letter to H. E. Roberto Rojas, minister of foreign affairs and worship of Costa Rica, May 31, 2001. The letter stipulates the following:

With a view toward an end to the impasse, I wish to outline five elements which I am confident will foster an end to this situation. I urge the international community to support this initiative as symbol of its solidarity with a burgeoning democracy.

1. I am now in a position to inform you that the seven contested Senators have resigned as evidence of their patriotic commitment to ending the electoral controversy surrounding the May 21, 2000 elections.

2. I commit to appoint a new Provisional Electoral Council (CEP) by June 25, 2001. This CEP would be composed of nine members nominated by the Executive, Judiciary, political parties—including the Convergence, Fanmi Lavalas, and other political parties—and churches, both Catholic and Protestant.

I will uphold the integrity of the new CEP as a functionally independent entity.

It should be clear that if any of the above groups fail to nominate its assigned member(s), the undesignated member(s) would be selected from among the other sectors identified above.

3. The new CEP will, after appropriate consultations, set the date for elections of the contested seats in the Senate and proceed to organize these elections in a timely manner. I am convinced that it would be in the country's best interest if the elections to fill the vacated seats were to occur before the end of the year 2001, and would encourage this result.

4. The new CEP would also organize early elections to replace all members of Parliament elected May 21, 2000, in accordance with the government's proposal outlined at the March 14, 2001, session of the OAS Permanent Council, the terms of the parliamentarians elected on May 21, 2000 would be reduced by two years, in order to regularize the cycle of renewal for the seats in the Haitian Parliament as provided for in the Constitution. Finally, the CEP would organize complementary elections that are necessary to bring about the establishment of a Permanent Electoral Council.

5. To increase confidence in these measures, I seek your support for the establishment of a Special OAS/CARICOM Mission whose mandate would be to facilitate dialogue with civil society and political parties, and to strengthen democratic institutions. The mission's functions would include the observation of human rights conditions and support for the proper functioning of the electoral process, including freedom of expression and security for all concerned.

39. "Breakthrough Reported in Montana Hotel Talks," Center for International Policy, July 17, 2001; see also "Haïti/Crise: Fanmi Lavalas et la Convergence Démocratique ont Fait des Avancées Significatives dans les Dernières Négotiations," Agence Haïtienne de Presse en Ligne, July 16, 2001; "Visite Officielle d'Aristide à Cuba dans un Contexte Difficile pour les Deux Pays," SICRAD, Série 2, No. 110, July 17, 2001; "New Elections OK'd in Haiti," *Miami Herald,* July 17, 2001.

40. As quoted in "New Elections OK'd in Haiti."

41. "Armed Men on Haiti Rampage," BBC News, July 28, 2001; "Armed Men Attack Police Academy and Jail in Haiti, Killing Three Policemen," Associated Press, July 28, 2001; "What Lies Behind Last Weekend's Assaults," *Haïti Progrès,* August 1–7, 2001.

42. CD leaders denied initially that the attackers had sought exile in the Dominican Republic, but they had to acquiesce to that reality when Hugo Tolentino Dipp, the Dominican foreign minister, acknowledged publicly the presence of the Haitian military officers in his country. See "Former Haitian Officers Seeking Asylum," *Miami Herald,* August 3, 2001.

43. "Haiti Opposition Denies Plot Charge," Associated Press, July 29, 2001; see also "What Lies Behind Last Weekend's Assaults."

44. "Les Attaques Meurtrières de Samedi: Un Coup Monté Selon la Convergence," Radio Métropole, July 30, 2001; see also "Réactions aux Attaques Perpétrées Contre la PNH," Agence Haïtienne de Presse en Ligne, July 30, 2001; "What Lies Behind Last Weekend's Assaults."

45. Ibid.; "Que Voulaient les Assaillants," *Haïti Progrès,* August 1–7, 2001.

46. "Haiti Arrests 35 Suspects in Attacks on Police," Reuters, July 30, 2001.

47. "Haiti: Opposition Calls on Government to End 'Environment of Persecution,'" BBC Monitoring Service, August 9, 2001, text of report by Haiti's Radio Métropole on August 8, available online at the website of the *Financial Times;* see also "La Oposición Haitiana Denuncia 'Campaña de Terror' de Lavalás," *Listín Diario* (Santo Domingo), August 2, 2001.

48. "Haiti: Opposition Calls on Government."

49. "L'Ambassadeur Américain Appuie les Conditions Posées par la Convergence pour Reprendre les Négociations," Radio Métropole, August 9, 2001; "Haitian Police Charged with Treason, Killings," Reuters, August 9, 2001.

50. As quoted in Isaac Deutscher, *The Unfinished Revolution: Russia 1917–1967* (New York: Oxford University Press, 1967), p. 97.

8

Conclusion

In this book, I have contended that the democratization of Haiti was fundamentally dependent upon the explosion of popular civil society and the balance of class forces. The collapse of the Duvalier dictatorship would have never materialized without the former; but because the latter underwent little change, the fundamental structures of Haitian society remained virtually unaffected. The political convulsions of the past fifteen years have generated a permanent crisis rather than a revolutionary order. It is true that popular civil society voiced its grievances and had some success by crystallizing in the original Lavalas movement that brought Aristide to power in 1991. In spite of its huge mass following, however, it was poorly structured and had only the weapon of rhetorical exhortation in its confrontation with the dominant class, who in contradistinction controlled the force of arms. The conflict of classes was thus lopsided. On the one hand, the poor and overwhelming majority could count only on the power of numbers; on the other hand, the dominant class had at its disposal significant material resources and the military as its praetorian guard.

Fearing that Lavalas was turning the world upside down and threatening their fundamental corporate interests, the army and its allies in the privileged sectors unleashed a violent coup against Aristide. In the polarized conditions that prevailed at the time, neither institutions nor political statecraft could have changed the political calculus. The overthrow of Aristide was the inevitable outcome of the structural constellation of power. Not surprisingly, his restoration to the presidency demanded another moment of brute military intervention, albeit of foreign origin. Without it, the junta and the dominant class would have never relinquished their hold on the state.

The U.S. occupation was full of contradictions. While it reinvigorated the *political* fortunes of Lavalas and curtailed the armed power of the dominant classes, it thoroughly deradicalized the *economic* project of Aristide's

197

regime. The balance of class was relatively equalized; but it was indeed a very relative equality. It implied at most the demilitarization of the predators and their supporters; by no means did it portend fundamental structural changes and the disappearance of the lingering authoritarian legacy. With the peaceful transfers of presidential power in February 1996 from Aristide to René Préval and back again to Aristide in February 2001, the process of changing regimes electorally may now be on firmer foundation, but the transformation—let alone the democratization—of the state remains a project in the making.

While electoralism opened up the political space for struggling for such a transformation, it created also the terrain for the fraudulent control of public office with which to acquire the prebendary sinecures of power. It is this appetite for monopolizing the state apparatus that ultimately generated the internecine conflicts that fractured Lavalas. In a country where wealth and privilege are rare and can seldom be attained through private venues, the state becomes the prime arena for the acquisition of resources. Politics is thus an entrepreneurial vocation, particularly for members of the relatively poor and marginalized petite bourgeoisie. They know that public office is their ticket to individual wealth and patronage. The emergence of a new class of *grands mangeurs* betrays the ugly reality that in a destitute country like Haiti, an individualistic *sauve-qui-peut* mentality is an easy detour in the democratizing journey. The detour is not necessarily proof of utter moral depravity—though it can be—but rather a traumatic response to a social structure that offers little hope for a collective escape from overwhelming poverty. The rigors of a life of political integrity are difficult to sustain in an environment where public honesty is a sign of madness and corruption a symbol of power. Opportunism tends to reign supreme.

The Lavalas cadres have suffered a fate similar to that of Jean-Marie Doumergue, elected president of the devastatingly poor (fictional) Caribbean island of Ganae. Brian Moore's novel *No Other Life* gives this description:

> [The] history of Ganae is like a cheap gramophone record. The new tune plays for a while, then the needle sticks in the groove and the player-arm slumps back and slips off the disc. Every Ganaen leader begins his term by promising to change things. Most of them don't even try. But the few who do—well, it's like the gramophone record. The needle sticks in a groove. There are many grooves—the elite, the Army, foreign business interests, the people's illiteracy—you name it—there's no way that progress or democratic ideals can work here. And so the leader becomes a strong man, trying to force his ideas through. Enemies have to be disposed of. Coups must be anticipated and crushed. The leader becomes a tyrant. Doumergue is simply a victim of this country's history.[1]

The question, however, is whether Haitians are condemned to be inevitable victims of their own history. In spite of constraining political and economic structures, there is no reason to believe that there is no alternative to the current crisis. The collapse of the Duvalier dictatorship clearly demonstrated that Haitians were capable of trespassing rigid boundaries and moving toward new horizons. Human agency, as it were, can cause history to take the most surprising course. Politics has thus an indeterminate quality, encapsulated in the "crucial ambivalence of our human presence in our own history, part-subjects, part-objects, the voluntary agents of our own involuntary determinations."[2]

This is not to say that history is a totally undetermined series of events and that people are free to do as they please. In fact, the indeterminacy of history is rooted in the unintended effects of rather predictable choices. Throughout these pages I have emphasized the centrality of class, how human beings organize to defend and promote their corporate interests. I have argued that Haiti's predatory democracy reflects a class structure based on an extremely weak economic foundation and therefore lacking both a classical bourgeoisie and a large working class. The result is a *politique du ventre*, generating a class of *grands mangeurs* bent on monopolizing public power to advance their private interests. Such politics represented an unlikely terrain for the implantation of liberal democratic forms of representation. In this environment, competition for office becomes a zero-sum game characterized by the emergence of militarized gangs loosely attached to different political blocs, fraudulent and violent elections, and the executive supremacy of a presidential monarch. The rituals of electoralism, which regularly impose limitations on the authoritarian tendencies of the system, mitigate these dysfunctional patterns. In addition, the existence of a free press and of a vigorous civil society preserve a space of liberty, nourishing resistance to the rise of any absolute power. While this space of freedom privileges the organizations and voices of the privileged, subordinate classes use it to defend and promote their interests.

To that extent, democratization engenders ferocious processes of class formation and reconfiguration without emasculating the power of those who had hitherto constituted the dominant class. These class conflicts are the very stuff of politics; they are the "given" of social change, they are indeed predictable, but their consequences are never certain. In Haiti, they have generated a systemic crisis and thus a conjuncture replete with dangers as well as opportunities.

The danger is that the current impasse will deteriorate into open violent conflict between Lavalas and the opposition. In the absence of a compromise, it is likely that the war of words will escalate into a "low-intensity" civil war. Compromise, however, need not erase all the divisions between

Aristide and his opponents; in fact, there is little chance of this happening. A more probable scenario is a fracture of the opposition induced by the negotiating process itself. It is clear that Lavalas's control of the state apparatus gives it immense advantages: it can dispense favors and jobs to important segments of the opposition. By doing so, Aristide can hope to attract the soft-liners into his government and marginalize the hard-liners. Hence, a strategy of selective inclusion can perhaps neutralize the opposition; it is probably Aristide's preferred alternative. It involves little political cost and preserves Lavalas's supremacy. It might well bring stability and peace to the country, but it guarantees neither meaningful democratic practice nor sustained economic development. In fact, it may undermine the rational allocation of resources by redirecting expenditures to unproductive forms of patronage.

A type of reconciliation based on the co-optation of critical members of the opposition is therefore quite possible. This would entail the incorporation of some of the "big men" into the cabinet and into the top echelons of the state administration. The key assumption behind this scenario is that the ideology and program of the opposition and of Lavalas differ little, making possible a pact based on the prebendary redistribution of state resources. In return, the opposition would have to accept the supremacy of Aristide's presidentialism. Political stability entails therefore the creation of an enlarged presidential "community of disciples," small enough to adequately satisfy its prebendary appetite but big enough to neutralize the opposition's hard-liners.

Rooted in the common search for predictable, safe, and "nourishing" relations, this enlarged community of disciples can derive significant gains by "routinizing" Aristide's charismatic authority. As Max Weber explained long ago, such a process of routinization responds to two fundamental motivations:

> (a) The ideal and also material interests of the followers in the continuation and continual reactivation of the community, (b) the still stronger ideal and also stronger material interests of the members of the administrative staff, the disciples, the party workers, or others in continuing their relationship. Not only this, but they have an interest in continuing it in such a way that both from an ideal and a material point of view, their own position is put on a stable everyday basis.[3]

To this extent, the "community of disciples" is seeking the establishment of more accountable forms of governance; this does not imply, however, that it necessarily espouses democratic rule. In fact, it may fear that truly democratic forms of representation might spell its own demise. To that extent, the opposition may find in the type of secretive, closed-door negotiations advocated by "civil society" the perfect means for advancing its interests. The routinization of Aristide's rule could therefore be mutually beneficial to both Aristide himself and the opposition.

This is not to imply, however, that a pact will be reached easily. Negotiations are marred by the reality that the contending parties distrust each other utterly; they are also dangerous because they are likely to fragment the unity of the respective blocs. A successful compromise is liable to fracture the opposition and generate internecine struggles within Fanmi Lavalas. This is so because not all the disparate members of the opposition will be satisfied by Aristide's concessions and be ultimately included in the pact. In addition, some key constituents of Fanmi Lavalas will be frustrated by having to share power with their adversaries and thus forced to accept a reduced share of prebendary resources. It is this *politique du ventre* that explains the failure of the negotiations sponsored by "civil society," rather than the opposition's alleged desire for "a real democracy—[and] not a piece of the government," as Micha Gaillard, a delegate of Convergence Démocratique, put it.[4]

It seems clear now that the issue is not a deepening of democratic practice, but rather a historic "arrangement" between the competing blocs of the Haitian political class. It is a matter of regulating and indeed "civilizing" the appetite and eating habits of this class. That in itself would be no small achievement. It would grant international legitimacy to Aristide's rule and thus enhance prospects for foreign investments and aid, making Haiti's integration into world markets more productive. This strategic arrangement would by no means substantially reduce the conditions of absolute misery confronting 80 percent of the population, but it would be an improvement over the current dismal situation. The government might then succeed in achieving some of the ambitious objectives set by Aristide in his inauguration speech.

In this speech, Aristide maintained that his program of "investing in human beings" can be integrated into the larger macroeconomic reforms advocated by the major international financial institutions. He expected that his administration would be able to increase the growth of the GDP to about 4 percent; limit the rate of inflation to less than 10 percent; and reduce unemployment to 45 percent by augmenting investments by at least 50 percent. Finally, he called for the creation of approximately 500,000 stable jobs in the public and private sectors. Aristide also hoped to eliminate the massive shortage of electricity that has plagued the country. Additionally, he promised to raise the level of food self-sufficiency by 30 percent and make drinking water accessible to 70 percent of the rural population and to 80 percent of urban dwellers. Moreover, the president vowed to improve and rehabilitate more than 3,000 kilometers of minor and tertiary roads and 2,000 kilometers of primary roads. Finally, he would undertake the refitting of five national airports and the rehabilitation of the international airports of Port-au-Prince and Cap-Haïtien. According to Aristide, this economic program is feasible through the development of a partnership between the public and the private sectors. As he himself acknowledged, however, "We are just waiting for our future partners."[5] He knew that to lure these partners into his orbit, he would have to extricate the country from its long political crisis. That in turn required significant concessions to the opposition and the international community.

Paradoxically, then, the success of Aristide depended more on his capacity to steer his enemies into his camp than on his ability to satisfy the immediate desires of his mass constituency. In this sense, democratization had obdurate class boundaries. As Guillermo O'Donnell and Philippe Schmitter put it,

> All previously known transitions to political democracy have observed one fundamental restriction: it is forbidden to take, or even to checkmate the king of one of the players. In other words, during the transition, the property rights of the bourgeoisie are inviolable. This player may be forced to give up pawns and even be deprived of its rooks, . . . but its king cannot be placed in direct jeopardy. This is a fundamental restriction which leftist parties must accept if they expect to be allowed to play in the central parts of the board. . . . [The] game leaves few places and moves open for new players. The democratic forces . . . may be allowed only a few weak and vulnerable pieces on the board.[6]

Aristide learned this lesson the hard way; his overthrow by the military in 1991 clearly delineated the outer perimeters of the "permissible." Thus, the Haitian case shows not only the limits of democratization as a political process, but also its inadequacies as a theory. In reality, democratization theory constitutes an impaired and benign paradigm.[7] It is impaired because it accepts the naturalness and necessity of markets as a precondition for the realization of democracy and rational economic efficiency. It does so on the basis of a benign interpretation of capitalist democracy within which it was born and caged. It is incapable of a visionary transcendence; at best it seeks to improve life in the cage by humanizing its wardens and unchaining its inmates. It advocates democracy but cannot conceive of it without the preservation of a lingering authoritarian legacy. Ultimately it serves to "protect the advantages of the advantaged."[8] O'Donnell and Schmitter put it very bluntly:

> For a transition to political democracy to be viable in the long run, founding elections must be freely conducted, honestly tabulated, and openly contested, yet their results cannot be too accurate or representative of the actual distribution of voter preferences. Put in a nutshell, parties of the Right-Center and Right must be "helped" to do well, and parties of the Left-Center and Left should not win by an overwhelming majority. . . .

> The Left is called upon to underutilize its immediate symbolic advantage and to sacrifice, or at least to postpone for an undefined period, the goal of a radical, "advanced democratic" transformation.[9]

The democratization paradigm transforms the harsh realities of continued class oppression and inequalities into benign necessities. This phenomenon is inextricably connected to the conscious or unconscious co-optation of "organic intellectuals" whose science turns mercenary under the weight of financial sponsors, especially international banking institutions and nongovernmental as well as governmental organs of imperial nations, whose mission is to preserve the current order of things.[10]

Instead of developing in resolute independence from such stifling pressures and "speaking truth to power," the democratization paradigm operates within the constraining discursive parameters of major international financial institutions and imperial think tanks from which it obtains major portions of its funding and information. The paradigm is thus thoroughly consistent with the conservative adjustment of existing structures of power. It rests comfortably on an elite vision of change. It posits privileged members of the political class negotiating democratic pacts among themselves that are best arrived at when insulated from popular pressures. It studies existing social and political structures and describes their workings, but it rarely challenges the harsh realities of class power, which it tends to take as given and immutable.

If we were to regard social life as a game, as Charles Lindblom has contended, political science would need to do more than merely "[assist] the game officials, and [study] the rules of the game, how it might be improved, and how to take care of game injuries." Our discipline would have to provide much more to the players. Players "need to know how the game came to be structured as they find it, how they were induced to take for granted that they should play, whether any other game exists, and how they might find and learn to play another game."[11] The vocation of a truly liberating political science is thus to reject the benignity of existing arrangements of power and wealth, provide historical alternatives, and offer a transcending vision of the "good life" for which we would aim and with which we could measure the extent of current imperfections, injustice, and misery. The paradigm of democratization fails on all of these scores; enmeshed in the status quo, it is in dire need of its own democratization. It does not go beyond an embrace of electoralism, which is often a facade masking authoritarian politicians, dubious procedures, and fraudulent outcomes. It promises a new world but it recreates the old. If democratization is to hold its promise, it must develop, as Edward Said has emphasized, in "a spirit in opposition, rather than in accommodation, because the romance, the interest, the challenge of intellectual life is to be found in dissent against the status quo at a time when the struggle on behalf of underrepresented and disadvantaged groups seems so unfairly weighted against them."[12]

At this time, however, Haiti's *moun andeyo* have little to celebrate—they face a bleak future even if they are overwhelmingly convinced that Aristide's return will be their salvation. In a moment of utter bluntness, Préval told a group of peasants in the town of Marmelade that the situation was so desperate that they should be prepared to "najé pou soti" [swim to get out]. Haitians drew the inevitable conclusion that their own president was telling them he had nothing to offer and that the quest for a better life entailed embarking on the dangerous journey of boat people to reach the shores of Florida. The "exit option" betrayed the massive failures of the Préval administration. It is true that when it assumed power in 1995, it inherited a devastated country and had little time and resources to *changer la vie;* but five years later, Haiti seemed to be nearer the abyss leading to a fall into hell.

The fall, however, is not inevitable. Haitians still enjoy the social space necessary to build the popular civil society that had been so brutally squelched under the junta.[13] Community organizations of poor peasants and urban dwellers, rather than a thoroughly discredited and opportunistic opposition, are the best hope for consolidating the democratizing process and blocking any attempt at restoring authoritarianism. As Beatrice Pouligny has emphasized,

> While the political class is generally incapable of thinking out a political project, members of those small organizations continue to reflect, in very concrete terms, on the meaning of being a Haitian citizen, on their "right to exist and to inhabit the country"—the basic principle associated with the concept of "democracy." In spite of its serious weakness, this network of popular organizations continues to be a space where people are striving to make sense of what is changing and are inventing means of survival that defy all conceivable clichés about Haitian misery.
>
> The Haiti of popular organizations has no other choice but to unleash a rich imagination. This capacity to imagine is the most promising sign that no one has the right to lose hope for the country, and it might be the source from which might emerge a new political class, formed for a new political culture.[14]

Haitians have therefore a chance to reestablish and consolidate fragile democratic structures while emasculating those institutions that had historically kept the overwhelming majority destitute. The abolition of the armed forces was President Aristide's single most important contribution to the empowerment of *le peuple,* preventing the threat of coups from hanging like a sword of Damocles over Haitians and restraining the despotic power of the bourgeoisie from reasserting itself. Finally, the possibility of struggling for a more equitable pattern of economic development is not completely foreclosed. And for the vast majority, the controversial reelection of Aristide has rekindled hopes for a better future.

Such hopes, however, should not mask the enormous obstacles confronting those dreaming of a more democratic and egalitarian Haiti. The country still hovers on the verge of political catastrophe; it faces economic ruin, ecological destruction, and mass starvation of the poor. The dominant class, bewildered and confused by the U.S. intervention, is now encouraged by the Republican ascendancy in Washington and the Bush presidency. It has not surrendered; on the contrary, it is regrouping and is capable of blocking any strategy of development that it deems antagonistic to its interests. Promises of massive international assistance do not guarantee economic growth, let alone social equity. In fact, Lavalas's ambiguous and hesitant conversion to the magic of the market and privatization reflected the reality that such policies generate huge social dislocations that may well undermine its popular support.[15] The return to electoral politics and the partial disarmament of the repressive organs of the state have not been sufficiently institutionalized to ensure the success of democratic consolidation. The moral dilemma of seeking national reconciliation while at the same time establishing the rule of justice has remained a Gordian knot.[16] The return to social normalcy has been uneasy; it has meant accepting the presence of unpunished torturers and murderers. It is a compromise that may have bought temporary peace but which ultimately portends future victims. Moreover, armed groups of Macoutes, criminal thugs, and Chimères have taken advantage of the withdrawal of U.S. and UN troops and their replacement by an ill-prepared, incompetent, and increasingly corrupt Haitian police to unleash a new cycle of violence and unbalance the precarious stability of the Lavalas regime. The new police force has also shown signs of becoming the Trojan horse of the old predatory coalition; many of its "commanding officer positions" have been assigned to former members of the "discredited and brutal Haitian army."[17] Finally, the ambiguities of the U.S. role in Haiti as both supporter of the dominant class and forceful restorer of Aristide's presidency bode poorly for a genuine democratic *déchoukaj*.

The future is thus full of uncertainties. The class conflicts, which had been momentarily subdued by the U.S. presence and by Aristide's reluctant transformation from radical priest into would-be conciliator, have crystallized again with added tensions. The reemergence of this historical clash between *le pays en dehors*—the marginalized—and the privileged few reflected the persistent fact that little had changed in the distribution of power and that a new class of *grands mangeurs* has emerged. The coexistence of ostentatious wealth amid acute poverty inevitably dampened the short-lived euphoria of Aristide's 1994 return to power. But will the specter of a hellish war of all against all prove capable of permanently assuaging the obdurate antagonisms of class? Or will it merely cause a temporary deceptive calm before the storm? Only time will tell. For the moment, the signs of economic recovery and democratic renaissance are so ambiguous, fragile, and contradictory that they are overwhelmed by morbid symptoms of political opportunism, mass misery, and criminal delinquency.

*   *   *

As this book goes to press, Haiti's systemic vicissitudes have been dramatically underscored by what appears to have been an attempted coup d'état launched by disgruntled members of the disbanded army.[18] In the early morning hours of December 17, 2001, about thirty heavily armed commandos stormed the National Palace in pickup trucks. While there are conflicting reports, the surprise attack seems to have been aimed at over-throwing, and possibly assassinating, Aristide. Aristide and his family were at their private residence in Tabarre and were unharmed. Special presiden-tial security forces assisted by the national police SWAT team and large groups of Chimères aborted the coup and forced the commandos to flee the palace.

The violent episode resulted in at least eight deaths—five commandos, two policemen, and one civilian. Pro-Lavalas crowds in Thomazeau killed four of the five commandos, and presidential security guards shot the fifth during the assault. In the town of Terre Rouge, Aristide's supporters cap-tured Pierre Richardson, a former soldier who had participated in the attack on the palace. Placed under police surveillance, Richardson told reporters that the coup d'état had been planned in the Dominican Republic by former military and police officers Guy Philippe, Jean-Jacques Nau, and Guy François.[19] According to Richardson, the commandos' goal was to take the National Palace and overthrow Aristide with the help of backup forces organized by François. When these forces failed to materialize, the com-mandos fled the palace and sought to escape to the Dominican Republic.

Richardson stated that he did not believe that Convergence Démocratique was involved in the botched coup. Clearly, the Chimères and large Lavalas crowds that took to the streets to defend Aristide on the morning of December 17 did not share this belief. With cries of "Aristide or death," they went on a rampage burning to the ground the headquarters of the CD as well as three buildings belonging to other opposition parties. The homes of anti-Lavalas leaders Gérard Pierre-Charles and Victor Benoit were also set ablaze.[20] This swift retaliatory violence prompted the CD to argue that the attempted coup was not a coup at all, but rather an event staged by Lavalas itself in an effort to find a pretext to destroy the opposi-tion and silence dissent. The CD contended that Aristide "fabricated" the coup to generate a crisis in a desperate effort to reestablish his waning popularity, regroup his increasingly divided Fanmi Lavalas, and stop the political ascendancy of the opposition. Indeed, during the weeks preceding the attempted coup, major figures within Lavalas had accused each other of incompetence and corruption, a public war of words that highlighted the fissures and antagonisms within Aristide's regime.[21] Moreover, on December 3, 2001, the vicious murder of radio reporter Brignol Lindor by Lavalas partisans led to an upsurge of antigovernment unrest that culminated in riots in the city of Petit Goâve.[22] According to the CD, the besieged Aristide had no option but to plan December 17 as a means to neutralize and eliminate an increasingly assertive opposition.

However farfetched, the CD's explanation of the coup has its logic. That a president in trouble would orchestrate a coup against his own persona in order to uncover and destroy real or imaginary opponents is not new; François Duvalier used the same technique. The war of personalities and, to a lesser degree, ideological and programmatic differences between Aristide and his erstwhile allies of the CD have produced a reciprocal demonization, a pattern of increasing rhetorical vilification from which neither side can extricate itself. Thus, in the eyes of the opposition the attempted coup of December 17 was a criminal machination of Aristide, while for Lavalas and its Chimères it was a conspiracy engineered by the CD. The evidence in this situation is immaterial; Richardson's claim that he was engaged in a coup plotted by former military officers and that the CD had no role in the affair will not change the perspective of either camp.[23] Moreover, it is highly unlikely that the government's appointment of Judge Bernard Sainvil as a special prosecutor charged with investigating the attack on the palace and the ensuing violence of Lavalas' Chimères will modify the situation.[24]

Similarly, the "message of peace" that Aristide addressed to the nation in the wake of the attempted coup fell on deaf ears. Anti-Lavalas forces saw only prevarication in his call for all Haitians to "walk straight on the road to democracy and to continue to mobilize peacefully under the flag of peace."[25] Gérard Pierre Charles expressed the collective opinion of the opposition when he denounced Aristide as a "liar" bent on "establishing a ferocious dictatorship."[26] There is little reason to believe that the attempted coup and the ensuing violence of the Chimères have cowed the opposition; in fact, the attacks may have generated more international support for the parties challenging Lavalas.[27] Far from solidifying Aristide's posture in his negotiated confrontation with the CD, the coup has only intensified external pressures on him for more concessions.[28]

It is true that the events of December 17 have confirmed Lavalas' continued capacity to mobilize its supporters and unleash its Chimères against opponents. The aborted coup and its aftermath, however, have demonstrated the precarious nature of Aristide's hold on power and underscored the virtual absence of structured, functioning governmental institutions. These events have shown that the abolition of the army may have made coups an affair of the past. In the absence of the military, forces bent on overthrowing a regime can no longer depend on the centralized monopoly of coercion required to launch a successful putsch. December 17 has also proved that in spite of internal divisions and a declining popularity, Lavalas is still the dominant political force of the country. The situation, however, is close to the abyss. Unless the fear of mutual destruction compels the major actors into forging a historic compromise, Haiti could easily descend into a civil war. The era of euphoria and hope is long gone; it has given way to uncertainty, cynicism, and gloom. The country is dangerously close to the scenario described in W. B. Yeats' famous poem *The Second Coming:*

> Things fall apart; the centre cannot hold;
> Mere anarchy is loosed upon the world,
> The blood-dimmed tide is loosed, and everywhere
> The ceremony of innocence is drowned;
> The best lack all conviction, while the worst
> Are full of passionate intensity.[29]

The collapse of the Duvalier dictatorship and the rise of Lavalas opened the possibility of another pathway, albeit uncertain, to a way of life freed from the legacy of authoritarianism, injustice, and destitution. Those forging the pathway, however, have taken unfortunate detours leading to multiple and obscure dead ends. Their journey has heightened the reality that the corrupt structures of the past do not die easily; always lurking in the shadows, they continue to shape the new forms that are struggling to be born. Haiti has thus entered what Bertolt Brecht once described as "the time of struggles between the new and the old."[30] We must wait to see whether the promise of the new will flourish or degenerate into the ugly vulgarities of the old. While the current situation invites at best a moderate pessimism, Haitians continue to struggle against all odds. Like William Morris they know how people "fight and lose the battle, and the thing that they fought for comes about in spite of their defeat, and when it comes turns out not to be what they meant, and other [people] have to fight for what they meant under another name."[31]

Notes

1. Brian Moore, *No Other Life* (New York: Nan A. Talese, 1993), pp. 23–24.

2. E. P. Thompson, *The Poverty of Theory and Other Essays* (New York: Monthly Review, 1978), p. 88.

3. Max Weber, *Economy and Society,* edited by Guenther Roth and Claus Wittich (Berkeley: University of California Press, 1978), p. 246.

4. "Talks Break Down Between Haiti's Opposition and Aristide's Party," Associated Press, February 6, 2001.

5. "Discours d'Investiture d'Aristide: Des Objectifs Très Ambitieux," SICRAD, February 7, 2001.

6. Guillermo O'Donnell and Philippe C. Schmitter, *Transitions from Authoritarian Rule: Tentative Conclusions About Uncertain Democracies* (Baltimore: Johns Hopkins University Press, 1986), p. 69.

7. Charles E. Lindblom, *Inquiry and Change* (New Haven: Yale University Press, 1990).

8. Ibid., p. 204.

9. O'Donnell and Schmitter, *Transitions from Authoritarian Rule,* pp. 62–63.

10. As Robert Cox (with Timothy J. Sinclair), *Approaches to World Order* (Cambridge: Cambridge University Press, 1996), p. 379, has forcefully argued,

> Intellectual production is now organized like the production of goods or of other services. The material basis of networks is provided by formal (usually nongovernmental) organizations as mobilizing and coordinating agencies with research directors and funds (from sources sometimes more, sometimes less, visible) for commissioning studies, financing conferences, and symposia or informal luncheon discussions. The materially independent scholar is a rarity, though perhaps not quite extinct. The material basis of networks allows for a selection of participants which guarantees a certain homogeneity around a basic core of orthodoxy. However, since the object of the exercise is consensus building, narrow orthodoxy or exclusiveness would be a self-defeating criterion, and the activators of each network extend their search to those whose ideas reach the outer boundaries of what might ultimately be acceptable. Above and beyond material support, the organized network holds out to the intellectual the prospect of political influence, of being listened to by top decision makers and even of becoming part of the decision making team.

See also Colin Leys, *The Rise and Fall of Development Theory* (Bloomington: Indiana University Press, 1996); and William Robinson, *Promoting Polyarchy* (Cambridge: Cambridge University Press, 1996), pp. 41–72.

11. Lindblom, *Inquiry and Change,* p. 279.

12. Edward W. Said, *Representations of the Intellectual* (New York: Pantheon, 1994), p. xvii.

13. Human rights observers have estimated that the military or their auxiliaries murdered at least 3,000 people. In addition, some 300,000 people went into hiding fearing the violence of the junta.

14. Béatrice Pouligny, "Haïti: Deux ou Trois Raisons d'Espérer," *Libération,* February 13, 2001. Translated from the original French by Carrol Coates:

> [Alors que la classe politique dans son ensemble est incapable de penser un projet politique, les membres de ces petites organisations continuent à réfléchir, en des termes très concrets, sur ce que signifie être citoyen haïtien, sur leur "droit à exister et à habiter ce pays," première signification associée à la notion de "démocratie." Même affaibli, un tel réseau continue à être un espace où l'on tente de donner du sens à ce qui change et d'inventer, jour après jour, les termes d'une survie dont les visages dépassent tous les clichés que l'on peut avoir sur la misère du peuple haïtien.
>
> Ce Haïti-là n'a pas d'autre choix que de déployer des trésors d'imagination. Il est le plus prometteur, celui qui fait que l'on n'a pas le droit de perdre espoir pour ce pays, celui d'où pourrait émerger une nouvelle classe politique, formée à une nouvelle culture politique.

15. Michel-Rolph Trouillot, "Aristide's Challenge," *New York Review of Books*, November 3, 1994, pp. 39–40.

16. National Coalition for Haitian Rights (NCHR), *No Greater Priority: Judicial Reform in Haiti* (New York: NCHR, 1995).

17. William G. O'Neill, "Building a New Haitian Police Force and Justice System," *Haiti Insight* 6, no. 1 (October-November 1995): 8.

18. See "Une Journée Chaude: Attaque Contre le Palais National, Lavalas Reprend le Contrôle," *Haïti en Marche*, December 19–24, 2001, pp. 1–6; "Coup d'Etat! Commandos Storm Palace in Failed Attempt to Overthrow Aristide," *Haitian Times*, December 19–25, 2001, pp. 1–15; "Déroulement et Avatars d'un Complot," *Haïti Progrès*, December 26, 2001–January 1, 2002; "Haitian Commandos Attack Palace Before Being Routed," *New York Times*, December 18, 2001; "Five Dead in Haiti Coup Attempt," *BBC News*, online at http://news.bbc.co.uk/hi/english/world/americas/newsid_1715000/1715515.stm, December 18, 2001; Michel Karshan, foreign press liaison of Haiti's government offers the official version of events in an e-mail release on December 21, 2001 entitled "Details on the Attempted Coup d'Etat on Haiti's National Palace on December 17, 2001." The new Web page of Le Palais National de la République d'Haïti, online at www.palaisnational.org, offers a similar version in French entitled "Le Film des Evénements du Coup d'Etat Avorté du 17 Décembre 2001."

19. See Michel Karshan, "Details on the Attempted Coup d'État on Haiti's National Palace on December 17, 2001"; "Le Film des Evénements du Coup d'État Avorté du 17 Décembre 2001," Le Palais National de la République d'Haïti; "Ex-Soldier Details Haiti Coup Plans," *Associated Press*, December 21, 2001; "Envahisseur Capturé Passe Aux Aveux," *Haïti en Marche*, December 26, 2001–January 2, 2002, pp. 1–6, 17.

20. "Mobs Used as Political Tool," *Haitian Times*, December 26, 2001–January 1, 2002, pp. 1–17; "Violence Mars Outlook for Resumed Negotiations," *Haitian Times*, December 26, 2001–January 1, 2002, p. 4; "Noël: La Sincérité des Voeux de Paix d'Aristide Mise en Doute," *SICRAD* 2, no. 128, December 26, 2001; "17 Décembre: Retour au Dechoukaj," *Haïti en Marche*, December 19–24, 2001, pp. 6–7; "Mobs Torch Haiti Opposition Offices After Aristide Survives Coup Attempt," *Independent.co.uk*, online at http://www.independent.co.uk/, December 18, 2001.

21. Prime Minister Jean-Marie Chérestal and his own minister of the interior, Henry Claude Ménard, traded public accusations of corruption. A similar dispute erupted between Chérestal and Lavalas parliamentarians. See "Inquiétudes Au Sein de Lavalas Sur la Crédibilité du Gouvernement," *SICRAD* 2, no. 120, October 29, 2001.

22. "Haïti: un Journaliste Tué à Petit-Goâve," *AFP International*, December 4, 2001; "Mise à Jour d'Alerte: RSF Exprime son Indignation Suite à l'Assassinat d'un Journaliste par des Partisans Présumés du Pouvoir," *Reporters Sans Frontières*, December 5, 2001; "Une Organisation Populaire Reconnaît le Meurtre d'un Journaliste Haïtien," *AFP International*, December 6, 2001; "Dans un Pays Dévasté, le Président Haïtien Attaque la Presse," *Le Monde*, December 10, 2001; "Violence at Reporter's Funeral," *Associated Press*, December 12, 2001; "Violence Eroding Aristide's Rule," *Miami Herald*, December 13, 2001.

23. Richardson was also involved in the earlier violent incident of July 28, 2001, when armed commandos stormed the headquarters of the police academy and fled to the Dominican Republic. Jean-Dady Simeon, the national police spokesman, indicated that the "same people" were involved in the two plots. Guy Philippe, the alleged leader of the attempted coup of December 17, is the former police chief of

the northern city of Cap-Haïtien, who also escaped to the Dominican Republic last year after being accused of conspiring to overthrow then-president René Préval. Philippe, who has denied any involvement in the coup, was detained in Ecuador and deported to Panama. He found his way back to Santo Domingo only to be arrested by Dominican police on December 27. As of early January 2002, security forces at a private residence were holding Philippe. It is unclear whether the Dominican Republic will hand him over to Haitian authorities, as there is no extradition agreement between the two nations. See "Alleged Gunman in Haiti Linked to Police Academy Attack," *Miami Herald,* December 20, 2001; "Alleged Haiti Coup Leader Behind Bars in Dominican Republic," *Associated Press,* December 28, 2001; "Dominicans Arrest Alleged Haitian Coup Plotter," *Reuters,* December 29, 2001.

24. "Haitian Government to Probe Post-Coup Mob Violence," *Reuters,* December 27, 2001.

25. "Noël: La Sincérité des Voeux de Paix d'Aristide Mise en Doute," *SICRAD;* Aristide's speech, "Message de Paix du Président Jean-Bertrand Aristide à la Nation Haïtienne Après l'Échec du Coup d'État Tenté par des Commandos Armés Contre le Palais Présidentiel dans la Nuit du 16 au 17 Décembre 2001," can be accessed online at the website of Le Palais National de la République d'Haïti; "Le Président Aristide Prêche la Tolérance Envers les Partis Politiques de l'Opposition: La Convergence Sceptique," December 31, 2001.

26. "Noël: La Sincérité des Voeux de Paix d'Aristide Mise en Doute," *SICRAD;* See also "Au Lendemain d'un Coup d'État Manqué, l'Opposition Crie au 'Montage,'" *AFP International,* December 18, 2001; "La Convergence Parle d'un Coup Monté," *Haïti en Marche,* December 26–January 2, 2002, pp. 10–11; "La Convergence Démocratique Qualifie de Scénario, Les Événements Survenus en Haïti," *Flash InterVsion2000,* December 21, 2001.

27. "Haiti: Amnesty International Condemns Attacks," Amnesty International, *AI Index: AMR 36/015/2001,* December 18, 2001; "U.S. Condemns Pro-Government Rampages in Wake of Alleged Failed Haitian Coup," *AFP International,* December 18, 2001.

28. For instance, the Inter-American Commission on Human Rights issued a press communiqué following the attempted coup of December 17 that demanded that pluralism be respected in Haiti ("Inter-American Commission on Human Rights Concerned About Violence in Haiti," Organization of American States, no. 34/01, December 18, 2001):

> The Executive Secretary of the IACHR emphasized "the need to restore a climate of democracy in Haiti and the importance of the rule of law." The challenges of democracy-building make it imperative that all sectors of society be able to participate in strengthening democracy without risking reprisal. The Executive Secretary reaffirms his rejection of any action that would threaten the welfare of persons. "Democracy must be built in a climate of tolerance, with all sectors of society participating," said Dr. Cantón.

See also "L'UE Demande aux Autorités Haïtiennes de 'Condamner Fermement' les Violences," *AFP International,* December 26, 2001; "Lean on Haiti to Negotiate Free and Fair Elections," *Newsday,* December 21, 2001; "Where is Haiti's Lifeline?" *Miami Herald,* December 19, 2001.

29. W. B. Yeats, *The Collected Poems of W. B. Yeats* (New York: Macmillan Company, 1956), pp. 184–185.

30. Bertolt Brecht, *Poems 1913–1956,* edited by John Willett and Ralph Manheim, with the cooperation of Erich Fried (New York: Methuen, 1979), p. 424.

31. As quoted in Thompson, *The Poverty of Theory,* p. 88.

Acronyms

AC	Assemblé de Concertation
ALAH	L'Alliance pour la Libération d'Haïti
CATH	Centrale Autonome des Travailleurs Haïtiens
CD	Convergence Démocratique
CEP	Conseil Électoral Provisoire
CHR	Conférence Haïtienne des Religieux
CNG	Conseil National de Gouvernement
CONACOM	Congrès National des Mouvements Démocratiques
CTH	Confédération des Travailleurs Haïtiens
EC	Espace de Concertation
FL	Fanmi Lavalas
FNC	Front National de Concertation
FNCD	Front National pour le Changement et la Démocratie
FOS	Fédération des Ouvriers Syndiqués
FRAPH	Front pour l'Avancement et le Progrès d'Haïti
HNP	Haitian National Police
HRC	Honneur Respect Constitution
IMF	International Monetary Fund
JPP	Jeunesse Pouvoir Populaire
KID	Confédération Unité Démocratique
KONAKOM	Kongré Nasyonal Mouvman Démokratik
MDN	Mouvement pour le Développement National
MIDH	Mouvement pour l'Instauration de la Démocratie en Haïti
MKN	Mouvman Kombit Nasyonal
MOCRENHA	Mouvement Chrétien pour une Nouvelle Haïti
MPP	Mouvement des Paysans de Papaye
MPSN	Mouvement Patriotique pour le Sauvegarde National
NACLA	North American Congress on Latin America
NCHR	National Coalition for Haitian Rights/Refugees

NIC	newly industrialized country
OAS	Organization of American States
ONG	organisations nongouvernementales
OPL	Organisation du Peuple en Lutte
OPL	Organisation Politique Lavalas
PADEMH	Parti Démocrate Haïtien
PAIN	Parti Agricole Industriel National
PANPRHA	Parti National Progressiste Haïtien
PDCH	Parti Démocrate Chrétien Haïtien
PSCH	Parti Social Chrétien d'Haïti
RDNP	Rassemblement des Démocrates Nationalistes et Progressistes
SAP	structural adjustment program
SICRAD	Service d'Information du Centre de Recherche et d'Action pour le Développement
SSP	Service Sécurité Président
TKL	Petite Commaunauté de l'Église de Saint Jean Bosco
TNH	Télévision Nationale d'Haïti
UNR	Union for National Reconstruction
USAID	U.S. Agency for International Development

Glossary

bo tab la	to the dinner table
changer la vie	make life better; change life for the better
chef	leader/head/boss
Chimères	violent, intimidating gangs
déchoukaj	uprooting
déplumé	fleeced
dérive totalitaire	drift toward totalitarianism
doublure	rule by non-officeholders
en ba tab la	under the dinner table
grands mangeurs/gran manjers	big eaters
groupuscules	very small groups working for the benefit of a *chef*
gwoupman	peasant cooperative
houngan	male vodou priest
kombit	working together
la politique du ventre	politics of the belly
lapè nan tet, lapè nan vant	peace in the head, peace in the belly (Aristide's 2000 campaign slogan)
lavalas	flood (symbolizing mass movement of the destitute)
le pays en dehors	the marginalized
le peuple	the people; the masses
légliz sé nou, nou sé légliz	the church is us, we are the church
loa	vodou spirits
magouilles	fraud; wheeling and dealing
mambo	female vodou priest
marronage/mawonaj	resistance through elusiveness

moun andeyo	marginalized masses, excluded outsiders
nou pran pouvwa, nou pran'l net	we have taken power and will keep it forever
ouverture	opening up
Père Lebrun	"Necklacing"; victims are forced into tires that are set afire with gas
sans non	without a name
sauve-qui-peut	every man for himself
télédjol	rumors
ti léglize	little church; radical wing of the Catholic Church
ti soldat	little soldier; lower-ranked military
Tontons Macoutes/tonton-makout	boogeymen; Duvalier private security force
tout moun se moun	every human being is a human being
tout sa ou wè, sé pa sa	everything you see is an illusion
voudouisant	follower of Vodou-based religion
Zinglendos	violent, intimidating gangs

Bibliography

Abbott, Elizabeth. *Haiti: The Duvaliers and Their Legacy*. New York: McGraw-Hill, 1988.

Agence Haïtienne de Presse en Ligne, http://www.ahphaiti.org/.

Amsden, Alice H. *Asia's Next Giant: South Korea and Late Industrialization*. New York: Oxford University Press, 1989.

Arana, Ana. "Impunity, Haiti: The Case of Jean Léopold Dominique." Inter American Press Association, January 2001. Available online at http://www.impunidad.com/cases/jeanleopoldE.html.

Aristide homepage, unofficial, http://www.unofficialaristide.homepage.com/.

Aristide, Jean-Bertrand. *Aristide: An Autogiography*. MaryKnoll, N.Y.: Orbis, 1993.

———. *Dignity*. Charlottesville: University Press of Virginia, 1996.

———. *Eyes of the Heart*. Monroe, Maine: Common Courage Press, 2000.

———. *In the Parish of the Poor*. New York: Orbis, 1991.

———. *Tout Moun Se Moun, Tout Homme est un Homme*. Paris: Seuil, 1992.

Aristide, Marx V., and Laurie Richardson. "Haiti's Popular Resistance." In James Ridgeway, ed., *The Haiti Files: Decoding the Crisis*. Washington, D.C.: Essential Books, 1994, pp. 64–71.

———. "Haiti's Popular Resistance." *NACLA* 27, no. 4 (January-February 1994): 34–35.

Attinger, Joel, and Michael Kramer. Interview with Aristide, "It's Not If I Go Back, But When." *Time,* November 1, 1993, p. 28.

Avril, Prosper. *Vérités et Révélations: L'Armée d'Haïti, Bourreau ou Victime?* Port-au-Prince: Le Natal, 1997.

"Background and Analysis on the May 28th Confrontation at Champ de Mars." *Haïti Progrès,* July 21–27, 1999, pp. 9–20.

Ballard, John. *Upholding Democracy: The United States Military Campaign in Haiti, 1994–1997*. Westport, Conn.: Praeger, 1998.

Barthélémy, Gérard. "Le Discours Duvalieriste Après les Duvalier." In Gérard Barthélémy and Christian Girault, eds., *La République Haïtienne*. Paris: Karthala, 1993, pp. 179–189.

———. *Les Duvalieristes Après Duvalier*. Paris: L'Harmattan, 1992.

———. *Le Pays en Dehors*. Port-au-Prince: Éditions Henry Deschamps, 1989.

Bauduy, Jennifer. "Haiti's Aristide Presents Party Platform." *Sun-Sentinel* (Fort Lauderdale, Fla.), December 15, 1999.

Bayart, Jean François, *The State in Africa: The Politics of the Belly.* New York: Longman, 1993.

BBC News, http://news.bbc.co.uk/.

Berins Collier, Ruth. *Paths Toward Democracy.* Cambridge: Cambridge University Press, 1999.

Bonnardot, Martin-Luc, and Gilles Danroc. *La Chute de la Maison Duvalier.* Paris: Karthala, 1989.

Bourdieu, Pierre. *In Other Words: Essays Towards a Reflexive Sociology.* Stanford: Stanford University Press, 1990.

Branch, Taylor. "Clinton Without Apologies." *Esquire,* September 1996.

Brecht, Bertolt. *Poems 1913–1956,* edited by John Willett and Ralph Manheim, with the cooperation of Erich Fried. New York: Methuen, 1979.

Bresser Pereira, Luiz Carlos, José María Maravall, and Adam Przeworski, eds. *Economic Reforms in New Democracies: A Social-Democratic Approach.* Cambridge: Cambridge University Press, 1993.

Burton, Michael, Richard Gunther, and John Higley. "Elites and Democratic Consolidation in Latin America and Southern Europe: An Overview." In Richard Gunther and John Higley, eds., *Elites and Democratic Consolidation in Latin America and Southern Europe.* Cambridge: Cambridge University Press, 1992, pp. 323–348.

Carey, Henry F. "Electoral Observation and Democratization in Haiti." In Kevin J. Middlebrook, ed., *Electoral Observation and Democratic Transitions in Latin America.* San Diego: Center for U.S.-Mexican Studies, 1998, pp. 141–166.

Castaneda, Jorge G. *Utopia Unarmed.* New York: Vintage, 1994.

Catanese, Anthony V. *Haitians: Migration and Diaspora.* Boulder: Westview Press, 1999.

Center for International Policy, http://www.ciponline.org/.

Centre Haïtien de Recherches et de Documentation (CHRD), http://www.chrd. org/.

Chamberlain, Greg. "Haiti's Second Independence: Aristide Seven Months in Office." In NACLA, ed., *Haiti: Dangerous Crossroads.* Boston: South End Press, 1995, pp. 51–56.

———. "Le Héros et le Pouvoir." In Gérard Barthélémy and Christian Girault, eds., *La République Haïtienne.* Paris: Karthala, 1993, pp. 226–228.

———. "An Interregnum: Haitian History from 1987 to 1990." In NACLA, ed., *Haiti: Dangerous Crossroads.* Boston: South End Press, 1995, pp. 35–39.

Chapman, Audrey R., and Patrick Ball. "The Truth Commissions: Comparative Lessons from Haiti, South Africa, and Guatemala." *Human Rights Quarterly* 23 (2001): 1–43.

Charles, Etzer. *Le Pouvoir Politique en Haïti de 1957 à Nos Jours.* Paris: Karthala, 1994.

Charles-Antoine, Gabriel. "Une Lecture de la Crise." *Haïti en Marche,* November 19–25, 1997, pp. 3–18.

CNN News, http://www.cnn.com/WORLD.

Cohen, Youssef. *Radicals, Reformers, and Reactionaries.* Chicago: University of Chicago Press, 1994.

Commission Nationale de Vérité et de Justice. Rapport de la Commission Nationale de Vérité et de Justice. Haiti Online, 1998.

Conaghan, Catherine M., and James M. Malloy. *Unsettling Statecraft.* Pittsburgh: University of Pittsburgh Press, 1994.

Cox, Robert, with Timothy J. Sinclair. *Approaches to World Order.* Cambridge: Cambridge University Press, 1996.

Crozier, M., Samuel Huntington, and J. Watanuki, eds. *The Crisis of Democracy.* New York: New York University Press, 1975.

Dahl, Robert. *A Preface to Economic Democracy.* Cambridge, England: Polity Press, 1985.

Dahomay, Jacky. "Où en Est la Démocratie en Haïti? Haiti Online, January 14, 2001.

Dahrendorf, Ralph. *Class and Class Conflict in Industrial Society.* Stanford: Stanford University Press, 1959.

Danner, Mark. "The Fall of the Prophet." *New York Review of Books,* December 2, 1993.

Danroc, Gilles. "Imbroglio, Précarités et Démocratie." Diffusion de l'Information sur l'Amérique Latine, Dossier 2358, March 1–15, 2000, pp. 1–2.

Davis, Wade. *Passage of Darkness: The Ethnobiology of the Haitian Zombie.* Raleigh: University of North Carolina Press, 1988.

Deibert, Michael. "Notes from the Last Testament," windowsonhaiti.com, May 1, 2001.

Delince, Kern. *Les Forces Politiques en Haïti.* Paris: Karthala, 1993.

Deutscher, Isaac. *The Unfinished Revolution: Russia 1917–1967.* New York: Oxford University Press, 1967.

Di Palma, Guiseppe. *To Craft Democracies.* Berkeley: University of California Press, 1990.

Downs, Anthony. *An Economic Theory of Democracy.* New York: Harper and Row, 1957.

Doyle, Kate. "Hollow Diplomacy in Haiti." *World Policy Journal* 11, no. 1 (spring 1994): 50–58.

Dupuy, Alex. *Haiti in the New World Order.* Boulder: Westview Press, 1997.

Elkin, Stephen L., and Karol Edward Soltan, eds. *A New Constitutionalism.* Chicago: University of Chicago Press, 1993.

Elster, Jon, "Introduction." In Jon Elster and Rune Slagstad, eds., *Constitutionalism and Democracy.* Cambridge: Cambridge University Press, 1993, pp. 1–17.

———. *Making Sense of Marx.* Cambridge: Cambridge University Press, 1985.

Embassy of Haiti in Washington, http://www.haiti.org/index.html.

Evans, Peter. *Embedded Autonomy.* Princeton: Princeton University Press, 1995.

Farmer, Paul. *The Uses of Haiti.* Monroe, Maine: Common Courage Press, 1994.

Fass, Simon. *Political Economy in Haiti.* New Brunswick, N.J.: Transaction, 1990.

Fatton, Robert Jr. "The Impairments of Democratization: Haiti in Comparative Perspective." *Comparative Politics* 21, no. 2 (1999): 209–229.

———. *The Making of a Liberal Democracy: Senegal's Passive Revolution, 1975–1985.* Boulder: Lynne Rienner, 1987.

Fauriol, Georges A. "Searching for Haiti Policy: The Next Ninety Days." *The Center for Strategic and International Studies* 9, no. 3 (June 19, 2001). Available online at the Center for International Policy.

Ferguson, James. *Papa Doc, Baby Doc: Haiti and the Duvaliers.* New York: Basil Blackwell, 1987.

Fick, Carolyn E. *The Making of Haiti.* Knoxville: University of Tennessee Press, 1990.

Flash InterVision2000, http://www.intervision2000.com/.

Fouchard, Jean. *Les Marrons de la Liberté.* Port-au-Prince: Éditions Henry Deschamps, 1988.

Franck, Thomas. "The Emerging Right to Democratic Governance." *American Journal of International Law* 86 (1992): 46–91

Fukuyama, Francis. *The End Of History and the Last Man.* New York: Free Press, 1992.

Gambetta, Diego. *The Sicilian Mafia.* Cambridge: Harvard University Press, 1993.

Garrison, Lynn. *Voodoo Politics.* Los Angeles: Leprechaun, 2000.

George, Susan, and Fabrizio Sabelli. *Faith and Credit: The World Bank's Secular Empire.* Boulder: Westview Press, 1994.

Gibbons, Elizabeth. *Sanctions in Haiti: Human Rights and Democracy Under Assault.* Westport Conn.: Praeger, with the Center for Strategic and International Studies, Washington, D.C., 1999.

Gramsci, Antonio. *Selections from the Prison Notebooks,* edited and translated by Quintin Hoare and Geoffrey Nowell Smith. London: Lawrence and Wishart, 1971.

Greene, Anne. *The Catholic Church in Haiti.* East Lansing: Michigan State University Press, 1993.

Gros, Jean-Germain. "Compensation as a Justice Tool in the Post-Conflict Era." In Peter Cross and Guenola Rasamoelina, eds., *Conflict Prevention Policy of the European Union, Yearbook 1998/99.* Baden-Baden: Nomos Verlagsgesellschaft, 1999, pp. 195–208.

———. "Haiti's Flagging Transition." *Journal of Democracy* 8, no. 4 (1997): 94–109.

Hadenius, Axel. *Democracy and Development.* Cambridge: Cambridge University Press, 1992.

Haggard, Stephan, and Robert R. Kaufman. *The Political Economy of Democratic Transitions.* Princeton: Princeton University Press, 1995.

Haïti en Marche, http://www.haitienmarche.com/sommaire.html.

———. "Carnaval Grands Mangeurs," February 12–18, 1997, pp. 1–8.

———. February 19–25, 1997, p. 12.

Haiti Global Village, http://www.haitiglobalvillage.com/.

Haiti homepage, unofficial, http://www.uhhp.org/.

Haiti Info, http://www.haitiinfo.com/.

Haiti Online, http://www.haitionline.com/.

Haïti Progrès, http://www.haiti-progres.com/.

Haiti Reborn Home, http://www.quixote.org/haiti/index_main.html.

Haïti Solidarité Internationale. *Haïti Elections 1990: Quelle Démocratie?* Port-au-Prince: Jean-Yves Urfie, 1990.

Haiti Support Group, http://www.gn.apc.org/haitisupport/.

Haitian Information Bureau. "Chronology." In James Ridgeway, ed., *The Haiti Files: Decoding the Crisis.* Washington, D.C.: Essential Books, 1994, pp. 205–240.

Haitiwebs.com, http://www.haitiwebs.com/cgi-bin/gazette/news.cgi.

Harrison, E. "Voodoo Politics." *Atlantic Monthly,* June, 1993, pp. 101–107.

Held, David. *Models of Democracy.* Cambridge, England: Polity Press, 1987.

Horblitt, Stephen. "Barriers to Nonviolent Conflict Resolution." In Georges A. Fauriol, ed., *Haitian Frustrations: Dilemmas for U.S. Policy.* Washington, D.C.: Center For Strategic and International Studies, 1995, pp. 129–142.

House International Relations Committee, "Gilman, Helms and Goss Issue Statement on Haitian Election." Washington, D.C., December 8, 2000.

Human Rights Watch/Americas. *Thirst for Justice: A Decade of Immunity in Haiti.* New York: Human Rights Watch, 1996.

Human Rights Watch, Human Rights Watch Backgrounder. "Aristide's Return to Power in Haiti." February 2001. Posted on the website of the Center for International Studies.

Huntington, Samuel. *The Third Wave.* Norman: University of Oklahoma Press, 1991.

Hurbon, Laennec. *Comprendre Haïti.* Paris: Karthala, 1987.

———. *Culture et Dictature en Haïti.* Paris: L'Harmattan, 1979.

———. "The Hope for Democracy." *New York Review of Books,* November 3, 1994.

———. *Voodoo: Search for the Spirit.* New York: Abrams, 1995.

Ives, Kim. "The Lavalas Alliance Propels Aristide to Power," in NACLA, ed., *Haiti: Dangerous Crossroads.* Boston: South End Press, 1995, pp. 41–49.

———. "The Unmaking of a President," in NACLA, ed., *Haiti: Dangerous Crossroads.* Boston: South End Press, 1995, pp. 65–87.

Jallot, Nicolas, and Laurent Lesage. *Haïti: Dix Ans d'Histoire Secrète.* Paris: Éditions du Félin, 1995.

Janvier, Louis Joseph. *Les Constitutions d'Haïti (1801–1885).* Paris: C. Marpon et E. Flammarion, 1886.

Jean, Jean-Claude, and Marc Maesschalck. *Transition Politique en Haïti.* Paris: L'Harmattan, 1999.

Joanis, Susan. "Haiti: Hopes for Democracy Rest on Police." *Compass, a Jesuit Journal* 13, no. 6 (January-February 1996).

Karl, Terry Lynn. "Dilemmas of Democratization in Latin America." *Comparative Politics* 23, no. 1 (1990): 1–21.

Kumar, Chetan. *Building Peace in Haiti.* Boulder: Lynne Rienner, 1998.

Kurzban, Ira. "A Rational Foreign Policy Toward Haiti." Haiti Online, February 6, 2001.

Labelle, Micheline. *Idéologie de Couleur et Classes Sociales en Haïti.* Montreal: Les Presses de l'Université de Montréal, 1978.

Laguerre, Michel S. *The Military and Society in Haiti.* Knoxville: University of Tennessee Press, 1993.

———. *Voodoo and Politics in Haiti.* London: Macmillan, 1990.

Lane, Charles. "Cop Land." *New Republic,* September 29, 1997, p. 23.

Lemarchand, René. "Political Clientelism and Ethnicity in Tropical Africa: Competing Solidarities in Nation-Building." In Steffen W. Schmidt, James Scott, Carl Landé, and Laura Guasti, eds., *Friends, Followers, and Factions.* Berkeley: University of California Press, 1977, pp. 100–123.

Le Monde, http://www.lemonde.fr/.

Le Monde Diplomatique, http://www.monde-diplomatique.fr/en/.

Le Nouvelliste, http://www.inhaiti.com/forms/NOU-v-home.html.

Lewin, Moshe. *The Gorbachev Phenomenon.* Berkeley: University of California Press, 1988.

Leys, Colin. *The Rise and Fall of Development Theory.* Bloomington: Indiana University Press, 1996.

Lindblom, Charles E. *Inquiry and Change.* New Haven: Yale University Press, 1990.

Linz, Juan J. "Presidential or Parliamentary Democracy: Does It Make a Difference?" In Juan Linz and Arturo Valenzuela, eds., *The Failure of Presidential Democracy*. Baltimore: Johns Hopkins University Press, 1994, pp. 3–87.

———. "Transitions to Democracy." *Washington Quarterly* 13, no. 1 (1990): 143–164.

Linz, Juan J., and Arturo Valenzuela. "Preface," in Juan Linz and Arturo Valenzuela, eds., *The Failure of Presidential Democracy*. Baltimore: Johns Hopkins University Press, 1994, pp. ix–xvi.

———, eds. *The Failure of Presidential Democracy: Comparative Perspectives*, vol. 1. Baltimore: Johns Hopkins University Press, 1994.

Lipset, Seymour Martin. "Some Social Requisites of Democracy: Economic Development and Political Legitimacy." *American Political Science Review* 53, no. 1 (1959): 69–106.

Loveman, Brian. *The Constitution of Tyranny: Regimes of Exception in Spanish America*. Pittsburgh: University of Pittsburgh Press, 1993.

Lundahl, Mats. *Peasants and Poverty: A Study of Haiti*. London: Croom Helm, 1979.

Maguire, Robert. *Bootstrap Politics: Elections and Haiti's New Public Officials*. Baltimore: Hopkins-Georgetown Haiti Project, No. 2, February 1996.

———. "Demilitarizing Public Order in a Predatory State: The Case of Haiti." The North South Agenda Papers, No. 17, December 1995.

Mahon, Arthur. "Haïti: Une Dictature Rampante." *Rouge*, December 7, 2000.

Maingot, Anthony. "Haiti and Aristide: The Legacy of History." *Current History*, February 1992, pp. 65–69.

Malone, David. *Decision-Making in the UN Security Council: The Case of Haiti*. Oxford: Oxford University Press, 1998.

Malval, Robert. *L'Année de Toutes les Duperies*. Port-au-Prince: Éditions Regain, 1996.

Marshall, T. H. *Class, Citizenship and Social Development*. Westport, Conn.: Greenwood Press, 1973.

Martin, Ian. "Haiti: Mangled Multilateralism." *Foreign Policy*, no. 95 (summer 1994): 80–85.

Marx, Karl, and Frederick Engels. *The German Ideology*. New York: International Publishers, 1947.

———. *Karl Marx: Selected Writings in Sociology and Social Philosophy*, translated by T. B. Bottomore, edited by T. B. Bottomore and Maximilien Rubel, with a foreword by Erich Fromm. New York: McGraw-Hill, 1964.

———. *The Marx-Engels Reader*, 2d ed., edited by R. C. Tucker. New York: Norton, 1978.

McGowan, Lisa. *Democracy Undermined, Economic Justice Denied: Structural Adjustment and the Aid Juggernaut in Haiti*. Washington, D.C.: Development Group for Alternative Policies, 1997.

Meiksins Wood, Ellen. *Democracy Against Capitalism*. Cambridge: Cambridge University Press, 1995.

———. *Retreat from Class*. London: Verso, 1986.

Merrill, John. "Vodou and Political Reform in Haiti: Some Lessons for the International Community." *The Fletcher Forum of World Affairs* 20, no. 1 (winter-spring 1996): 31–52.

Métraux, Alfred. *Voodoo in Haiti*, with new introduction by Sidney Mintz. New York: Schocken, 1972.

Métropole Haïti, http://metropolehaiti.com.

Miami Herald, http://www.miami.com/herald/.

Michel, Manno. "Les Élections du 21 Mai 2000." August 2000, online at Windows on Haiti.

Midy, Franklin. "Aristide: Entre le Prophète et le Prince." *Haïti en Marche,* December 26, 1990–January 1, 1991.

———. "Changement et Transition." In Gérard Barthélémy and Christian Girault, eds., *La République Haïtienne.* Paris: Karthala, 1993.

———. "Qui Êtes-Vous, Père Aristide?" *Haïti en Marche,* October 26–November 2, 1988.

———. "What Is Blocking Haiti." Online at Center for International Policy, 1999.

Miliband, Ralph. *Marxism and Politics.* Oxford: Oxford University Press, 1977.

Mintz, Sidney. *Caribbean Transformations.* Chicago: Aldine, 1974.

Moïse, Claude. *Une Constitution dans la Tourmente.* Montreal: Éditions Images, 1994.

———. *Constitutions et Luttes de Pouvoir en Haïti.* Vol. 1, *La Faillite des Classes Dirigeantes (1804–1915).* Montreal: CIDIHCA, 1988.

———. *Constitutions et Luttes de Pouvoir en Haïti.* Vol. 2, *De l'Occupation Etrangère à la Dictature Macoute (1915–1987).* Montreal: CIDIHCA, 1990.

Moïse, Claude, and Émile Ollivier. *Repenser Haïti.* Montreal: CIDIHCA, 1992.

Montas, Michèle. "An Open Letter to My Husband, Jean Léopold Dominique." Center for International Policy, May 3, 2001.

Moore, Barrington Jr. *Injustice: The Social Bases of Obedience and Revolt.* White Plains, N.Y.: M. E. Sharpe, 1978.

———. *Social Origins of Dictatorship and Democracy.* Boston: Beacon Press, 1966.

Moore, Brian. *No Other Life.* New York: Nan A. Talese, 1993.

Morrell, James. "Haiti: Success Under Fire." Online at Center for International Policy, January 1995.

———. "Snatching Defeat from the Jaws of Victory." International Policy Report, August 2000. Online at Center for International Policy.

Morrell, James R., Rachel Nield, and Hugh Byrne, "Haiti and the Limits to Nation-Building." *Current History,* March 1999, pp. 127–146. Online at Center for International Policy.

MSNBC, http://www.msnbc.com/news/.

Nairn, Alan. "He's Our S.O.B." *The Nation,* October 31, 1994, pp. 481–482.

———. "Our Man in FRAPH." *The Nation,* October 24, 1994, pp. 458–461.

National Coalition for Haitian Rights (NCHR). *No Greater Priority: Judicial Reform in Haiti.* New York: NCHR, 1995.

New York Times, http://www.nytimes.com/.

———. "Political Feuds Ravage Haiti: So Much for Its High Hopes." October 18, 1998.

Nicholls, David. *From Dessalines to Duvalier,* rev. ed. New Brunswick, N.J.: Rutgers University Press, 1996.

Nield, Rachel. *Policing Haiti: Preliminary Assessment of the Civilian Police Force.* Washington, D.C.: Washington Office on Latin America, 1995.

Nield, Rachel, ed., Juan L. Guiller, trans. *Demilitarizing Public Order: The International Community, Police Reform and Human Rights in Central America and Haiti.* Washington, D.C.: Washington Office on Latin America, 1995.

North, Douglass. *Structure and Change in Economic History.* New York: Norton, 1981.

O'Donnell, Guillermo. *Counterpoints.* Notre Dame: University of Notre Dame Press, 1999.

———. "Delegative Democracy?" *Working Paper No. 173,* Helen Kellogg Institute. Notre Dame: University of Notre Dame, March 1992.

———. "On the State: Democratization and Some Conceptual Problems: A Latin American View with Glances at Some Postcommunist Countries." *World Development* 21, no. 8 (1993): 1355–1370.

O'Donnell, Guillermo, and Philippe C. Schmitter. *Transitions from Authoritarian Rule: Tentative Conclusions About Uncertain Democracies.* Baltimore: Johns Hopkins University Press, 1986.

O'Neill, William G. "Building a New Haitian Police Force and Justice System." *Haiti Insight* 6, no. 1 (October-November 1995). Online at *Haiti Insight,* www.nchr.org/insight default.htm.

OPL. "OPL Press Communique." Port-au-Prince, June 2, 1999.

Orenstein, Catherin. "Aristide, Again." *The Progressive* 65, no. 1 (January 2001). Online at *The Progressive,* www.progressive.org.

Ostrom, Elinor. "Covenants, Collective Action, and Common-Pool Resources." In Karol Edward Soltan and Stephen L. Elkin, eds., *The Constitution of Good Societies.* University Park: Pennsylvania State University Press, 1996, pp. 23–38.

Peck, Raoul. *Monsieur le Ministre . . . Jusqu'au Bout de la Patience.* Port-au-Prince: Éditions Velvet, 1999.

Perusse, Roland I. *Haitian Democracy Restored: 1991–1995.* New York: University Press of America, 1995.

Petras, James, and Morris Morley. *Latin America in the Time of Cholera.* New York: Routledge, 1992.

Pezzullo, Lawrence. "The Challenge of the Negotiation Process." In Georges A. Fauriol, ed., *Haitian Frustrations: Dilemmas for U.S. Policy.* Washington, D.C.: Center For Strategic and International Studies, 1995, pp. 98–102.

Pierre-Charles, Gérard. "Fondements Sociologiques de la Victoire Electorale de Jean-Bertrand Aristide." In Gérard Barthélémy and Christian Girault, eds., *La République Haïtienne: État des Lieux et Perspective.* Paris: Karthala, 1993, pp. 213–225.

Polanyi, Karl. *The Great Transformation.* Boston: Beacon Press, 1957.

Pouligny, Beatrice. "Haïti: Deux ou Trois Raisons d'Espérer." *Libération,* February 13, 2001.

Powell, Colin. *My American Journey.* New York: Ballantine, 1995.

Przeworski, Adam. *Democracy and the Market.* Cambridge: Cambridge University Press, 1991.

———. "Democracy as a Contingent Outcome of Conflicts." In Jon Elster and Rune Slagstad, eds., *Constitutionalism and Democracy.* Cambridge: Cambridge University Press, 1993, pp. 59–80.

———. *Sustainable Democracy.* Cambridge: Cambridge University Press, 1995.

Putnam, Robert. *Making Democracy Work.* Princeton: Princeton University Press, 1993.

Regan, Jane. "A.I.D.ing U.S. Interests in Haiti." *Covert Action,* no. 51 (winter 1994–1995): 7–58.

Reporters Sans Frontières. "Who Killed Jean Dominique? 3 April 2000–3 April

2001." Online at Center for International Policy, http://www.ciponline.org/ Haiti/March-May%202001/rsf.htm, March 2001.

Reuters. "Fights Disrupt Haiti Election Rally." November 30, 1999.

———. "Haiti Approves New Elections." July 20, 1999.

Ridgeway, James, ed. *The Haiti Files: Decoding the Crisis.* Washington, D.C.: Essential, 1994.

Robinson, William. *Promoting Polyarchy.* Cambridge: Cambridge University Press, 1996.

Rueschemeyer, Dietrich, Evelyne Huber Stephens, and John D. Stephens. *Capitalist Development and Democracy.* Chicago: University of Chicago Press, 1992.

Said, Edward W. *Representations of the Intellectual.* New York: Pantheon, 1994.

Sandbrook, Richard. *The Politics of Africa's Economic Recovery.* Cambridge: Cambridge University Press, 1993.

Sartori, Giovanni. *Comparative Constitutional Engineering,* 2d ed. New York: New York University Press, 1997.

Schmidt, Hans. *The United States Occupation of Haiti, 1915–1934.* New Brunswick, N.J.: Rutgers University Press, 1971.

Schmitter, Philippe C. "Transitology: The Science or the Art of Democratization?" In Joseph S. Tulcin with Bernice Romero, eds., *The Consolidation of Democracy in Latin America.* Boulder: Lynne Rienner, 1995, pp. 11–41.

Schulz, Donald, "Whither Haiti?" *Strategic Studies Institute,* April 1, 1996.

Schumpeter, Joseph A. *History of Economic Analysis.* New York: Oxford University Press, 1954.

Scott, James C. *Domination and the Arts of Resistance.* New Haven: Yale University Press, 1990.

Shacochis, Bob. *The Immaculate Invasion.* New York: Viking, 1999.

———. "There Must Be a God in Haiti." In Edward Abbey, ed., *The Best of Outside: The First 20 Years.* New York: Vintage Departures, 1998, pp. 293–306.

Shin, Doh Chull. "On the Third Wave of Democratization: A Synthesis and Evaluation of Recent Theory and Research." *World Politics* 47, no. 1 (1994): 135–170.

SICRAD (Service d'Information du Centre de Recherche et d'Action pour le Développement), http://rehred-haiti.net/membres/crad/sicrad/index.html.

Slavin, J. P. "The Elite's Revenge: The Military Coup of 1991." In North American Congress on Latin America, ed., *Haiti: Dangerous Crossroads.* Boston: South End Press, 1995, pp. 57–61.

Smarth, William. "Une Page de l'Église des Pauvres: Le Père Jean-Bertrand Aristide, Président d'Haïti." In Gérard Barthélémy and Christian Girault, eds., *La République Haïtienne.* Paris: Karthala, 1993, pp. 55–62.

Soltan, Karol Edward. "Introduction: Imagination, Political Competence, and Institutions." In Karol Edward Soltan and Stephen L. Elkin, eds., *The Constitution of Good Societies.* University Park: Pennsylvania State University Press, 1996. pp. 1–18.

Sorensen, Georg. *Democracy and Democratization.* Boulder: Westview Press, 1993.

Stepan, Alfred. *Rethinking Military Politics.* Princeton: Princeton University Press, 1988.

Stepan, Alfred, and Cindy Skach. "Constitutional Frameworks and Democratic Consolidation." *World Politics* 46, no. 1 (1993): 1–22.

Stotzky, Irwin P. *Silencing the Guns in Haiti.* Chicago: University of Chicago Press, 1997.

Tarrow, Sidney. *Power in Movement,* 2d ed. Cambridge: Cambridge University Press, 1998.

Taussig, Michael. *The Nervous System.* New York: Routledge, 1992.

Télévision Nationale d'Haïti, http://www.haiticulture.net/tnh/index.htm.

Thompson, E. P. *The Poverty of Theory and Other Essays.* New York: Monthly Review Press, 1978.

Trouillot, Michel-Rolph. "Aristide's Challenge." *New York Review of Books,* November 3, 1994.

———. "Haiti's Nightmare and the Lessons of History." In North American Congress on Latin America, ed., *Haiti: Dangerous Crossroads.* Boston: South End Press, 1995, pp. 121–132.

———. *Haiti: State Against Nation.* New York: Monthly Review Press, 1990.

———. "The Way I See It: Traps and Trappings of Haitian Democracy." *The Gazette* (Johns Hopkins University), July-September 1997, pp. 3–4.

Turnier, Alain. *Quand la Nation Demande des Comptes,* 2d ed. Port-au-Prince: Éditions Le Natal, 1990.

United Nations. "United Nations International Civilian Support Mission in Haiti, Report of the Secretary-General." Fifty-fifth session, A/55/618, November 9, 2000.

Valenzuela, Samuel. "Democratic Consolidation in Post-Transition Settings: Notion, Process, and Facilitating Conditions." In Scott Mainwaring, Guillermo O'Donnell, and J. Samuel Valenzuela, eds., *The New South American Democracies in Comparative Perspective.* Notre Dame: University of Notre Dame Press, 1992, pp. 57–104.

Vanberg, Viktor J., and James M. Buchanan. "Constitutional Choice, Rational Ignorance and the Limits of Reason." In Karol Edward Soltan and Stephen L. Elkin, eds., *The Constitution of Good Societies.* University Park: Pennsylvania State University Press, 1996, pp. 39–56.

Wade, Robert. *Governing the Market: Economic Theory and the Role of Government in East Asian Industrialization.* Princeton: Princeton University Press, 1990.

———. "Japan, the World Bank, and the Art of Paradigm Maintenance: The East Asian Miracle in Political Perspective." *New Left Review* 217 (May-June 1996): 3–36.

Wargny, Christophe. "The Country That Doesn't Quite Exist: Haiti's Last Chance." Online at *Le Monde Diplomatique,* July 2000.

Washington Office on Haiti, http://www.igc.org/wohaiti/index.html.

Washington Post, http://www.washingtonpost.com/wp-srv/front.htm.

Weber, Max. *Economy and Society.* Guenther Roth and Claus Wittich, eds. Berkeley: University of California Press, 1978.

Weinstein, Brian, and Aaron Segal. *Haiti: The Failure of Politics.* New York: Praeger, 1992.

White, Robert E. "Haiti: Democrats vs. Democracy." *International Policy Report,* Center for International Policy, November 1997.

———. "Haiti: Policy Lost, Policy Regained." *Cosmos: A Journal of Emerging Issues* 6. Online at Center for International Policy.

Wilentz, Amy. "Aristide in Waiting." *New York Times Magazine,* November 5, 2000.

———. "It's a New Day for Haiti, If U.S. Would Accept it." *Los Angeles Times,* June 4, 2000.

———. *The Rainy Season.* New York: Touchstone, 1989.

Windows on Haiti, http://windowsonhaiti.com.

World Bank. *Governance and Development.* Washington, D.C.: World Bank, 1992.

———. *World Development Report 1997: The State in a Changing World.* Oxford: Oxford University Press, 1997.

———. *World Development Report 1999/2000: Entering the 21st Century.* Oxford: Oxford University Press, 2000.

Wucker, Michele. *Why the Cocks Fight.* New York: Hill and Wang, 2000.

Yahoo, Haiti News, http://fullcoverage.yahoo.com/fc/World/Haiti/.

Index

About the Book

The collapse of the Duvalier dictatorship in 1986 gave rise to optimism among Haitians in all walks of life—to hopes for a democratic journey leading to economic development, political renewal, and social peace. The reality of the subsequent years, however, has not been so sanguine. Robert Fatton analyzes the vicissitudes of politics in Haiti from the demise of Duvalier through the events of 2001.

Despite a relatively stable period since Jean-Bertrand Aristide assumed the Haitian presidency for the second time, in 1994, Fatton reveals a country in which the imperfect trappings of liberal democracy coexist with violent struggles to monopolize the few sites of public power with any access to wealth and privilege. *Haiti's Predatory Republic*, while recognizing the possibilities of a happier future, tells a somber story of an apparently endless transition to democracy.

Robert Fatton Jr. is professor in the Department of Government and Foreign Affairs at the University of Virginia. His numerous publications include *Predatory Rule: State and Civil Society in Africa* and *The Making of a Liberal Democracy: Senegal's Passive Revolution*.